Stage Management Basics

Stage Management Basics, second edition, offers a deep dive into the basics of stage management for theatre, dance, and opera productions.

Without assuming any intrinsic prior knowledge of the theatrical field and its associated, specialized terminology, this book covers every aspect of stage management, from reading a script, meeting with a director and theatre staff, and running auditions to communication best practices and opening night protocol. This new edition features brand new chapters on opera, dance, and unions, information on working with intimacy and fight directors, updated tips and tricks, and vibrant color images.

Using simple language and detailed explanations, this book is the perfect primer for the beginning stage management student.

The companion website contains blank form templates, chapter comprehension tests, a suggested reading list, glossary term flashcards, and more.

Emily Roth is a freelance AEA production stage manager currently living and working in New York City. She holds a BA from Coe College in Theatre with an emphasis in Design and Technology. Her career has taken her through a wide variety of experiences; from early beginnings in her local community theatre to six years of professional summer stock, from educational theatre to Off-Broadway and touring. She has found herself working on productions ranging between musicals, straight plays, new works, and theatre for young audiences. Like many, Emily discovered stage management somewhat by accident and, like many, is largely self-taught. Through this experience, she felt the need for a text that breaks the job down into its bare-bones basics and guides new stage managers step-by-step through a production.

Jonathan Allender-Zivic, MFA, is a lifelong educator and theatrical artist who has been teaching and working in the industry for over 18 years primarily as Professor, Lighting, Projection and Sound Designer, as well as Technical Director. Jonathan has been mentoring stage managers as part of his academic responsibilities since 2010. Jonathan is Associate Professor of Theatre heading the lighting, sound, and stage management emphases at the University of South Dakota. He has over 125 professional and academic credits in the past 5 years, keeping an active hand in the professional arena; designing regionally when he is not teaching. Jonathan received his MFA from Western Illinois University. He maintains an active role in the United States Institute for Theatre Technology (USITT) and the Kennedy

Center American College Theatre Festival (KCACTF). In 2018, he branched out into product development when he invented and patented the Cable Munkey® and founded Cable Munkey LLC.

Katy McGlaughlin has been working in and around theatre her whole life; mostly stage managing and a little bit of everything else. She has worked all across the United States on productions ranging from new works to large-scale musicals and dance. Katy holds a BFA from Webster University, where she specialized in stage management and technical direction, as well as an MFA in stage management from the University of Iowa. She is currently the production manager for the theatre department at the University of Northern Iowa. She is a proud member of the Actors' Equity Association, the Stage Managers Association, the Association for Theatre in Higher Education, and USITT.

Stage Management Basics
A Primer for Performing Arts Stage Managers

Second Edition

EMILY ROTH, JONATHAN ALLENDER-ZIVIC, AND
KATY MCGLAUGHLIN

Routledge
Taylor & Francis Group

NEW YORK AND LONDON

Cover photo by Jonathan Allender-Zivic

Second edition published 2022
by Routledge
605 Third Avenue, New York, NY 10158

and by Routledge
4 Park Square, Milton Park, Abingdon, Oxon, OX14 4RN

Routledge is an imprint of the Taylor & Francis Group, an informa business

First edition published by Routledge 2017

Library of Congress Cataloging-in-Publication Data
Names: Roth, Emily, author. | Allender-Zivic, Jonathan, author. |
McGlaughlin, Katy, author.
Title: Stage management basics: a primer for performing arts stage
managers / Emily Roth, Jonathan Allender-Zivic, Katy McGlaughlin.
Description: Second edition. | New York: Routledge, 2022. | Includes index.
Identifiers: LCCN 2021027471 (print) | LCCN 2021027472 (ebook) | ISBN
9780367678326 (hardback) | ISBN 9780367678319 (paperback) | ISBN
9781003133049 (ebook)
Subjects: LCSH: Stage management--Handbooks, manuals, etc.
Classification: LCC PN2086 .R68 2022 (print) | LCC PN2086 (ebook) | DDC
792.02/5--dc23
LC record available at https://lccn.loc.gov/2021027471
LC ebook record available at https://lccn.loc.gov/2021027472

ISBN: 978-0-367-67832-6 (hbk)
ISBN: 978-0-367-67831-9 (pbk)
ISBN: 978-1-003-13304-9 (ebk)

DOI: 10.4324/9781003133049

Access the companion website: www.routledge.com/cw/roth

To all those who will come after us, keep the art alive and keep the play in the work.

Contents

Figures

Acknowledgments

To all those people throughout our lives and careers that have guided, mentored, taught, and influenced us.

Foreword

Stage management is a rich, complex, ephemeral art that can require the talents of a great diplomat. It is also a craft that can be, at times, purely clerical in nature. Although essential to the production process, to the audience, the stage manager is invisible, or at best, misunderstood. Therefore, the person taking on the role of the stage manager may be doing so with only the vaguest sense of what will be required of them.

Jonathan, Katy, and Emily have written a thorough description of the role of the stage manager throughout the production process. One that is both accessible and detailed, a veritable handbook to guide one on their journey into stage management. A light in the darkness to guide one through the murky waters, if you will.

The complexities in the art and craft of stage management are rooted in the great varieties of ways it can be practiced. Every director, producer, and theatre may have different work flows and procedures they prefer. The personalities of the collaborators we work with from performers and crew to designers and directors each require unique, individualized, and artful touch to communicate effectively with.

These skills are laid out in the first chapter of *Stage Management Basics* where many of the qualities of great stage managers are described. These traits often fall into the category of "soft skills" and the greatest stage managers have them in abundance. These skills however, are built on a solid foundation. Stage managers need to know their role in every phase of the theatrical production process. *Stage Management Basics* does just that. By the end of the book, the reader will have a strong base upon which to build a great career and an understanding of the further development and growth that will and should continue.

When I started out stage managing, as a student at UCSD, a text like this would've been a great asset. There is so much that goes into the job, specific roles and responsibilities the stage manager plays in the production process, key questions to be asked during preproduction, detailed reports to send in rehearsals, and vital communications to manage a successful run. All are laid out in a clear, simple, and instructive manner.

No text will ever cover the many diverse of ways to stage manage. In my career, stage managing at the La Jolla Playhouse was different than at Ballet Iowa, and both were different than Broadway. *Stage Management Basics* breaks down the duties and responsibilities of a stage manager, describing what needs to get done and the questions to ask, at every step along the way. It also acknowledges the complexities and variables that come with different collaborators and different theatres. Along the way, Jonathan, Katy, and Emily also share many tips and tricks!

I am so honored to be asked to provide a preface for this book, as I'm a great believer in the ability of stage managers to have a powerful impact on the company and the show. I've spent over two decades stage managing on Broadway, a decade educating young stage managers at SUNY Purchase, and created the Broadway Stage Management Symposium (an annual conference for stage managers, more info at www.broadwaysymposium.com). I've seen how a thorough understanding of the basics provides a great foundation for continued growth, excellence in practice, and success in one's career.

A solid foundation is important for any great artist. Painters need to know about brushes and canvases. Sculptors need to know chisels and stones. A stage manager needs to understand the production process. It's upon these basics that the artistry is built. We stage managers play an essential role and if we do our job really well, no one in the audience will ever know. By providing a clear, concise, and instructive text, *Stage Management Basics* sets up the next great generation of stage managers for success.

Along with providing a fundamental understanding of the stage managers job, Jonathan, Katy and Emily demonstrate a powerful beating heart at the core of *Stage Management Basics*. It's not just the a,b,c's. It acknowledges the complexities and variations that will be found and how many of the soft skills required will continue to grow over time.

Anyone beginning their adventure into stage management will be well served by *Stage Management Basics*. For everyone reading this book, I welcome you to the wonderful, rewarding, challenging journey of stage management.

Matthew Stern,
Broadway stage manager and producer of
the Broadway Stage Management Symposium

Matthew Aaron Stern is the founder of the *Broadway Stage Management Symposium*, an annual conference for all stage managers. Stage Manager credits on 20+ Broadway productions include: *Finding Neverland, On The Town, Doctor Zhivago, Side Show, Spider-Man: Turn Off The Dark, Death of A Salesman, An Evening with Patti LuPone & Mandy Patinkin, The Little Mermaid, Wicked, Fiddler on the Roof, The Phantom of the Opera, Enchanted April, The Full Monty, Grease*; Tours: *Mandy Patinkin: Dress Casual* and Diaries, *John Lithgow's Stories By Heart, Billy Crystal's 700 Sundays, Les Miserables*. Other: *Radio City Christmas Spectacular, Blue Man Group at the Hollywood Bowl, Lord of the Rings Symphony Concerts*. Matthew has stage managed for numerous corporate events both online and onsite around the world. Corporate clients include the tech, auto, pharma, and financial industries, as well as with many non-profit companies. Matthew is an alumnus of UC San Diego, part of the faculty at SUNY Purchase, and serves on the Board of Directors of the Stage Managers' Association USA. For more info about Matt, his blog, or the Symposium visit www.broadwaysymposiuim.com

What's New in Edition Two

When putting together the second edition of *Stage Management Basics,* we really wanted to make the examples and figures more easily accessible so one of the biggest changes we implemented was to put all of the examples within the text itself, eliminating the appendices. We also felt strongly that there needed to be some reorganization and renaming of the chapter structure to allow the book to more precisely follow the typical production process from start to end. While we recognize that when a textbook is reorganized, it creates a bit more work for the faculty and teachers to rework and update their past coursework, we feel this reorganization will better facilitate teaching from the text and flow more smoothly through the process.

The 2nd edition also goes a bit more in depth noting differences between academic theatre practices and professional practices. The newly updated figures are directly from works we have stage managed with some necessary information scrubbing for privacy and copyright purposes. We rebranded those examples with the SMB logo for consistency.

- New chapters: 4 – The Stage Management Team, 13 – Unions, 14 – Opera, 15 – Dance.
- Updated color figures and examples throughout the book.
- Updated and revised content of the 1st edition chapters.
- Updated terminology and position titles to reflect more current trends.
- Updated resources on the companion website.
- Renamed Chapter 1 to better encapsulate the content and added additional traits.
- Added a more detailed discussion on communication.

Introduction

As a theatrical educator in both small and large academic institutions I believe that one of the most neglected fields of instruction is stage management. Good stage management is pivotal to a successful production process. Many programs produce stage managers, but not all of them truly train stage managers. In academia, it is often assumed that student stage managers know what is needed and expected of them from day one of the process. We expect them to execute and complete tasks with little to no training, guidance, or mentorship. This text has been created to help fill in the gaps for programs where a specific stage management track or emphasis does not exist or for anyone who wishes to get a good grasp of the basics.

The purpose of this book is to help beginning, young, and less experienced stage managers grasp the tasks that will be expected of them as the stage manager of a production. So often experienced theatrical practitioners forget that terms and processes that are second nature to them are not as clear and intuitive to the students that are often thrown into these positions. When laying out this book, we tried to go back to the basic building blocks, and explain everything as if this is your first time ever working in a theatre. This step-by-step approach will build a strong foundation for you to work from with a solid basis in terminology and processes. This book is not meant to focus specifically on either the professional or academic worlds, but to give a generic overview of the field, and should serve as guidelines and a starting place for inexperienced stage managers.

It is important to note that there are already many different textbooks in existence for the field of stage management. No single text will have the same information and method for accomplishing common tasks, because there isn't always a "right" way to do something, only what works best for that moment in time. There are many different types of theatres with many different artistic structures, all of which function differently. That said, this book is one view compiled from three different professionals who have worked in different theatres, positions, and environments, each with different training and experiences. We have pooled our knowledge to create a starting point for you to get your feet and maybe your knees wet, but not drown. The methods in this book are not the only correct methods, and everything in the theatrical environment needs to be flexible to a point. However, standardization is also important, so use your best judgment as you begin to grow as a stage manager to decide when to bend and change the "rules." The words "typically" and

DOI: 10.4324/9781003133049-1

"usually" are used a lot in this text because we are talking about best practices and our personal past experiences. Always remain open to trying and learning new things during what is hopefully an extremely collaborative process.

Stage management is not only a job, but also a state of mind. It's not for everyone. It requires dedication, passion, patience, a little neuroticism, and a whole lot of love for what you do.

Chapter One
Traits of a Stage Manager

The individual responsibilities of the stage manager vary from company to company, but at its core, you are creating art with a group of people that you will be spending large quantities of time with.

Being a good stage manager requires many skills. Organization and communication are often the most discussed facets of the job, however, maintaining paperwork and coordinating personnel are just a small portion of a stage manager's skill set. A large aspect of stage management is the personal interaction between the stage manager and all the other people involved in the **production** process. A stage manager is one of the few individuals with whom all members of the company interact and, as such, becomes a coach, a peacekeeper, and a collaborator.

These skills, like any other aspect of stage management, are acquired. With experience, you will improve and begin to learn how to read the people you work with and to better anticipate challenges and possible solutions. Some skills will come easier for you than others and some you will need to continue to improve upon throughout your career. Never be afraid to reach out to a friend or mentor if you need advice or are having trouble developing a skill.

Organization

Organization is one of the most obvious and easily identifiable traits necessary in a stage manager. When done well, it leads to an overall smoother and more efficient process. Organization is much more than just keeping paperwork up-to-date or coordinating schedules. As the stage manager, you will be coordinating crew assignments, scheduling meetings and rehearsals for the production team and cast, respectively, and many times helping to keep the rehearsal room on schedule and on track. Everyone organizes in different ways; figure out what works best for you. Keeping detailed lists, writing everything in a notebook or planner, or using an app are all good ways to help keep yourself organized.

DOI: 10.4324/9781003133049-2

Attention to Detail

Attention to detail is critical in making sure every element of the show is addressed properly and that the integrity of the show is maintained once it has opened. The stage manager must notice when a piece of furniture is off its **spike** (not in its correct position), if a light **cue** is incorrect, or if a performer is a few seconds late for an entrance, as it may affect the entire performance. In rehearsal, attention to detail allows you to assist the director with continuity and helps with tracking **props**, **costumes**, **scenery**, and performer entrances to create the show paperwork. Be aware of what is going on around you; notice when a shift is consistently late or problematic, and pay attention to when a cast member struggles with a section of text or **blocking**.

Attention to detail is not only about physical things. Being aware of the subtle shifts and changes of the company's mood and vibe will allow you to gauge tempers and notice when someone is "off" that day so you can reach out to check on them. This allows you to address needs before they become problematic, and keep the company and production running smoothly.

Timeliness

There is an old quote from *Letterman's Law of Private International Business, Volume 1*, which says "five minutes early is on time." In theatre, this is translated into the idea that "early is on time, on time is late, and late is unacceptable." One role of the stage manager is to be the timekeeper in rehearsal and production. You will be responsible for keeping track of the rehearsal time to ensure breaks happen at appropriate intervals and tracking runtimes to ensure the pace is consistent. It is important that stage managers themselves are timely. You set the expectation and behavior that is modeled for the rest of the cast and production team. If breaks routinely run long or rehearsals start late because you are not ready to start on time, it will set a bad precedent for the production. Make sure that you arrive with enough time to go through your entire preset and prep, and have a moment to breathe before rehearsal begins.

Efficiency

Combining organization, attention to detail, and timeliness will help you to work efficiently. The stage manager will always have many tasks on their to-do list and dawdling will extend your day unnecessarily. Planning when and how you will accomplish tasks, and learning to fit smaller tasks in between larger chunks of work will help you manage your time. Efficiency is important in many aspects of a stage manager's work, from completing reports and editing meeting minutes in a timely fashion to creating rehearsal **calls** and well-choreographed scene changes. Keeping lists and creating templates are both great tools to help you work more efficiently; we will talk about both later on.

Communication

The stage manager is the hub of communication during the entire production process. Many, if not all, show-related emails should include the stage manager so everyone is in the loop. Always ask to be included on email chains for side meetings and conversations if you can't attend in person. Having information is one of the things that allows you to be most effective at your job so you can communicate that information out to the necessary parties. Many people are not great note takers so having a stage manager present will ensure better communication of meeting content and ideas for the entire team.

As technologies change, best practices for communication also evolve. Knowing when to send an email versus text versus call is something you will get the feel for with practice and time. Knowing who will read an entire email from beginning to end or just the first sentence lets you know how and where to communicate necessary information to those people. There is such a thing as over communication, but err on the side of a bit too much rather than not enough.

Compassion

Along with administrative duties, the stage manager also steps into the role of psychologist, mediator, and confidant. Creating in collaboration with other people can be a very vulnerable undertaking. For this reason, compassion is a crucial part of a successful collaboration process. It is important to remember that respect is a large part of compassion; people need to know that they are safe and will not be judged. That said, your primary responsibility is to keep the production moving smoothly and this is more important than being friends with your cast and crew. Be compassionate but don't let people walk all over you.

Confidence

In order to gain the trust of the rest of the company members, stage managers must conduct their work with confidence. Maintaining the artistic choices of the production, the safety of the personnel, and the execution of many, specific, and detailed tasks are the stage manager's responsibility. Confidence in one's own work inspires confidence and trust from those working with you. This does not mean, however, that you need to have all the answers or do everything correctly the first time. As with everything in life, stage management is a continuous learning process and mistakes happen. However, uncertainty, doubt, and the inability to stick to your guns will only hinder your ability to connect with the company members in the ways necessary to facilitate a successful production. Any uncertainty regarding your job should be addressed on a one-on-one basis as much as possible, be it with the stage management team, the producer, the director, or a mentor unassociated with the production. It is fine to not have all the answers, and it is okay to ask questions, but it is better in the moment to make an informed decision, even if it turns out to be the wrong decision later. A lack of confidence can be viewed as a weakness and may severely limit the stage manager's ability to run the room. If you do make the wrong decision, it is important to admit you were wrong; owning your mistakes is a sign of maturity and will help you earn the respect of your company. Once you've gained confidence in the field, find a balance; don't become cocky and overconfident. Arrogance is not a strong leadership skill.

Assertiveness

The stage manager is the company's steadfast leader from the first rehearsal to the closing performance and the company needs to be able to trust you as such. The ability to show strong leadership is crucial, in everything from running meetings to maintaining focus in rehearsals to managing and running a successful performance night after night. Learn to find the balance between serious and fun, between compassion and discipline. Remember that being a tyrannical dictator is not the way to gain respect.

Assertiveness can be very light handed; conveying information in a structured, calm, and organized matter is just as assertive as barking commands. It is also imperative that the stage manager is willing to speak up on behalf of the cast or in questions of safety.

Poise

Whether in the stress of final dress when half the costumes are incomplete and the lead performer has yet to learn their **lines** correctly, or in rehearsal when a prop accidentally breaks while four people are asking you questions and you are trying to track down a missing performer, it is critical to have the ability to address issues calmly and rationally, without allowing strong emotions to take over. This ability will help you gain the trust of your company. The stage manager's role is, among other things, to provide stability and be a voice of reason in the company. If they see this waver or fall apart, it can quickly cause panic within the company. When first starting out, your inner composure may waiver, but try not to let that affect your outer composure. If, for some reason, you do lose your temper, recover it as quickly as you can; don't let it color the rest of the process. A lot can be gained by apologizing, publicly if necessary.

Adaptability

Many stage managers are control freaks, and often it is a helpful trait. However, the desire to control all of the details must be tempered with the ability to adapt. It is easy in the midst of a long tech week to get frustrated that the team fell short of the day's goal but a good stage manager will put aside that frustration and help re-evaluate the goals for the next day; a great stage manager will do it with humor and a smile. Shows are living, breathing creatures; things will inevitably change. You never know what is going to change but being able to assimilate the information and keep moving is critical. Having a good attention to detail will help you to anticipate changes and roll with them. This trait also shows itself in the stage manager's ability to work in different venues and with different companies – adapting to the different needs, styles, and personalities of your director, creative team, and cast will allow you to be in control of any situation and to become more marketable in the industry.

Neutrality

One of the more difficult qualities of being a good stage manager is the ability to remain neutral in any given situation and to hold your tongue. This can be especially difficult for those who come from a directorial, acting, or design background, who are used to making design/acting decisions. The stage manager's primary role is to support and facilitate the needs of the production, not to provide creative input. There are occasions when you will be asked for your input regarding a decision or your opinion about an artistic choice and, at that time, you can feel free to offer feedback. However, especially with directors, this is often a trust that is gained after a few instances of working together. You need to ensure that you have that kind of relationship before offering unsolicited input. Remember that any time you are asked your opinion regarding a design choice, an acting choice, or a directing choice, your response will be a judgment on someone's art. Don't be afraid to answer honestly, but take care in your approach and word choice. They can hurt! In matters of safety, it is important to speak up immediately, but do so diplomatically.

Performers may approach the stage manager when they are having issues with their fellow performers, the designers, or the director. Anticipate becoming the shoulder for them to cry on, someone to vent to, and a confidant of any personal troubles that may interfere with their work or the production. In all of this, you should be a source of comfort and confidentiality but remain neutral. It should be your goal to help them through an issue by listening and finding a compromise or a civil solution. Never gossip about fellow company members or encourage exclusion.

Diplomacy

Being able to diffuse a situation with confidence and tact is the hallmark of any great diplomat. As productions move through the process, tempers will inevitably flare, and you will need to be Switzerland to both parties. Stage managers need to know how to talk to, interact with, and collaborate with each member of the team. There will always be a mix of personalities and it is essential to know who you can joke with, who prefers extra formality, or who needs to be handled with care.

Discretion

Stage managers are often privy to lots of information that isn't necessarily meant for the general population. It is of the utmost importance that the company knows that the stage management team can be approached about anything and they will deal with it respectfully, quietly, and professionally. It is important to have a trusted person not related to the production or company with whom you can discuss ideas or challenges. Trust is hard won and easily lost; remember, discretion is the better part of valor.

A Sense of Humor

Theatre is very serious business … to those in the business of theatre. Plays can (and often do) expose the rawest of human emotions and so producing theatre can be an incredibly stressful process. A stage manager with a good sense of humor (and timing) helps to break the tension and remind everyone that they are doing this because it is fun. You are the voice of authority and will often have to be strict and unrelenting, but that doesn't mean you can't laugh along with the performers' jokes or throw out a teasing comment to the lighting designer during tech. There is a time and a place for humor; be aware of your situation, and remember that offensive humor is never okay.

Understanding Personality

Knowing who you are and how you will respond to a situation will go a long way to helping you succeed in the world of theatre. Finding and taking a personality test can be a starting point for learning more about yourself. The Myers Briggs Type Indicator® is perhaps the most widely known, but the results from any test will provide insights into your personality. Take these tests' results with a grain of salt but utilize the information you get from them. Are you introverted or extroverted, do you think more or feel more, how conscientious and agreeable are you? How much grit[1] and perseverance do you have? Employ this knowledge in the task of learning how you interact with different people and various scenarios. Take some time to consider the other personality types; you will run across a variety of them in your work and recognizing and understanding their traits may help you collaborate more efficiently.

Self-Care

Throughout any production process it is important to remember to take time for yourself. Relax a bit, take a breath. You can't work in theatre for long if you don't take care of your spirit, mind, and body. Tech week can be a long and grueling process, you must take care of yourself. Remember to eat (preferably something healthy, or at least semi-healthy); food is fuel, if you put crappy fuel in your car, it breaks down and your body is no different. Remember to sleep; there is so much to get done, mountains of paperwork, and long rehearsals, but you will be less efficient, tired, and run down if you are constantly sleep deprived. All of the traits discussed above suffer when you become tired or stressed or hungry, so take a moment or two to step out of the building and get some fresh air away from other people to rejuvenate yourself. Remember that, after all, what we do is rarely life or death, it is art, meant to be appreciated and enjoyed.

Personal Fulfillment in Your Work

Stage management is not a glamorous job, in any sense of the word. You will work an extraordinary number of hours, produce endless pages of paperwork and reports that people won't read, and put your heart and soul into a production with rarely a "thank you" uttered. You will be asked and required to handle situations you have never encountered and for which you haven't prepared. But, you will get to work with some of the greatest, kindest, most talented, and most generous people in the world. Satisfaction comes from the ability to guide a production from start to finish, with no injuries, from some text on paper to a full-fledged production. Do not expect applause or praise; if you are doing the job well, it is likely no one will notice it happening.

Stage management is finding the delicate balance of being organized, adaptable, neutral, confident, assertive, and diplomatic, with poise, discretion, compassion, and attention to detail, all while having a sense of humor, keeping people on schedule, and being on time.

Note

1. *Grit: The Power of Passion and Perseverance* Book by Angela Duckworth.

Chapter Two
The Theatre

Before diving into the nuts and bolts of stage management, it is important to have a basic understanding of some different types of theatre configurations as well as important rooms and features that you may run across. Additionally, this chapter offers thoughts about what to look for when first touring these spaces for a production.

Where to put it?
what to consider?

Theatre Configurations

Theatres come in a variety of shapes, sizes, configurations, layouts, and locations. Some of the most common configurations are **Proscenium**, **Thrust**, and **Arena**. There are also flexible spaces, called **blackbox** theatres, that allow for a variety of different configurations. Theatres may be found in buildings built expressly for the purpose of live theatre, or buildings that have been modified to be theatres. Theatre may also be **site-specific** or outdoors. Each configuration has its own advantages, challenges, and unique features (Figures 2.1–2.3).

Proscenium

Proscenium style theatres can be traced back to Ancient Greek theatre architecture. A **proscenium arch** is the primary defining feature and the configuration's namesake. Proscenium theatres have audience seating on one side of the action, with the arch creating a frame through which the action is viewed straight-on. This layout allows for large scenic elements, big dance numbers and lots of locations for entrances and exits. The area downstage of the proscenium is referred to as the **Apron**. A head-on configuration that does not have a proscenium arch is sometimes called **Endstage.** — *Trans Recital Hall*

main stage

Thrust

A thrust stage typically has audience seating on either two or three sides of the stage with a playing space "thrust" out into the audience. Thrust style theatres tend to have smaller scenic elements because the audience needs to be able to see across the stage and large elements would obstruct the audience's view from either side. Some thrust theatres are converted proscenium theatres, and still have the arch and a lot of the upstage space that

DOI: 10.4324/9781003133049-3

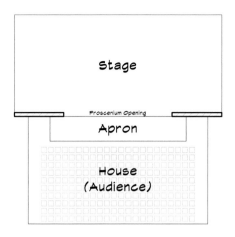

Figure 2.1 Proscenium Theatre

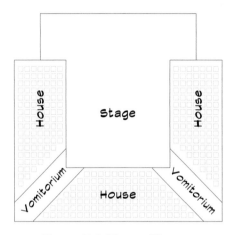

Figure 2.2 Thrust Theatre

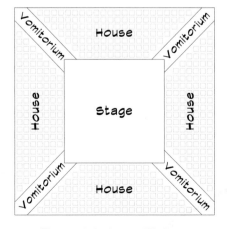

Figure 2.3 Arena Theatre

can be employed for larger scenic elements, entrances and exits, as well as storage. In the thrust environment, there may be entrances through the audience called **vomitoriums** (voms for short). Many thrust theatres allow for a more intimate playgoing experience, due to the proximity of the actors to the audience.

Arena

In arena style theatres (also called "theatre in the round"), the audience surrounds the entire stage. There is no "**upstage**" and "**downstage**" but rather the action takes place in 360 degrees. Arena configurations typically have minimal scenic elements so as not to obstruct the audience's view.

Blackbox

A blackbox theatre is typically a square or rectangular room painted completely black (hence the name). Blackboxes are designed to be "flexible" spaces, which can be set up in multiple configurations (e.g., thrust, arena). Many blackbox theatres are small and allow for a more intimate setting. Depending on the configuration, they can have a wide variety of scenic elements and, due to their flexible nature, tend to have quirks when it comes to entrances and exits, storage of scenic elements, dressing room access, and audience access.

Site-Specific or Environmental

Site-specific or environmental theatre is performed "on-location" in a venue that fits the style and vision of the production (e.g., a **play** that is set in a bar actually happening in the local bar). Site-specific theatre has its own complexities, and each site will bring new and different challenges. Site-specific locations rarely have the amenities expected in a traditional theatre (dressing rooms, private restrooms, **green rooms**, theatrical equipment of any kind) so it is important to take note of the needs of the production and discuss with the production team how those needs can be met within the desired location. A site visit should be planned early in the process.

Outdoor Theatre

Outdoor theatres offer just as much variety as indoor theatres and can range from large permanent structures to small temporary structures in any of the above configurations. Outdoor theatre comes with a unique set of challenges including weather, access to water and power, scenic and prop storage, ambient sound, and wildlife.

Stage Directions

In order to communicate effectively with the performers and the production team, everyone must be using the same vocabulary. In the theatre, we use **stage directions** to talk about where things happen on stage and which direction someone is moving. Stage directions

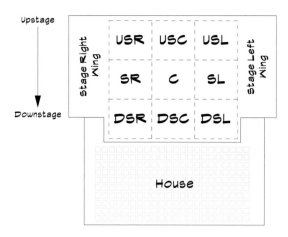

Figure 2.4 Basic Stage Directions

take a bit of getting used to at first, but after a few productions become second nature. The most important thing to remember about American stage directions is that they are always based on the performer's point of view looking toward the audience. Looking out toward the audience, the performer's left becomes stage left, their right, stage right. Stage right and stage left don't change when a performer faces away from the audience. When a performer moves away from the audience, that is called moving upstage and when they move closer to the audience, it is called moving downstage. This comes from the fact that, historically, theatres had **raked stages** with the higher section farthest from the audience, meaning performers literally walked uphill and down when travelling along this plane. Based on the configuration of the theatre and the size of the space, these directions can be further divided into downstage right, midstage right, upstage right, etc. (Figure 2.4). When working in-the-round (arena) sometimes it is helpful to designate a "downstage" to help facilitate consistency and understanding of where the performers and scenery are in a space. Using clock designations (or cardinal directions) also work well, with 6 o' clock (or south) being downstage and 12 o' clock (or north) being upstage and so on. Determine this early in the process with your director and then be sure to communicate it to everyone involved on the show to minimize miscommunication. These stage directions are different from descriptive stage directions within the **script**, which are addressed later (p. 48).

Tour of the Theatre

Early in the process, request a tour of the theatre and any other relevant spaces such as offsite rehearsal rooms, office space, and storage. The tour will provide a great deal of information, so it is in your best interest to take notes. Some questions you may want to ask or make sure are addressed on your tour include:

- What are the venue-specific emergency procedures and policies?
- What are the parking policies? Are there specific lots/spots reserved for patrons only?
  - Does this apply during rehearsal and performances or only performances?
- Is there Wi-Fi available? What are the network name (SSID) and password?

- Where is the rehearsal space?
- Is there a physical **callboard** or a common location for posting information? If so, where? If not, how does the stage manager communicate with the company? Is there somewhere one could be added or created?
- Is there an office or area that stage management can use for paperwork?
  - Also, determine if there is a printer and a copier on site that you will be able to use and if it is capable of color printing.
- What is the protocol for locking and unlocking the theatre? Who is responsible for these duties? If it is the stage manager:
  - Which doors need to be locked, which lights need to be double-checked, etc.?
  - If there are security personnel responsible for the building, gather their contact information.
- Where is the stage manager typically stationed to call the show? Is there a **booth** or back of house calling position or does the stage manager call from backstage?
  - If the stage manager calls from backstage, what systems are in place to see the stage and make calls (video monitors, audio monitors, etc.)?
  - How do you communicate backstage with the assistant stage manager and crew? Is there a headset system setup available? If not, how have past users of the space solved this issue?
- Are there **monitors** (audio and/or video feed from the stage) backstage or in the green room and dressing rooms?
- Does a **cue light** system exist? If so, how does it work?
- Where are the controls for the **work lights** and the **house lights**? How are they operated?
- What is the path from the dressing rooms to the stage? In some theatres, they may be on different floors, and, in site-specific theatre, possibly a different building.
- Locate **crossovers** (paths that performers can take backstage to get from stage right to stage left without being seen by the audience) and other possible performer paths. In some rare cases, this might be outside, which presents another set of challenges to work through.
- Where are the HVAC (Heat/AC) controls located? Who is responsible for making adjustments – stage management or the venue? What is the protocol for adjusting the HVAC? If someone from the venue is responsible, be sure to obtain their contact information.
- Are there any phones, alarms, or other things that make noise (e.g., shop air compressors, central air systems) that need to be turned off or disabled during performances?
- Are any of the spaces shared? Any spaces that are off limits? How will this affect the rehearsal and production process? Are there "quiet" hours? (Outdoor theatre especially may have noise restrictions)
- What is the policy for theatrical smoke and haze? Who needs to be notified if it is being used?
- What is the policy for smoking or open flame onstage? Does this need specific approval from anyone? What is the venue's policy regarding fire proofing?
- What is the policy for the use of weapons onstage? Is there somewhere to lock the weapons away securely?

- What is the policy on food and drinks in the rehearsal space, **house,** dressing rooms, and green room?
- Does the theatre have its own house manager and front of house staff? If so, gather the relevant contact information and meet them in person, if possible.
- Is there a secure place to lock up valuables?

This is not an exhaustive list of questions but it is certainly a good place to start.

Important Rooms and Features

The Stage (Performance Space)

This will be the main playing space for the show, also commonly referred to as "the **deck.**" As the stage manager, take the time to become as familiar with it as possible. Every space has its quirks, some of those will become apparent early in the process, others will only show themselves at very specific times and within very specific circumstances. Good things to start noticing:

- How best to keep the stage clean (mopping and sweeping patterns to get the most dust, where to vacuum, etc.)
- The best backstage spots to set props
- Entrances, exits, and performer pathways
- Audience sightlines to backstage
- Where the floor squeaks badly or is uneven
- Which doors squeak or slam or might accidentally lock
- Anything else that may help, impede, or otherwise impact the production

The more you know, the better the production can be shaped to fit in the space.

The House

The portion of the theatre that contains the seating area is referred to as the house. It is good to be familiar with the seating layout. If entrances and exits are being made through the house, it is particularly important to note any obstacles in the aisles and to figure out the paths from backstage to the house.

Front of House (FOH)

Front of house refers to all the areas of the theatre that are accessible to the **patrons** (lobby, box office, concession stand, etc.) and the personnel who attend to these areas.

Scene Shop

Depending on the layout and size of the theatre, the **scene shop** may be an important part of the rehearsal or production process; it could act as a rehearsal space during the rehearsal period or storage and a pass-through during production or you may never go near it. Determine the needs and usage of the shop space for the production (if any) and plan for time and staff to clean, clear, and maintain the scene shop as needed. In some cases, the scene shop is off-site and transporting the scenery to the theatre for **load-in** will have to be coordinated to accommodate the needs of the production team as well as any rehearsals scheduled in the space. All of this usually falls to the technical director or the production manager, but is good to be aware of for production logistics.

Costume Shop

The **costume shop** may or may not be an integral part of the production process. It may act as a dressing room or wardrobe space. Laundry facilities and supplies that will be used to perform costume maintenance during the run of a performance are typically housed in the costume shop. If the costume shop is used as a dressing room, determine what steps must be taken to keep the shop in working order when not in performance. Costume **fittings** may also be held in the costume shop, in which case be able to succinctly direct performers to its location.

Dressing Rooms

The dressing rooms should be kept neat and orderly throughout the entire production process. While it is the performer's personal space, it still needs to be kept clean and usable. Typically, (depending on the theatre's policies) no food or drinks are allowed in dressing rooms or anywhere near costumes (water in a sealed container is usually acceptable). Make sure to locate any monitors and monitor volume controls.

> Many modern dressing rooms have a separate switch that enables/disables the wall outlets by the makeup mirrors. Knowing where this switch is located will save you and your crew a headache when it accidentally gets flipped leaving the performers without power.

Green Room

The title may well be a misnomer (they aren't all green) but this is a good space to be aware of. It is an area, often located either near the dressing rooms or near the stage (sometimes both), in which the company can loiter when they aren't busy. Often they will have tables, chairs, and/or couches. Sometimes they have appliances like sinks, microwaves, and refrigerators for company use.

Booth (Control Room)

This is the room or place in the theatre where the lighting control console (light board) and sometimes the sound mixing console (sound board) are located. In many theatres, the booth is where the stage manager will be stationed during shows to call **cues** and oversee the performance. This area may also house the theatrical systems for the theatre (dimmer racks, amplifier racks, control computers, etc.). The booth is often one of the most secure areas of the theatre because of the amount of equipment it contains. Determine who has access to this room/area and how it is secured. Make sure you walk the route to and from the booth a few times to familiarize yourself with how to get there. In many theatres it is a very circuitous route, sometimes access is on a different floor or down an access corridor.

In venues where the stage manager calls from backstage, there will be a podium or station backstage, sometimes referred to as the calling desk (or prompt corner in the UK). This often includes a video and audio monitor, as audio and video are necessary to allow the stage manager to see and hear the cue lines. It may also include a cue-light system, if one is installed in the theatre.

Live Audio Mixing Position

In venues that utilize microphones for audio reinforcement, there is typically a location in the house where the sound mixing console is located. The location in the house will vary from venue to venue, but its proximity to the audience allows the person mixing audio to hear what the show sounds like from the audience's perspective, which generates a better sounding production. Depending on the venue, this may also be where the sound playback (effects/cues) will be triggered.

The Callboard

The callboard is where the company goes for important information regarding the production. It is often a corkboard or similar bulletin board and is placed in a centralized location easily accessible in the theatre. Common places are in the green room or right inside the stage door. The callboard should include a daily **sign-in sheet**, the rehearsal calendar, the daily/weekly rehearsal schedule, and important notifications or announcements. It should not have the **contact sheet** or other confidential information. In union productions, this will also include some paperwork required by the **Actors' Equity Association (AEA)**. Keep the information on this callboard up to date and consistent with any information distributed electronically or verbally. Performers can be forgetful and this gives them a place to check for correct information without having to contact you for that information. If a board doesn't already exist, scout out the best place for one and plan extra time and materials to make one before rehearsals start. When you load-into the theatre, the callboard should either travel with you or the information should be transferred to a board at the theatre. Some theatres are making the move to virtual callboards, but the premise is the same.

Rehearsal Space

In many cases, the performance space may not be available to use until tech week, so rehearsals will take place in a secondary location. Just as with the theatre, you will be responsible for preparing and maintaining this space.

If the rehearsal space is rented or used by multiple productions or classes, check with the staff or renter to determine the appropriate use of the space, as well as how the space needs to be left at the end of each rehearsal. Follow these rules carefully and maintain a strong and positive relationship with the owners and fellow users of the space. Doing so is not only courteous, but will also increase the likelihood of being invited back for future productions and being granted some favors (such as storage space for props, ability to leave tape on the floor, use of in-house props/furniture, etc.). Remember to treat rented spaces just like you would treat your own personal space (or better); many of these rentals have security deposits just like apartments and even small things may cost the company money.

If the rehearsal space is located off-site, it is important to set up a tour to see that location as well. Make sure to ask similar questions about access, parking, venue hours, etc. If you are regularly transitioning between locations, make sure to take travel times and traffic into account (for yourself and all traveling parties) and plan accordingly.

Once rehearsals are moved to the performance space, be sure to leave the rehearsal space in a clean, usable condition for the next production. This includes removing ("pulling") **spike tape**, sweeping and mopping, emptying trash, etc.

> **!** Remember, pulling up spike tape can pull up the floor finish underneath, so always test to make sure the tape will not damage the floor before putting it down.

Prop and Costume Storage

Most theatres have a storage area or facilities where their stocks of costumes, furniture, and **hand props** are stored. This is where **rehearsal props**, costumes, and furniture can be pulled. It is important to ascertain whose responsibility pulling items will be and the proper procedure to get access and check things out as required by the theatre staff. Often stage managers pull rehearsal props and furniture, but costume pieces are pulled by designers or staff. In many cases, storage facilities are off-site and arrangements for access and/or transportation of items may need to be made. Plan accordingly for this.

Keys

Typically, stage managers will be assigned a ring of keys or a key card to allow access to all necessary spaces. Determine whose responsibility it will be to lock up and what needs to be done to shut down after rehearsal (turn lights off, lock access doors, set out **ghost light**, shut down light and sound systems, etc.). In many places, it will be the stage manager's responsibility to make sure that all spaces are closed and locked once the last person leaves the building. Security is high priority, so keep careful track of keys and be diligent about checking all doors when locking up for the night (don't just visually confirm a closed door, make sure it is actually locked). The stage manager is often the first production staff member in and the last one out. If the building has security staff, it is important to meet them and introduce yourself, since you will often be there early and late. Occasionally (for instance when the venue is rented), the stage manager will not be issued keys. In these cases, the venue's house manager or security personnel is typically responsible for unlocking and locking the building. If this is the case, introduce yourself to these individuals and be sure to have their contact information. Keep them informed of the schedule and confirm what time you need the venue to be unlocked each day.

Cleaning Supplies

Basic upkeep of the space may also fall under the stage manager's purview in many theatres. This primarily includes sweeping and mopping the rehearsal/performance space, as well as keeping the theatre neat during the rehearsal and performance period. As such, be sure to locate brooms, dustpans, mops, vacuums, trash-cans, and utility sinks. Find out the location and accessibility of dumpsters. If renting a space, determine whether the theatre company or the venue will be responsible for providing supplies such as trash bags, bathroom items (soap, paper products), etc.

Chapter Three
The People

It takes a tremendous number of people to create a theatrical production. Understanding who they are and what they do is paramount to being a successful stage manager. As you meet the people you will be working with, take the time to ask questions, find out how things have been done in the past, and any expectations for the future or new paths to explore.

Stage management entails interaction with and coordination of all of the positions that will be discussed in this chapter. In order to better connect with and understand each of these team members, we highly recommend trying your hand at or shadowing as many of them as you can. Take courses in directing and acting. Ask to attend a fittings session with the costume designer and wardrobe manager. Take a break from stage managing and ask instead to assist with lights or sound. Put on your work gear and spend a Saturday in the scene shop building scenery or painting. Shadow the choreographer or music director in a class or workshop. Many of these people will love to share their knowledge with you and will appreciate that you take an interest in their passion. More than that, it will give you invaluable insight into what their work is like, allow you to learn the terminology, and better equip you to coordinate schedules, anticipate issues between departments, and truly be the connecting fiber for the whole production team.

Theatre Staff

Every theatre is unique in how many and what type of staff they employ at any given time. Staff positions tend to be a combination of full-time and part-time depending on the size and scope of the theatre's season. In many theatres, multiple jobs may be rolled into a single staff position. A few common positions and duties are listed below. Remember that titles and duties vary from theatre to theatre. In Figure 3.1, we introduce several of the positions that a stage manager is most likely to interact with and the typical flow of communication.

While you will likely not interact heavily with them, most theatre companies have full-time staff in finance, development, marketing, education, patron services, and ticketing.

DOI: 10.4324/9781003133049-4

Rehearsal Communication Flow Chart

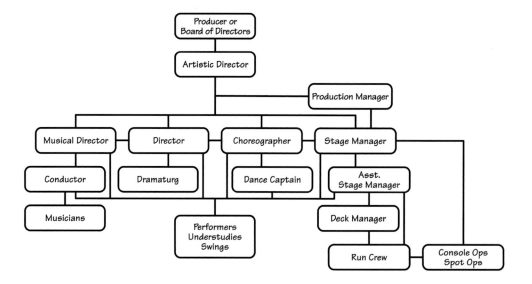

Production/Backstage Communication Flow Chart

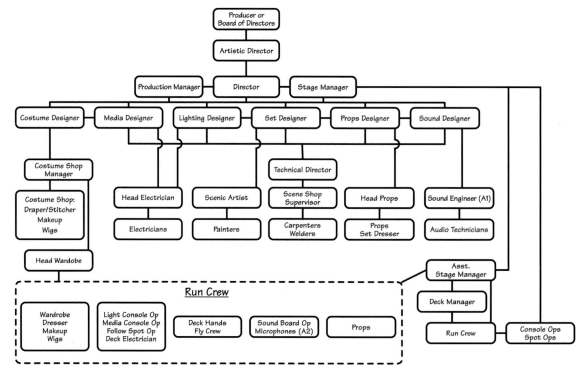

Figure 3.1 Diagram of Theatrical Relationships – this is not a comprehensive list, and may have some variation from theatre to theatre

Producer or Board of Directors

Producers manage the overall financial functions of a theatrical organization: they hire and fire, sign paychecks, and typically have final say over all decisions. Producers frequently also have a large hand in season selection and securing rights. Remember during all interactions with the producer that continued and future employment depends a lot on how you present yourself, how you handle the production process, and your overall attitude. In some organizational structures (especially Not-For Profit), instead of a single person acting as producer, there is a board of directors that fulfills the governing role of a producer. Most boards do not handle the specific day-to-day tasks like hiring and firing but entrust that instead to an artistic director. In academic environments, a department chair will typically fulfill some portion of this role.

Artistic Director (AD)

Artistic directors maintain the artistic vision of the theatre company's season and individual productions within the season. Often ADs direct or perform in productions, but when they are not directly involved, they will act as a resource for directors and the artistic staff. For companies that do not have a producer, the AD will typically fill many of the producer's roles like hiring and firing, season selection, signing paychecks, and obtaining rights.

Production Manager (PM)

Production managers are responsible for the implementation and realization of the creative team's artistic vision. The PM typically acts as the liaison between the designers and the director and will work hand in hand with the stage manager to ensure that the rehearsal process and production process flow smoothly. PMs are often responsible for managing budgets, personnel, and master production calendars for an entire season, which requires them to be knowledgeable and involved in every production a theatre produces. PMs will typically take on the hiring and firing responsibilities for technical and artistic staff. PMs are typically around during **technical rehearsals** (tech), but are not always physically in the theatre.

Technical Director (TD)

The technical director supervises and/or implements all technical aspects of a production. They also typically run the scene shop and all scenic construction in addition to scenic load-ins and **strikes**. If a PM is not present within the company, a TD may handle managing budgets, personnel, and production calendars, as well as act as the liaison between the stage manager and designers. TDs are typically present in all technical rehearsals and most **dress rehearsals** to troubleshoot any scenic/technical issues or answer any technical logistical questions.

Scene Shop Supervisor

Bigger theatres have a larger staff and there may be someone who is dedicated to supervising the day-to-day goings-on of the scene shop because the TD has other duties that prevent them from managing the shop. This person may be able to keep you informed on the progress of the build and pieces needed for rehearsal or be a conduit to communicate more easily with the shop. Always make sure you are aware of who has the authority to sign off on using a piece of **scenery**; just because the supervisor is fine with it doesn't mean the TD is.

Scenic Artist

Often larger theatres will have a separate paint department which will be headed by the scenic artist. This department is responsible for all paint treatment on the set, including floor treatment, scenic drops, etc. It is important to communicate with the scenic artist when determining things such as when spike marks will be transferred to the stage.

Costume Shop Supervisor/Manager

Costume shop supervisors/managers are the TDs of the costume shop. Shop managers run the day-to-day operations of the costume shop; building, pulling, altering, or renting costumes to realize the costume designer's vision. This position works closely with the stage manager to schedule fittings and provide rehearsal costume pieces (shoes, skirts, corsets, etc.). In an academic environment, shop managers may advise the wardrobe crew and sit in on the first few dress rehearsals to troubleshoot or take notes as needed.

House Manager

The house manager is the head of the front of house staff and is responsible for everything relating to the theatre patrons. For performances, stage management works in conjunction with the house manager to coordinate when to open and close the house, and to gather a house count (total number of people in the audience for a given performance; this is often different from the number of ticket sales) and any important information about the audience (injuries, latecomers, dogs, oxygen tanks, etc.).

The Production Team

Director

The director provides the artistic vision and acts as the guiding force of the team. They provide the inspiration and parameters within which the designers and performers create the world of the play. The director is the ultimate idea wrangler who creates a unified interpretation of the play. They are responsible for creating the **blocking** (movement patterns) for the performers. The stage manager works closely with the director throughout the rehearsal process. In technical and dress rehearsals, the director works with the cast and creative team to hone the production into the final work that will be presented to the audience.

Designers

Designers create the visual and aural world of the play. This process uses many different mediums, starting with visual and aural research, moving on to sketching, drawing, drafting, rendering, and models, finally culminating in a realized design that will be put on stage.

Scenic Designer

The scenic designer creates the visual world of the scenery (**set**), i.e., what the world surrounding the performers looks like (from an empty stage to the grand palace of the King of Siam). The scenic design heavily influences the blocking patterns of the production (where the furniture sits, where the doors and pathways are located, etc.). It is important to communicate with the designer throughout the rehearsal period as things are "discovered" in rehearsal and modifications may need to be made. Large scenic modifications cannot be made after the shop has begun the build process, so make sure the designer and director are communicating openly and clearly (this will make your life easier down the road). Small modifications such as furniture placement can happen throughout the process. The scenic designer is responsible for creating **groundplans**, **elevations**, **renderings**, and **models**. Always ensure you are working with the most current drawings in rehearsal. It will adversely affect the process if you are working off of out-of-date drawings.

Scenic designers will be in technical and dress rehearsals to take notes and clarify ideas and intentions of scenic flow. Some scenic designers may want to help choreograph scenic transitions or tweak furniture placement for a scene.

Costume Designer

The costume designer creates the visual world of the costumes, i.e., what each performer wears (clothing, jewelry, shoes, etc.). Just as with the scenic designer, what the costume designer chooses to dress the performers in will influence their movement around the stage. For example, if it is a **period piece**, the large skirts need to be taken into account in large group scenes. If a performer is in five-inch heels, they probably cannot run up stairs or perform really involved choreography. The costume designer can also play a vital role in helping the performers discover and embody their characters by putting them literally and emotionally "in the shoes" of their character.

The costume designer will be present for dress rehearsals to take notes on each actors' costumes' fit, flow, and usage. If there is a costume malfunction, they may help address it depending on the wardrobe crews' responsibilities.

Lighting Designer (LD)

The lighting designer lights the visual world created by the scenic and costume designers. They also add to and create parts of the visual world. LDs are sometimes more in the background of the design process at the start, as much of their work is dependent on the other designers. However, as productions become increasingly more full of glitz, glamour, media, LEDs, and spectacle, LDs may take a front row seat in the design process from the beginning. LDs are responsible for creating the **lightplot**, selecting **gel**/color and **gobos**, and creating a cue list notating placement of lighting cues. LDs will also collaborate with the team about the placement of fixtures on the deck or in the **wings**.

LDs will be present in technical and dress rehearsals. This will be some of their most active time. LDs will actively make level adjustments, set final looks, or run and rerun a section to solidify timing. LDs may work with a programmer who programs the show and operates the lighting console during technical rehearsals.

Sound Designer

The sound designer creates the aural world of the play (what the audience hears), whether that is the quiet ambience of a river in the distance, a distant thunderstorm that steadily grows closer throughout the production, or gunshots and car crashes. The sound designer finds, records, or creates the sound content and often acts as the programmer for the sound output computer. The sound designer is responsible for creating a sound cue list notating the placement of the sound cues. Sometimes the designer will also be responsible for creating and/or providing rehearsal sound cues.

The sound designer is present during technical and dress rehearsals to make adjustments to cues, take notes on necessary alterations or revisions, and help ensure the sound design is executed as intended.

Digital Media Designer

The digital media designer is responsible for creating and designing the content that will be seen on the projection and/or video surface(s). A relatively new field, digital media is quickly gaining traction as technology becomes more integrated in production. The digital media designer will furnish a cue list containing all called media cues.

The media designer will be present in technical and dress rehearsals. Often, media interacts with and affects sound and lights. The only time all three departments are together with all the technology fully implemented is tech so this is when the tweaking, editing, and adjusting happens for media.

Properties (Props) Manager/Designer

The props manager/designer creates, builds, buys, and/or finds hand props, furniture, and **set dressing** to round out the world being created by the production team. This position must coordinate closely with the other departments and designers to make sure that the props align with the cohesive vision of the production. It is important to communicate clearly and frequently with the props manager/designer – they need to know how things are being handled, what additions have been made since the original lists were created, and any other pertinent information (the chair needs to be strong enough to stand on, the hairbrush should be blue, etc.).

The props manager is typically available during technical and dress rehearsals, but not always in the building or room.

Music Director (MD)

Music directors work to teach and shape the music of a production. They are responsible for the singing and orchestral portions of a musical. This position helps make decisions about things such as cuts in a dance break or adding a few measures to a **vamp**. Sometimes the music director assists with the casting process, lending advice about vocal ability to help the director make final decisions. The MD will typically play piano for the rehearsals and give vocal/musical notes throughout the process. In some companies, the music director helps find and engage the **pit** musicians, and often are the orchestra conductor as well.

The music director is present in technical and dress rehearsals. This is the time when many parts of the productions are melded together and sometimes adjustments need to be made to the music. A costume piece or change may affect a singing moment or a transitional piece of music may need to be elongated to cover a scene shift. These things will either be addressed during the rehearsal or during the notes session.

Accompanist/Rehearsal Pianist

If the music director isn't playing during auditions or rehearsals, an accompanist or rehearsal pianist is used. It is important to take them into account when scheduling rehearsals and keep them in the loop about any scheduling changes or updates. Whenever possible, let them know what will be worked on each day as well. This is a nice gesture and will allow them to better prepare for rehearsal.

Choreographer

The choreographer creates the dances and movement patterns of the performers during musical numbers. Choreographers and directors work very closely during musicals. It is important that the design team understands the needs of the dance pieces (dancing on furniture, doing splits, etc.) so the costumes and set pieces can function as needed with the choreography. Depending on a director's skill set, the director may also act as the choreographer.

Choreographers are present during technical and dress rehearsals. They typically supervise **spacing rehearsals** of all musical numbers, making adjustments and alterations to the choreography as needed with the scenery, lights, costumes, sound, etc.

Fight Director

If the production includes any physical altercations (slaps, etc.), fights, or battle sequences (both armed and unarmed combat), a fight director should be hired to ensure the safety of all participants in the fight. The certifying organization for fight directors is The Society of American Fight Directors (SAFD). Depending on the extent of the fight(s), the fight director may only be present for a few rehearsals. Before leaving the production, they will assign a member of the cast to be the fight captain. It is extremely important to safely and properly choreograph any sort of physical violence to protect the performers from injury. Improperly choreographed violence can result in serious injury (even a slap).

Intimacy Director/Coordinator

If the production includes any physical, emotional, or implied intimacy, an intimacy director should be hired to coordinate and choreograph the intimate moments, as well as ensure the emotional and psychological well-being of all involved. They achieve this by implementing a system for choreographing such scenes in a way that is both specific and repeatable, that realizes the director's vision, but most importantly prioritizes the performers' safety and comfort while protecting the performers involved from harassment or harm. It is important to use a trained intimacy director; there are a number of organizations to choose from.

> **!** Fight, dance, and intimacy captains are members of the cast (or stage management) that are selected by the choreographer/director/coordinator of that specific area (fight, dance, intimacy) to maintain the safety of the performers and the integrity of the director's vision after the show has opened. Captains will lead fight/dance/intimacy calls before each performance to review all of the associated moments, and make any necessary safety or integrity adjustments.

Dramaturge

Dramaturges provide information about the script, time period, writer, and anything else relevant to the production. They may provide a glossary if there are a lot of unusual words or find articles that give context to any aspect of the play. Some dramaturges are heavily involved in the process and may be in the rehearsal room regularly, while others may only serve as a consultant for the director and will rarely be seen.

Associates and Assistants

Depending on the size of the production, there may be associates and assistants who are part of the process. Associates serve as the right hand to the director, choreographer, or designer they accompany; they typically are heavily involved in the process and can make executive decisions if the primary isn't present. Many associates take on tasks such as paperwork and logistics of the production, allowing the primary to focus on the artistic intricacies. If a show is a remounted production, a trusted associate may take on the entire process, freeing the primary to work on new projects. Assistants assist both the primary and associate. They interface with the team and staff a lot, run errands, and manage paperwork. Typically, they cannot make final decisions without the primary's approval. In academic environments, students fill the associate and assistant roles and their responsibilities may vary a bit.

Crew (Deck Crew/Fly Crew/Wardrobe Crew/Console and Spot Operators)

The crew work behind the scenes during tech week and for the run of the production to help create a seamless, smooth, and consistent show night after night.

The deck crew (also called "run crew") work backstage moving set pieces, setting props, facilitating costume changes, and anything else that must be done to make the production run smoothly. The assistant stage manager or the deck manager is responsible for leading this crew.

The fly crew is responsible for the operation of all **linesets** (**battens**). One of the harder and more precise jobs backstage, it requires crew members to move large, heavy pieces of scenery into place at a very specific time in order to avoid hitting cast and crew members maneuvering around during a scene change. Larger productions may have a large fly crew to allow for multiple lines to be moving at the same time. Theatre is the only industry in the world that allows people to pass under large, heavy objects while they are in motion. As such it is very important everyone knows their job, cue, route, and proper safety procedures to avoid any catastrophes.

Automation is the control of scenery and flies through mechanical methods and is becoming more prevalent as technology becomes more integrated into theatre. This technology has many specialized safety devices to ensure scenery can only move when it is safe to do so.

The wardrobe crew (sometimes called dressers) typically works in the dressing rooms rather than in the wings, except during **quick changes**. The wardrobe crew is responsible for helping with costume, hair, and makeup. They are also typically responsible for maintenance of the dressing rooms, as well as laundry. This crew works closely with the wardrobe supervisor.

Console operators run the lighting control console and the sound playback control console or device. Depending on the needs of the production, a live microphone mixer (sometimes referred to as the "Audio 1" or "A1" for short) may be hired to run mics. In some cases, the sound playback operator will be responsible for both playback and live sound. Depending on the theatre, they may be stationed in the house rather than the booth for acoustic purposes. If the production has a media design, sometimes a separate individual is hired to run this as well. These crew members work with the staff and/or designers to learn how to run the console, how to run system checks, and basic trouble-shooting techniques should anything go wrong.

Spot operators run the followspots. They work directly with the lighting designer or head electrician to learn their cues and spot techniques. Often, spot operators will take their own cues during performances.

The stage manager is responsible for calling all cues during the show. As such, they will be in direct contact with each of these operators: over headset, via cue light, or in the booth. Depending on the production, experience of the spotlight operators, and the complexity of the cues, the stage manager may call spot cues as well.

Communicating with the Production Team

Communication is a large part of what makes all theatrical productions successful. Ensuring clear, accurate, and concise communication with all members of the production team is extremely important. Be aware that what may seem to be a simple request or design change to one team member, may ruffle another's feathers. Because of this, careful phrasing of those questions or requests is important. Getting to know the different personalities quickly will save many headaches down the road.

Be mindful in all of your communications. Theatre is a very small, interconnected world, you may be working with the same people again in the future, or someone they have worked with before. Build a network of people, colleagues, and friends, don't burn bridges, words and actions travel fast in this community of artists. Networking is how to stay connected, move forward, and gain experiences and jobs.

Chapter Four
The Stage Management Team

The stage management team can take a variety of forms; it may be quite large or it could be just you. We will provide an overview of some of the different positions that could make up your team. We will also talk a little bit more about working as a team throughout the process.

Team Members

Production Stage Manager (PSM)

The production stage manager position may have a variety of responsibilities depending on the company. Often, they are the most experienced stage manager in a group of stage managers or they are the resident stage manager for a company that hires additional stage managers and assistant stage managers. In a situation where more than one show is in production at a time, the PSM is likely to oversee the teams assigned to each show and perhaps calling one of the smaller shows, or sometimes the most complex show. With a large enough team, the production stage manager will take turns with the stage manager calling the show so that the one not calling can watch and take notes to maintain the show. They may also have hiring/firing power within the stage management team. A PSM might be the primary stage manager on a show and then train someone to replace themselves as the calling stage manager so that the PSM can start rehearsing the next show in the season. As with the ASM (below), if there is no production stage manager, many elements of this role will fall to the stage manager.

Stage Manager

The stage manager is the team leader for a specific production. They are responsible for the completion of all of the tasks laid out throughout the rest of this book. If the stage manager is the only person on the team, they will be responsible for all stage management duties. If there are additional stage management personnel, duties will be divided based on the number of team members and specific needs of the production.

DOI: 10.4324/9781003133049-5

Assistant Stage Managers (ASM)

Assistant stage managers have distinctly different roles and responsibilities than the stage manager. The specifics will likely vary from theatre to theatre and even show to show, but they are most commonly responsible for everything on deck. During rehearsals, they are often in charge of prop and costume **tracking** and starting to plan for things such as costume changes and scenic transitions. They may also be **on book** or taking **line notes**. If there are multiple ASMs, those duties may be divided between them. During tech, dress, and performances, ASMs organize the backstage layout and run the deck. Depending on the company, assistants may be present through the entire process, once runs have started, or sometimes not until technical rehearsals start.

Production Assistant (PA)

This person often fills the more stereotypical role of an assistant. They may be responsible for tasks such as making copies or setting up and maintaining hospitality (coffee, water, etc.) for the rehearsal space. In other instances, they act as an additional ASM. In either case, they are an extra set of hands, eyes, and ears that make rehearsals run smoothly. Depending on the company, a PA may be a part of the entire process or they may leave the production at opening. On larger productions and in commercial theatre, a production assistant may instead assist the producer or a specific person affiliated with the production. They may be tasked with moving props across town or dealing with correspondence.

> **!** In the United Kingdom, titles and responsibilities are a little different from what is described in this chapter. Positions include the company stage manager, the deputy stage manager, the technical stage manager, and the stage manager, as well as ASMs. One key difference in job responsibilities is that the stage management team is responsible for creating/acquiring all of the props. UK stage managers are also not responsible for artistic maintenance of the show.

Working as a Team

It is important to remember that the entire stage management team is in fact a team in the truest sense of the word. Everyone has a role and differing responsibilities. Within this team, titles are often just a way to describe the job responsibilities and have little to do with actual hierarchical structure within the team. Each person will have areas of expertise and knowledge that are crucial to the production. Discover each other's strengths and lean into them. Though you are the leader, it is important to work together, trust each other, and build comradery to make it through the entire production process.

As a beginner stage manager, it is likely that you will do your first few projects as the solo stage manager on the production. After this, it can be difficult to work on a production with multiple team members as you will have gotten so used to handling the whole production alone. It can be hard to let go of control and trust others to handle tasks for you. Delegation is an important skill to learn; it will allow the team to be utilized to its fullest potential.

Common Division of Labor

Pre-Production

Most of the pre-production work will likely be done by the stage manager, although if ASMs or PAs are contracted, they may pitch in as well. The stage manager will handle tasks such as creating the rehearsal calendar and connecting with the production team, whereas ASMs will likely work on script and paperwork preparation. This is a great time and place to get to know your team's strengths and weaknesses, initiate discussions about work distribution (who is responsible for what, in rehearsal and during the show; e.g., prop tracking, line notes, blocking notes, sweeping, etc.), best practices/preferences, and any notes that should be shared from your meeting with the director. In the midst of all the preparatory work, be sure to engage with the team as people too, bonding as a group early will serve you later.

In Rehearsals

Typically, the stage manager will take blocking while the ASM(s) will track props, costumes, scenery, and performer entrances/exits. The ASM(s) will use this tracking information to create much of the paperwork needed for tech. ASMs will often take line notes and be on book, though working as a team for these tasks is helpful. Sometimes the stage manager will interact more with the director and the ASM will interact more with the cast – this isn't a set rule but it can be a helpful starting point. ASM(s) are also typically responsible for managing props and organizing/executing the scene changes during run throughs.

Tech and Beyond

During tech and performances, the stage manager is focused on calling cues and coordinating with the production team. The ASM will take over responsibility of the deck and be your link to the cast and crew.

Personnel Situations

Chapter Five

Safety

[handwritten annotation: Narcan / Evzio } for overdose / narcotic emergency, / in an emergency / situation.]

Safety is the most important factor in any production, no matter the size, scope, or scale, and should be the top priority for the stage manager. A stage manager needs to know all safety procedures/protocols for the space, as well as the location of all first-aid kits, fire extinguishers, emergency exits, naloxone, and automated external defibrillators (AED) as applicable. It is also important to know the emergency shelter locations of the venue. In most instances, the stage manager will be responsible (in coordination with the front of house staff) for implementing emergency procedures when the need arises. Make sure to review and familiarize yourself with those procedures early and ask questions to the appropriate parties if you have any; preparation is key. Remember, in this day and age, all decisions will eventually have to stand up to scrutiny and possible legal repercussions after the event is all said and done.

Occupational Safety and Health Administration (OSHA)

OSHA is a regulating body that sets and enforces safety standards. It is a part of the US Department of Labor and was established as part of the Occupational Safety and Health Act of 1970. Their mission is "to ensure safe and healthful working conditions for working men and women by setting and enforcing standards and by providing training, outreach, education and assistance.[1]" OSHA covers most private sector employers and their workers, but not state and local government workers (many public universities are part of the state government). Some states have State Plans which are OSHA approved, but operated by the individual states and cover state and local workers. State Plans must be as effective as OSHA requirements in protecting workers. www.osha.gov is a great resource to learn more about OSHA and to find out if the state you are working in has its own plan. If for any reason you have concern about your workspace, you can legally speak up and be protected from retaliation. OSHA also gives you the right to[2]:

- Be trained in a language you understand
- Work on machines that are safe
- Be provided required safety gear, such as gloves or a harness and lifeline for falls
- Be protected from toxic chemicals
- Request an OSHA inspection, and speak to the inspector

DOI: 10.4324/9781003133049-6

- Report an injury or illness, and get copies of your medical records
- See copies of the workplace injury and illness log
- Review records of work-related injuries and illnesses
- Get copies of test results done to find hazards in the workplace

It is important to remember that, as the stage manager, you are only responsible for the workspace(s) you are utilizing. You are not responsible for reporting safety concerns for other departments unless those concerns directly affect the health and safety of the stage management team or the performers within those spaces. OSHA is a resource and enforcement agency but make sure that you follow proper channels if there are issues or concerns. Report your concerns to the appropriate person or supervisor first (Production Stage Manager, Technical Director, Artistic Director, or Production Manager). If the concern is not adequately addressed and there is another level of supervisory structure (Producer, or Board of Directors), make sure to report your concerns to them before filing a report with OSHA.

Allergies and Sensitivities

People can have allergies or sensitivities to a wide range of substances and allergens. Each person will react differently and reactions can range from minor rashes to full-on anaphylactic shock. People may have a sensitivity to laundry detergents, cleaning products, food, airborne contaminants, medications, and many other things. Many theatres require that information to be disclosed on either audition paperwork or emergency medical paperwork. It is important to know what allergies and sensitivities people have, and have ready access to that information in case of an emergency. Be sure to notify appropriate staff members to avoid any of those items or substances. For example: if a performer is allergic to Febreze®, the costume shop and wardrobe crew need to be aware so as not to use it on or near their costume, or if someone has a severe peanut allergy it may be necessary to inform the company that a severe peanut allergy exists and not to bring any items into the rehearsal space or dressing rooms that may contain peanuts.

In the event of a medical emergency either related to the specific allergy/sensitivity or an unrelated emergency (serious injury, heart attack etc.), the stage manager should provide relevant information to the responding medical personnel concerning allergies and sensitivities. Some people with severe allergies may wear a medical alert bracelet, necklace, or similar which lets anyone who looks at it know what their allergy or condition is. There is a bit of difference in the design of the jewelry but most of them feature a Rod of Asclepius (Figure 5.1) in some way to signify their purpose.

Figure 5.1 Rod of Asclepius

> **!** Any information collected on a medical form should be treated as confidential and shared only as relevant to safety.

First Aid Kits

First aid kits are an important part of keeping everyone safe. Having an appropriately stocked first aid kit in close proximity to the rehearsal and performance spaces is important. Make sure to note where all first aid kits are located; find out who is responsible for their upkeep and re-supply (it might be the stage manager) and be sure they stay up to date in case of an emergency.

Weaponry

Society of American Fight Directors

Any shows requiring weaponry will require their own set of safety plans. An SAFD fight director will be able to assist in designing a safety plan as needed. All weapons will need to be secured in a locked area whenever they are not in use. Typically, they are given their own box, crate, or carrying case that can be locked. Keys are given only to the stage manager, props manager, and sometimes the fight director/fight captain. Any real weapons must be made performer safe (e.g., blades dulled) and should be inspected by the fight director before being used in rehearsal or performance. Anyone using or in close proximity to functioning (blank firing) firearms *must* be given safety training and follow proper protocol in regards to the loading, unloading, misfiring, and handling of the firearm(s). All safety steps in regards to weaponry must be taken very seriously and enforced among the company.

If a production will be utilizing weapons and/or gunfire, make sure the appropriate person in your organization notifies any security or law enforcement well in advance to ensure all parties are aware and to prevent a security incident.

When transporting weapons, especially through public spaces, make sure they are in locked and opaque cases to prevent a security incident.

Emergency Procedures

What to do in case of an emergency? Follow the emergency procedures and stay calm. You are setting an example for all others to follow and if you panic, others will panic too. Each emergency is different and stage managers must use their best judgment, but always err on the side of caution. The first meeting with the theatre staff is a great time to ask about the company's emergency procedures, where any written instructions and procedure documentation are located, and who is responsible for their implementation. Some questions you may ask in that meeting are:

- Is there a designated shelter area for the building? Is it the theatre? If so, what does that mean during a performance?

- Will you or the house manager be responsible for the audience in the case of an evacuation?
  - If you are responsible, arrange to get a house count for each performance as soon as one is available.
- Is there a policy in place for power outages?
  - How long do you hold the show in the event of an outage?
  - Is there emergency power?
- If you are working in an outdoor theatre, do you hold at the first sign of rain or push through until you see lightning or the stage becomes unsafe?
- If you have to hold for an emergency, how long do you wait before canceling the rest of the performance?
- What is the procedure if a company member becomes ill during a performance? What about a patron?
- Is there a procedure in place for an active shooter on the premises or bomb threats?
- Is there a security force associated with the theatre or performance space?

Some good general practices for some of the most common emergencies are outlined below. However, remember to always follow a venue's specific plan and use your judgment, as each situation will be unique.

Medical Emergency

Contact 9-1-1 if you feel emergency personnel are warranted. In conjunction with the house manager, attempt to quietly and calmly remove the person in question to an accessible location without disturbing the production to allow emergency personnel easy access and keep the audience calm. If necessary, make an announcement using the house address system (**god mic**) to hold the show and inform the audience calmly what is taking place and that the show will continue when possible. In instances where a security force or university police exist, make sure to notify the applicable department. While many companies and theatres request that local security (academic, building) be contacted first, this can delay the response time of emergency medical personnel, so it is best to make a judgment call that will best serve the person having the emergency.

Active Shooter

Contact 9-1-1 if the situation allows, evacuate/escape the theatre quickly and calmly. If evacuation/escape is not possible, lock down and barricade entrances into the theatre. Follow the directions of emergency personnel as they arrive. Sign up for active shooter training to better inform yourself of how to deal with an active shooter situation. ALICE training is one of the more widely accepted training methods. The Department of Homeland Security (dhs.gov) has a good active shooter response guide.

Weather or Natural Disaster

Remain calm, inform patrons of the issue, and follow the relevant emergency procedure. Typically, you will need to direct patrons to the appropriate shelter location in the building.

Fire

Contact 9-1-1, make an announcement to the audience, and direct them to quickly and calmly move to the nearest emergency exit. To the best of your ability, try to account for all of the people in the theatre (cast, crew, audience) once it has been evacuated.

Power Outage

In the event of a power outage, make an announcement to the audience to remain in their seats and stay calm. Depending on the duration of the power outage you may need to make additional announcements based on the specific procedures of the venue. The god mic may not work in this instance so be prepared to speak from the stage or have an ASM speak.

> If you are considering pursuing stage management as a career or a lifelong hobby, take a course in first aid and get CPR, AED, bloodborne pathogen, and mental health first certified. This is often expected of professional stage managers and will serve you extremely well when faced with the inevitable injuries or incidents that occur backstage, onstage, or in the rehearsal space.

Incident Reports

If a member of the team is injured during rehearsals, workdays, or performances, an **incident report** should be filled out. This documents the name of the injured person, the date, the circumstances and severity of the injury, and any necessary follow-up (ambulance called, doctor's visit required, etc.). This form can also sometimes be referred to as first report of injury. This information is a critical record keeping step for the company and workman's compensation claims (Figure 5.2).

> **INCIDENT VS ACCIDENT**
>
> It is important to distinguish between the two when filing a report. An accident is always an unintentional event caused by error or chance. Incidents can refer to both unintentional and intentional events, but are events in which something can or should have been addressed to prevent the same thing from happening again (proper safety procedures, or training).

Employee's Report of Injury Form

Instructions: Employees shall use this form to report all work related injuries, illnesses, or "near miss" events (which could have caused an injury or illness) – no matter how minor. This helps us to identify and correct hazards before they cause serious injuries. This form shall be completed by employees as soon as possible and given to a supervisor for further action.

I am reporting a work related:	☐ Injury ☐ Illness ☐ Near miss
Your Name:	
Job title:	
Supervisor:	
Have you told your supervisor about this injury/near miss? ☐ Yes ☐ No	
Date of injury/near miss:	**Time of injury/near miss:**
Names of witnesses (if any):	
Where, exactly, did it happen?	
What were you doing just before the incident/ near miss occurred? Describe the activity, as well as the tools, equipment or material you were using. Be specific. Examples: "climbing a ladder while carrying electric drill"; "mopping the backstage wings" (continue on the back if necessary):	
What happened? Tell us how the injury occurred. Examples: "When ladder slipped on wet floor, I fell 20 feet"; "Worker developed soreness in wrist over time."	
What was the injury or illness? If a near miss, how could you have been hurt? Examples: "strained back"; "cut on left foot"; "carpal tunnel syndrome."	
Did you see a doctor about this injury/illness? ☐ Yes ☐ No	
If yes, whom did you see?	**Doctor's phone number:**
Date:	**Time:**
Has this part of your body been injured before? ☐ Yes ☐ No **If yes, when?**	
Your signature:	**Date:**

Figure 5.2 Incident Report

Notes

1. Mission statement from https://www.osha.gov/aboutosha
2. Rights information from https://www.osha.gov/workers/

Chapter Six
Pre-Production

Auditions

Before Auditions

The stage manager's role in the audition process will vary depending on the production and the theatre company. Sometimes, there is no stage manager on contract yet so the producers and artistic directors set up and take care of many of the details for auditions. It is important to determine the expectations of your involvement in the audition process. Remember that every audition process is unique.

Meet with the Producer, Artistic Director, and Director

Once you determine who is responsible for making the decisions and announcements about auditions, schedule a meeting with the appropriate people to find out details of the audition and callback days (dates, times, location, schedule, dance call). If there is a **dance call**, check in with the choreographer about their needs prior to the call. *[may be held on a separate day and/or location.]*

During these meetings, find out what the auditionees will need to prepare.

- Will it be a **cold reading** (the performers will not see the audition material prior to the audition)? *[this is not usual. Usually means a reading from the script.]*
- Will they need to prepare specific materials?
- Get a detailed list of the **sides** needed for the auditions, if sides will be required.
- If it is a musical, what/how much music will they need to bring/prepare?
- Will they need to demonstrate any other talents (riding a unicycle, juggling, etc.)?
- Will **nudity** or appearance alterations (haircut, style, color, etc.) be required for the production? *[union has specific requirements]*

This is also the time to ask any other questions you may have about auditions, equipment, or personnel needs.

- For musicals, is an accompanist needed for music auditions? A piano? Sound equipment to play musical tracks?

DOI: 10.4324/9781003133049-7

- Where are auditions taking place and who is responsible for reserving the space?
- Will the director be reading individuals, groups, or pairs?
- Should the auditionees stay after their initial read?
- Will the dance call be on the same day in the same place?
- Are you responsible for setting up the room (tables, keyboards, etc.)?
- Does the director want you in the room or will you be coordinating the auditionees from the lobby/hallway? *or an assistant/PA or*

Prep Audition Material

If the stage manager is responsible for audition announcements, it may also fall to them to make announcement posters, web listings, or advertisements. Sign-up sheets, audition information forms, a **character breakdown**, and sides may also be required.

Audition Schedule

With input from the director and/or producer, set an expected length of material (if using sides, time a read of them to estimate the needed time; if performers are preparing monologues, a length should be specified, often 90 seconds or two contrasting 1-minute monologues). Next, schedule auditionees into appropriate time blocks (in the instance above, a 3-minute window gives time for them to walk in, slate [say their name and the name of the pieces they are using], take a note, and leave). There should be a timer in the audition room to warn the auditionee when they have 30 seconds remaining (e.g., by raising a hand) and to stop them when they have reached their allotted time (a firm "thank you" is standard).

Audition Form

Theatres may have a stock audition form, but if you are creating one it should include legal name, stage name, pronouns, phone numbers, preferred email address, height, hair color, age range, vocal range, previous experience, special skills, and scheduling conflicts. Some theatres require a **headshot** and/or resume to be attached as well (Figure 6.1). Check with the director at your audition meeting to determine any additional information or questions they may want to include.

Sides

Sides are scenes selected from the play to be used as audition material. These scenes are chosen in advance of auditions by the director so you can make copies and have them available for distribution with the sign-up sheets and audition forms. These copies should be neat and easy to read so that auditions can run smoothly. Always print a few more than you think you will need.

Preliminary Rehearsal Schedule

This should outline the general rehearsal period, tech week (e.g., required rehearsals), and performance dates. This will allow the performers to plan around the rehearsal period and not be surprised by required production dates. This will also give them a chance to report any known conflicts to you so that the rehearsal schedule can be made accordingly. Provide a place on the audition sheet for auditionees to list these conflicts.

SMB
STAGE MANAGEMENT BASICS

Audition Information Form

Personal Information

Name_____

Address_____

Cell Ph.#_____ E-mail_____

Age_____ Height_____ Hair Color_____ Eye Color _____

- If cast, please do not alter your appearance in any way unless otherwise directed (this includes cutting or dying your hair, tanning, shaving, getting visible tattoos, etc.)

Skills

Do you have any stage combat experience? YES or NO. Which weapons & to what extent?_____

_____

What is your vocal type/range if known? _____ to_____ SOPRANO MEZZO ALTO TENOR BARITONE BASS

Do you play any musical instruments? If so, which and for how long?_____

What other specialty skills (e.g. juggling, magic, gymnastics) do you have? _____

Are you proficient with any dialects? YES or NO. Which?_____

Do you have any previous injuries that might affect your ability to move or dance? YES or NO. What? _____

_____

Do you have dance experience? YES or NO. Which styles/how many years? _____

_____

Schedule

Please identify the times when you are **UNABLE** to rehearse due to class, work, or other commitments. Please specify the type of conflict

	Monday	Tuesday	Wednesday	Thursday	Friday	Saturday	Sunday
12 noon							
1 pm							
2 pm							
3 pm							
4 pm							
5 pm							
6 pm							
7 pm							
8 pm							
9 pm							
10 pm							
11 pm							

Please **identify any date-specific conflicts** you have which would prevent you from attending rehearsal between now and the performances. This includes rehearsals and performances for other events and trips out of town on business, for school activities, or to visit family. **Use the back of this sheet if necessary.**

Show Specific Questions

Would you be willing to cut and/or grow out and/or color your hair?   YES or NO

Are you comfortable with staged intimacy?   YES or NO

Are you aware of and comfortable with the content of the script?   YES or NO

Are you willing to simulate smoking and/or drug use on stage?   YES or NO

Experience: Please attach your headshot and resume to this form. If you don't have a resume, please list on the back a few roles you have played.

Figure 6.1 Audition Form

Make it clear that conflicts listed on the conflict sheet will be worked around as much as possible. Accommodations for any conflicts not disclosed at auditions or the time of hiring are usually decided on a case-by-case basis by the director and/or producer.

Character Breakdown

Character breakdowns provide basic information regarding the characters in the show: name, relationship to other characters in the play, age, and brief description. This information is often provided within the script, available from the publisher, or created by the director. If available, post this information somewhere that the auditionees can look at it. Auditionees can use this information to decide which roles they want to audition for or to gain insight into the relationships in the sides they are reading.

At Auditions

It is important to come prepared with extra sides, pens/pencils/highlighters, paper, a folder for audition forms, blank audition forms, clipboards, a stapler, a copy of the audition schedule, copies of the preliminary production calendar (if available), and a positive attitude. There will be little time to gather any of these items during auditions, so make sure they are easily accessible when needed.

Many times performers may read for multiple roles. Keep track of who reads what part and who reads in what groups, so later that information is available if needed to make decisions for callbacks or as a reminder of what took place during the audition process.

Staying on schedule is important, but often almost impossible. It is the stage manager's job to do their very best to keep auditions running on time. There may be times when the director opts to work with the auditionees after they have presented their pieces. In these cases, give them gentle reminders when someone's time is up, but remember that it is important that the director gets the time they need with each auditionee.

> With musicals and larger productions, it may be helpful to have an assistant to keep order outside the audition room and to wrangle the auditionees or work as a timer in the audition room. If possible, recruit a potential assistant stage manager or a colleague to help.

Callbacks

After the initial culling of the herd (large group auditions are often called cattle calls), the director, choreographer, and/or music director come up with a list of people they would like to "callback" or invite to an additional, more concentrated audition. These typically take place within a few days of the initial auditions. A callback list needs to be generated and posted on the callboard and any other locations where the theatre posts information. They may also be emailed to the auditionees as a courtesy.

While auditions are designed to get a feel for the talent of one individual, callbacks are typically meant to form the best ensemble from the selected talent pool. The director will likely compile a list of characters that they would like each performer to read (this can be when all of those notes you took about who read what and with whom will be helpful to refresh the director's memory). They may have additional sides or selections for callbacks that are different from the audition sides. These will need to be made available to the performers at callbacks.

Often performers will be called for the full callback time, released only when instructed by the director. The performers will be split into smaller ensemble groups and assigned according to the needs of the sides, allowing each performer the chance to read for all of the roles the director is considering them for. For your sanity, it is important to keep close track of who reads for which role to make sure that no one is overlooked accidentally.   (Help the director.

Cast List

Sometimes it will be the responsibility of the stage manager to post the cast list. Speak with the director or artistic director to find out how cast lists are typically distributed (via email, posting on a callboard, carrier pigeon). Thank everyone who auditioned and include the date, time, and location of the first rehearsal, as well as your contact information.

Getting Organized

Once the show has been cast and the production team has been selected, there is some preparation that must be done before beginning the production process. Once the production is underway, things will be hectic, constantly changing, and time will slip away quickly. The best way to prepare for this inevitability is to take steps to over-prepare as much as possible before rehearsals begin. This process, often referred to as "**prep week**," involves creating the promptbook, preparing paperwork, creating the rehearsal schedule, preparing the space for rehearsals, and restocking the stage manager's kit. Depending on your process, schedule, and contract, this may happen more than a week before or last longer than a week. It is important to take time to properly prepare, read the script, prep forms and templates, meet with the director, and get organized so you are ready for the production process to begin. Especially early in your career, it can be incredibly helpful to make a Prep Week Checklist for yourself. This outlines all the tasks that need to be done and all the paperwork that needs to be created and distributed during this week (Figure 6.2).

Personnel	Task	Time
Full Team	**Discussion:** Team Dynamics	10 minutes
Full Team	**Discussion:** Safety - Physical Safety - Emotional Safety	5 minutes
Full Team	**Discussion:** Director Meeting - Working with Designers/Company/Dramaturg	10 minutes
Full Team	**Discussion:** Daily Schedules Copies and Postings	10 minutes
Full Team	**Discuss,** Stock and Organize SM Kit Report to SM what is missing or low	5 minutes
Full Team	**Discussion:** Rehearsal & Performance Reports - Summary and notes	20 minutes
Full Team	**Discussion:** Actor Packets Order Show paperwork	10 minutes
Full Team	**Discussion:** Rehearsal Studio(s) Cleaning duties Monitoring food and drink Transfering to different room Maintenance of prop tables and floor tape Director/Playwright Table Set-up Stage Management Table Set-Up Prop Table and Furniture Set-Up	45 minutes
Full Team	**Discussion:** Taping the Groundplan Pick a date and time	20 minutes
ASM	**Paperwork** - Contact Sheet	45 minutes
SM	**Paperwork** - Rehearsal Calendar	75 minutes
SM	**Paperwork** - Daily Schedule for First Day of Rehearsal	30 minutes
ASM	**Paperwork** - Character-Scene Breakdown	60 minutes
SM	**Paperwork** - Prompt Book Cover Page	45 minutes

SMB
STAGE MANAGEMENT BASICS

Prep Week Checklist

ASM	**Paperwork** - Weekly Sign-in Sheets	60 minutes
ASM	**Paperwork** - Voting Slips	15 minutes
ASM	**Paperwork** - Props List	60 minutes
SM	**Paperwork** - Blocking template	20 minutes
ASMs	**Paperwork** - Run Sheets (Google Doc?)	120 minutes
ASM	Measure GP for Taping	75-120 minutes
SM	**Paperwork** - Call Board Headers - "Today" - "Sign-In" (not posted until tech) - Show Title	30 minutes
SM	**Paperwork** - Empty Rehearsal Reports	90 minutes
SM	**Paperwork** - Empty Performance Reports	90 minutes
ASM	**Paperwork** - Contact Cards	30 minutes
Full Team	Assemble Actor Packets: - Table of Contents - Actor/Scene Breakdown - Wallet Cards - Contact Sheet - Rehearsal Calendar - Emergency Forms - Directions to Studio Arts & Halsey	45 minutes
Full Team	Sweep/Clean Rehearsal Studio(s)	45 minutes
Full Team	Tape Rehearsal Studio(s)	75-90 minutes
SM	Check out Prop & Costume Cabinets	5 minutes
ASMs	Set up Prop & Costume Cabinets	45 minutes
SM	Assemble Call Board: - Show title(s) - Today's Rehearsal Schedule - Tomorrow's Rehearsal Schedule - AEA Postings - Rehearsal Calendar	30 minutes
Full Team	Prompt Book Assembly	90 minutes

Figure 6.2 Prep Week Checklist

This is one example, although you may add or eliminate certain items depending on your particular production.

Script

The script will typically be provided to you by the company. Most stage managers prefer a single-sided copy of the script. If you are trying to get a head start on prep work prior to receiving the official script, double check which version of the script your production will be using and make sure you are working out of the correct version. Many plays and musicals have different translations or versions and can be dramatically different.

Commonly, the stage manager is responsible for organizing and distributing scripts amongst the company. Sometimes this happens prior to the start of rehearsals, although they may also be handed out at the first rehearsal. In professional theatre, some performer contracts require memorization before rehearsal begins, so early script distribution must take place and is the responsibility of the company rather than stage management.

For some productions, especially musicals, the scripts and **scores** are rented and must be returned (in good condition). If they are to be returned, make sure the date of return is clear. Number each script and/or score in pencil somewhere erasable and

SMB Cabaret Actor Script/Score Sign Out Sheet					
Name	Score Number	Script Number	Sign Out	Sign In	Notes
Alex O.	20	20	9/12/19		
Bradley K.	19	19	9/12/19		
Maycie S.	18	18	9/13/19		
Noah H.	17	17	9/13/19		
Devin Y.	16	16	9/13/19		
Tatiana S.	15	15	9/13/19		
Erika B.	14	14	9/13/19		
Zoella S.	13	13	9/13/19		
Richard C.	12	12	9/13/19		
Thayne L.	11	11	9/16/19		
Caroline H.	10	10	9/16/19		
Jaden H.	9	9	9/16/19		
Madelyn H.	8	8	9/16/19		
Rachel W.	7	7	9/16/19		
Justin M.	6	6	9/17/19		
Andrew O.	5	5	9/17/19		
Liz M.	4	4	9/17/19		
Abigail C.	3	3	9/17/19		

Figure 6.3 Script Sign-Out Sheet by Kaitlyn Vasey

have company members sign them out in order to keep track of who has which script (Figure 6.3). Keep a copy of this information in your **promptbook** and a secondary copy with the packing list provided in the shipment of the scripts. Additionally, remind performers (and musicians, when applicable) that only light pencil marks are allowed on all rented scripts/scores and all marks MUST be erased before return. It is usually your responsibility to double-check that all scripts/scores have been erased once returned and prior to shipping.

Whenever possible, keep an extra copy of the script in the rehearsal room for when a new team member suddenly comes on board or when someone forgets their script. Make sure this script is kept updated with all script changes, if any occur.

Reading the Script

The more knowledge a stage manager has about the script (and score, when applicable), the better prepared they will be for the upcoming production. As such, one of the very first steps after being contracted for a show is to obtain a copy of the script and start reading. It is important to read the script a minimum of three times, ensuring intimate familiarity with the script and enabling the stage manager to best serve the production.

The First Read – For Literary Purposes

This is the time to read the script purely for its literary value, enjoyment, and to get an overall feel for the scope and mood of the text as the audience will receive it. During this first read, don't think too much about the requirements of the script or production; that is what later readings are for.

The Second Read – Preliminary Production Analysis

This is the time to take preliminary notes, including which sections might be challenging, any quick costume changes, complicated set/prop/costume requirements, sound effects, etc. These notes will be compiled in a piece of paperwork called the **Production Analysis** (Figure 6.5). A production analysis is a detailed overview of the full script, taking into account all aspects of the show (scenery, lights, sound, props, media, and costumes). Note-taking is different for everyone, but you can write directly in the script, on a separate notepad, or using the app of your choice (depending on whether it is the only copy of the script, a rented script, an electronic copy, or a full-sized copy). Note anything and everything that could impact rehearsals or the production. Be sure to look in both the text and the stage directions; indications of these things can be given in either location. Always include the page number, act, and scene in these notations. You will thank yourself later on when you don't have to go searching through your script again. Color coding the notes by department can also be helpful.

> **! TEXTUAL STAGE DIRECTIONS**
>
> In addition to navigating the stage, the term "stage directions" can also refer to anything in italics in a script. These may have been written directly by the playwright with the intention that they be followed. However, just as likely, they were written by the stage manager of the first production and relate specifically to that original production. Unless you are working on a brand new work or have the playwright in the room, there is no guarantee that any information given in the stage directions was originally intended by the playwright or that it will be used by your director. For this reason, be sure to keep careful track of whether something has been indicated in the text or in the stage directions. The place to indicate this would be in the "Notes" section of your production analysis.

Of Mice and Men

Act I

Scene 1

Thursday night[1]. A sandy bank of the Salinas River sheltered with willows-one giant sycamore up R. The stage is covered with dry leaves[2]. The feeling is sheltered and quiet. Stage is lit by a setting sun[3].

Curtain rises on an empty stage[4]. A sparrow is singing. There is a distant sound of ranch dogs barking aimlessly and one clear quail call. The quail call turns to a warning call and there is a beat of the flock's wings[5]. Two figures are seen entering - L or R, it makes no difference - in single file, with GEORGE, the short man, coming in ahead of LENNIE. Both men are carrying blanket rolls[6]. They approach the water. The small man throws down his blanket roll, the large man follows, then falls down and drinks from the river[7], snorting as he drinks.

GEORGE: (*irritably*) Lennie, for God's sake, don't drink so much. (*He leans over and shakes LENNIE.*) Lennie, you hear me! You gonna be sick like you was last night.

LENNIE dips his whole head under[8], hat[9] and all. As he sits on bank, his hat drips down the back.

LENNIE: That's good. You drink some, George. You drink some, too.

GEORGE: (*Kneeling, dipping his finger in water*) I ain't sure it's good water. Looks kinda scummy to me.

LENNIE: (*Imitates, dipping his finger also*) Look at them wrinkles in the water, George. Look what I done.

GEORGE: (*drinking from his cupped palm*) Tastes all right. Don't seem to be runnin' much, though. Lennie[10], you oughtn' to drink water when it ain't running. (*Hopelessly.*) You'd drink water out of a gutter if you was thirsty. (*Throws a scoop of water into his face, rubs it around with his hand[11], pushes himself back and embraces his knees. LENNIE, after watching him, imitates him in every detail.*)

KEY:
Direction / Actors
Scenic
Lighting / Electrics
Sound
Costumes / Hair & Makeup
Props

1. Lighting, **Sound** - day & time

2. **Scenic** - describes setting. (NOTE: Is the water in the river fake or real?)

3. Lighting - Further indication of time of day, as well as lighting angles & color choices

4. Direction - Actors will likely start the show offstage

5. **Sound** - Gives direction as to the soundscape the designer may create. Might also create cues for either the SM or the actors based off of specific sounds

6. Props - indicates at least 2 blanket rolls will be needed

7. **Scenic** - Water will likely need to be real, may need to be drinkable

8. Direction, **Scenic**, Costumes / Hair & Makeup, and **Sound** - This moment is going to require a conversation between the director, scenic, costumes, hair & makeup, and sound (if mics are being used) to ensure this action can happen successfully.

9. **Costumes** - indicates that Lennie might need a hat

10. **Scenic, Sound** - Water source is either stagnant or barely running

11. Direction, **Scenic**, Costumes / Hair & Makeup, **Sound** - Same as previous; all these departments will need to collaborate to make this moment happen successfully.

Figure 6.4 Of Mice and Men by John Steinbeck

The excerpt above demonstrates how just a few paragraphs can contain a world of information for the stage manager and creative team to work with (Figure 6.4).

When creating the production analysis, all notes should be based purely on the script. Do not yet take into account any preliminary designs that may exist for your production. This step will act as a double check to make sure nothing important to the action was

OF MICE AND MEN
Production Analysis

Director: Kenn S.

Act. Scene	Page	General	Scenic	Props	Lights	Costumes	Sound	Cast	Questions
1.1	1	Sheltered and Quiet	Sandy river bank, Giant Sycamore, willows, Lennie drinks from the river	Dry leaves, Blanket rolls (Bindle?, thrown down, later rolled out into "bed")	Setting Sun, willows/Sycamore Both sit on the ground/sand	Lennie has a hat - it gets dunked in water	Sparrow Singing, Ranch dogs barking aimlessly, quail call/warning call, beat of the flock's wings	George (Shorter than Lennie), Lennie	Actual Water? Mics & Water?
	2					George has a hat - handled roughly			
	3			dead mouse - comes from Lennie's coat pocket; Thrown		Lennie has a coat w/ a side pocket			
	5		Leaves are blown by wind		The light is going fast		A little wind whirls, dog howls		
	6			3 cans of beans - 2 get opened and eaten; Can opener A few small willow sticks; Second Mouse as backup			A little sound of splashing comes from Lennie's exit		
	7		Fire	Matches? (Fire lighting mechanism)	Light has continued to go out, when the fire it lit it is the major light				Fire?
	8			Pocket knife - dulled, used to eat beans -probably 2					
	12					Lennie is a messy eater			
	13				Light dies slowly out of the fire until only the faces of the two men can be seen; almost complete darkness		A night owl far off, coyote howl, dogs barking (all the dogs in the county)		
	14						Coyote howls		
1.2	14	Late Morning	Bunkhouse Interior - whitewashed board and bat, floors unpainted, at least 1 window, door w/ latch Bunk beds with boxes nailed over them Hanging light over table - round dim reflector	Heavy square table, boxes/crates (used as chairs - 4 around table w/ several additional throughout); Items for boxes over bunks (soap, talcum powder, razors, pulp magazines, medicine bottles, combs, neckties) Blanket rolls (repeat from 1.1) Big push broom	Late Morning, Sun streaking through the windows Hanging light over table - round dim reflector	Candy - blue jeans and a denim coat (pocket)	Many alarm clocks ticking	George, Lennie, Candy - a stoop shouldered old man right hand gone at the wrist	Candy missing a hand Blanket rolls - double or quick reset

V 1 Updated: 1/3/2019   KBM   Page 1 of 6

Figure 6.5 Production Analysis

accidentally missed by the designers or the director. Once the analysis is complete, you can review it with your production team for any discrepancies and determine if they are being omitted or changed purposefully for your production. The final analysis should reflect your production, including any additions or changes made by the designers.

Scenic

Take note of any and all textual stage directions, lines, etc. that would have an effect on the scenery (including year, season, presence of doors, etc.). Additionally, take note of set pieces that need to be **practical** or functional (e.g., a window that opens or a closet that needs to hide three people and have an escape hatch).

Lights and Sound

Take note of any and all stage directions, lines, etc. that may inform lights and/or sound (including time of day, year, date, windows, ambience, etc.). Note use of any practical lights or sounds onstage (lamps, flashlights, phone rings, radio noise, etc.). Also, note any scripturally indicated lighting shifts (e.g., Steven turns on a lamp, "We've been chatting so long, I didn't notice the sun had set!"). Remember that some things affect multiple aspects of design (e.g., an open window might also require sound effects of street noise). If the script refers to the directionality of the light or sound, note this as well.

> **!** It is especially important to note, both in your analysis and in your script, any sound cues that you will need to simulate or play during rehearsal. Typically, this is any sound that affects the action of the scene (e.g., a phone ring, a doorbell, a gunshot, etc.). Ambient background sounds or **soundscapes** are not generally required for rehearsals.

Props and Costumes

List any props and costumes indicated either in the text or in the stage directions. Include which character(s) handles the prop or wears the costume piece and when it moves onstage and offstage. If multiple characters handle the same prop or costume piece, make a note to determine whether this will be the exact same piece or if there might need to be multiples to avoid messy tracking of the items later. Take particular note of hand props and **personal props** that are used. Also, keep an eye out for places where quick changes (costume change that must happen in under 1 minute), **handoffs**, **catches**, or tracking may occur and take note of these as well. Quick changes may happen between scenes or in the middle of a scene.

> **!** A key task for stage managers during the rehearsal process is prop and costume tracking. This refers to the act of noting where props and costumes must be at all times during the show, including where they enter, exit, and where they travel while onstage. This notation will assist with setup for rehearsals, and preset for performances as well as highlighting moments when a performer or crew member will need to be tasked with getting a prop or costume from one place to another during the run of a show.

What are Props?

Props are considered to be anything movable or portable on a set. Any item that cannot be classified as scenery, **electrics**, or wardrobe falls under this category. Furniture is considered a prop in most theatres, although there are some exceptions. Props that are handled by the performers (e.g., cups, books, pencils) are known as hand props. Props that are kept in a performer's dressing room and handled exclusively by that performer (e.g., a pocket protector with pens, pocket watches, fans, canes) are known as personal props. Items that are usually untouched by the performers (e.g., mirrors, vases, picture frames, window dressing, rugs) are known as set dressing.

Some personal props may also be considered costume pieces and will be handled by the costume designer depending on the theatre and the item. Similarly, depending on the production and the items, set dressing may fall to the scenic designer. Electronic items such as lamps and radios will likely be sourced by the props department and rigged to function by the lighting or sound department. If it is uncertain which department an item falls under, make note of it and address it during a **production meeting**. Establish early on who will be responsible for obtaining that item. Stay on top of these items. If a particular team isn't given responsibility for the item, it will likely fall through the cracks or be forgotten until the last minute. If it falls to multiple teams, remind both parties of it often and make sure it is being addressed.

Typically, props are the aspect of the script that will be customized the most to fit each particular production. Since most of these changes are decided in rehearsals, the stage manager will need to keep careful track of them and make sure all changes are clearly communicated to the props department. The stage manager is responsible for tracking the props as they move around and onstage/offstage during the show and sometimes even responsible for obtaining and keeping track of rehearsal props. Schedule regular check-ins with the props manager throughout the process to confirm that the prop list is accurate and up-to-date (Figure 6.6).

> **!** After the preliminary prop list is made, it is important to go over it with the director (who may have a list of their own) and props department. Sometimes the director can tell you right away whether they are planning to use something or not and also if they have added additional props based on their vision for the production. Also, during this meeting, have the director highlight which props are top priorities to have in the rehearsal room.

Expendables (Consumables)

Make note of expendable props that will require multiples throughout the run. Always ensure that there will be extras; if the text calls for one shattered vase, make sure that there are enough for all performances as well as a few for rehearsals and accidents. Alert the props department of any expendable props as soon as possible to make sure that they are accounted and planned for.

Some examples of expendables are:

- Paper props (e.g., letters, shopping lists, certificates, contracts)
- Perishables (food and beverages)
- Breakables (not everything that could break, but things intentionally broken or disfigured during each performance, e.g., vases that need to be shattered or books that need to be torn).

> In some scripts, there will be a props list provided at the end of the text. This is a list that has usually been compiled by the stage manager of a particular production, meaning that while it can provide a good starting place for your list, it should by no means be relied upon to be complete or correct for the script. It may skip some props or add some according to the needs of that particular production. As such, always make and maintain your own list based on the text.

Pout Pout Fish

Preliminary Props List

NOTE: *C/S stand for Costumes or Set Props   *R stands for Rehearsal Props & A stands for Actual Props

Page	Prop	Qty	C/S	Character	Notes	R	A
1	Blue silk	2	C?				x
1	Seagull				Puppet		x
1	Fish				Puppet		x
1	Large Boat				Needs clip for water silk		x
1	Telescope				Real or mimed?		
2	Rocks/Coral		S				
2	School of fish	2		Ana/Maria	Puppet		x
2	Manta Ray				Puppet		x
2	Pout Pout Fish				Puppet		x
2	Bass			Sheldon	Puppet		x
3	Eel			Ana	Puppet		x
3	Goldfish			Sheldon	Puppet		x
3	Glasses		C		Placed on S3 to make "Clownfish"		
3	Clown nose				Placed on fish to make "Clownfish"		
5	Glitter		C?	Miss Clam	Appears & disappears in "Cloud of glitter"		
5	Miss Clam				Puppet		x
7	Mirror		S	PPF	Pull tab that changes happy/sad PPF		
9	Lightbulb			PPF	Literal or metaphorical lightbulb?		
9	Seashells				Used to make "smile mask"		
9	Smile Mask		C?				x
10	Seaweed curtain		S		Dark red & brown w/ fish skulls & skeletons		x
10	Old Pot			Bully	Pot from a ship, for "Fish Stew"		x
10	Bully Shark			Sheldon	Puppet		x
11	Barracuda				Puppet		
13	Cake Base Pedestal		S?	Miss Clam	With colorful sea sponges		x
13	Pearl				Puppet?		x
19	Octopus				Puppet		x
26	Whale (Miss Blue)			Miss Blue	Puppet/Set		
32	Worms				Puppet		
33	Conductor's baton			Storyteller			
34	Gradation Mesh		S		To indicate descent into Big Big Dark		
34	Seaweed curtains	3			"Big Big Dark"		
34	Seaweed Potluck			Scary Fish	is or includes bowl of seaweed salad		
34	Scary Fish	2		Ana/Maria	Puppets		
34	Bob the angler fish			Sheldon	Puppet, has functional light		
37	Big Dark sign		S		reads "The Big, Big Dark. Not that big. Not that dark."		

Figure 6.6 Properties (Props) List

The Third Read – Revised Production Analysis

This is the point when you add specificity to your preliminary production analysis (e.g., not only do you need a newspaper but the headline should read "Extra, Extra").

The production analysis is a living document. Keep it updated throughout the rehearsal process as things change to fit this particular production. Later in the process, you will be able to use this document to more easily create other paperwork such as **run sheets**, **preset lists**, and **costume plots**, which are discussed in Chapter 7.

Scene Breakdowns (Character/Scene Breakdown)

The next piece of paperwork you need to create is a **scene breakdown**. A scene breakdown outlines each act and scene as it is divided in the script and details which pages it is on, the locale of the scene (if indicated), which characters are onstage (or speaking/singing offstage), and a brief description of the action. For musicals, it also details which musical numbers are in each scene. This step will assist in the scheduling of rehearsals (by identifying who needs to be called for each scene), planning costume changes, backstage tracking, etc. It also gives you a simplified visual breakdown of the show to help keep things straight while you are still familiarizing yourself with the script (Figure 6.7).

Depending on the script and on your rehearsal needs, you may find it useful to make a **French scene breakdown**. French scenes are delineated by any entrance/exit of a performer (there may be multiple French scenes in a single script scene). This type of breakdown is

SMB
STAGE MANAGEMENT BASICS

PROOF
Scene Character Breakdown

Act/Sc	Pages	Time/Day	Characters	Actors
I.1	5-20	Present Day, Sept 4th 2000, Night	Catherine, Robert, Hal	Jenna, John, Jayson
I.2	21-28	Present Day, Sept 4th 2000, Morning	Claire, Catherine, Hal	Cadden, Jenna, Jayson
I.3	29-34	Present Day, Sept 4th 2000, Night, Party	Catherine, Hal	Jenna, Jayson
I.4	34-41	Present Day, Sept 5th 2000, Next Morning	Catherine, Hal, Claire	Jenna, Jayson, Cadden
INTERMISSION				
II.1	42-50	4 years earlier, Sept 4th 1996, Afternoon	Robert, Catherine, Hal	John, Jenna, Jayson
II.2	51-55	Present Day, Sept 5th 2000, an instant after end of Act I	Hal, Catherine, Claire	Jayson, Jenna, Cadden
II.3	56-58	Present Day, Sept 6th 2000, late morning/early afternoon	Hal, Claire	Jayson, Cadden
II.4	59-63	3 1/2 years earlier, December 1996	Robert, Catherine	John, Jenna
II.5	64-71	Present Day, Sept 13th 2000	Claire, Catherine, Hal	Cadden, Jenna, Jayson

Figure 6.7 Scene Breakdown

SMB — STAGE MANAGEMENT BASICS

French Scene Breakdown

Character (*Performer*)	**I.1** 5	6	7	8	9	10	11	12	13	14	15	16	17	18	19	20	**I.2** 21	22	23	24	25	26	27	28
Catherine (*Jenna K*)	x	x	x	x	x	x	x	x	x	x	x	x	x	x	x	x	/x	x	x	x	x	x	x	x/
Robert (*John W*)	x	x	x	x	x	x	x	x/																
Hal (*Jayson S*)								/x	x	x	x	x	x	x	x	x/								/x/
Claire (*Cadden J*)																	x	x	x	x	x	x	x	x

Character (*Performer*)	**I.3** 29	30	31	32	33	**I.4** 34	35	36	37	38	39	40	41
Catherine (*Jenna K*)	/x	x	x	x	x	x	x	x	x	x	x	x	x
Robert (*John W*)													
Hal (*Jayson S*)	/x	x	x	x	x	/x	x/					/x	x
Claire (*Cadden J*)							/x	x	x	x	x	x	x

Character (*Performer*)	**II.1** 42	43	44	45	46	47	48	49	50	**II.2** 51	52	53	54	55	**II.3** 56	57	58	**II.4** 59	60	61	62	63
Catherine (*Jenna K*)	/x	x	x	x	x	x	x	x	x/	x	x	x	x	x/				/x	x	x	x	x
Robert (*John W*)	x	x	x	x	x	x	x	x	x										x	x	x	x
Hal (*Jayson S*)						/x	x	x	x	x/	x	x	x	x	x/	/x	x	x				
Claire (*Cadden J*)										x	x	x	x	x	x/	/x	x	x				

Character (*Performer*)	**II.5** 64	65	66	67	68	69	70	71
Catherine (*Jenna K*)	/x	x	x	x	x	x	x	x
Robert (*John W*)								
Hal (*Jayson S*)					/x	x	x	x	x
Claire (*Cadden J*)	x	x	x	x/				

KEY:
x = character onstage
/x = character enters
x/ = character enters

Figure 6.8 French Scene Breakdown

useful for shows that are not broken down into acts and scenes, or have a lot of entrances and exits, like farces (Figure 6.8).

Once complete, share the production analysis and scene breakdown with the rest of the production team. This will give them an opportunity to compare notes and make sure that no elements are overlooked.

First Meeting with the Director

This is a very important step in the process, as it is the stage manager's primary job to ensure clear communication in order to best realize the director's vision. In order to do that effectively, the first step is to establish clear communication with the director and to gain as deep an understanding as possible of their vision for the world of the play. Plan this meeting as early as possible. Communication between the two of you will be much easier once this first meeting has occurred and you will be much more effective at your job once you have a grasp on their process. This meeting does not need to be in person (video chat or phone calls will also work very well), but this should not take place over email. An important element of this conversation is getting to know each other as co-workers and it will not be as effective without verbal communication. Take detailed notes during this meeting.

WORLD OF THE PLAY

The world of the play sets a production in a specific context with particular rules, established by the director, to govern this specific production's concept and vision. The world of the play dictates a lot about the play, including the style (e.g., realism, expressionism, etc.) and the rules or "guidelines" (e.g., do ghosts exist?, can characters interact with them?, or are they only visible to the audience?). i.e., Disney's *Alice in Wonderland* vs. Tim Burton' s *Alice in Wonderland* are the same story set in very different worlds.

Discussion Points

- What does the director expect from you?
  - How do they prefer to be addressed (first name, last name, pronouns, nickname)?
  - What is the best way to reach them (email, cell/office/home phone, call vs. text, face-to-face meetings)?
  - What is the best way to reach them for information that involves quick turnaround (sick/injured performer, space availability issues)?
  - Are there any restrictions on communication (no calls after 10 pm, email only during work hours, etc.)?
  - What role should you play in the rehearsal room? (Do they want or expect input from you or the room (cast)? Do they want you to start/end rehearsals? Are you expected/allowed to give notes? Should you give line or blocking corrections during scene work or after?)
  - Do they want to start immediately on time or have a couple of minutes of friendly chat at the top of the day?
- Who will be making the rehearsal schedule? (Will it be made after the day's rehearsal for the next day or a week at a time? Does the director have a schedule for the entire process? How much should be sent to the performers? Will the director give you a list of things that they want to work and let you figure out when they fit into the day or do they want to work chronologically? Will rehearsals be split? Do they want to announce an **off-book** (line memorization) date?)
- When would they like to start using rehearsal props? (Day one, after initial blocking, or once scripts are out of hands?)
- When and how often do they want to build in breaks during rehearsal?
  - Many companies use the standard breaks outlined by Actors' Equity Association: a 10-minute break after every 80 minutes of rehearsal or a 5-minute break after 55 minutes of rehearsal.
  - How would they like you to get their attention when it's time for a break (slide them a note, stand up, give a 2-minute warning, etc.)?
- Do they have any pet peeves (breaking mid-moment, performers that aren't in the scene entering/exiting the rehearsal space, gum chewing, performers not wearing closed-toed shoes)?

- Discuss the director's concept.
    - Have an in-depth discussion about the play. Make sure to discuss the plot, concept, and specific needs of this production. (For this reason, it is crucial that you come into this meeting having read the play and with an understanding of the characters.)
    - Make sure you have an in-depth understanding of the director's vision of the world of the play. Once the show opens, it will be your responsibility to maintain the artistic integrity of the show as envisioned by the director, so a clear understanding of their vision and concept is critical.
        - Academic productions typically differ in this respect because the director is usually present during the entire process, so the stage manager may not be responsible for maintaining the integrity of the show. This is also true for UK productions, where there is commonly an associate director who is responsible for maintaining artistic integrity throughout the run.
- Determine rules for rehearsals and the company.
    - Food and drink policies, noise and guests, sign-in procedures, emergency procedures, late policies, etc.
- Discuss what you expect from the director.
    - What is the best method for them to communicate with you?
    - Are there any restrictions on communication?
    - Expectation to be included on all future communication regarding design decisions, scheduling changes, new team members, etc. so as to remain as up-to-date and informed on all production aspects as possible.
- Establish a plan to meet briefly after every rehearsal. This is a good, consistent time when you will both be available to check in about the process and to discuss any issues or questions that arose during rehearsal. Daily communication is key to a successful director/stage manager working relationship. If post-rehearsal meetings are too difficult, find another consistent time when you can both check in.

> **!** Remember that directors and stage managers are co-workers and teammates (even in an educational environment). Don't be demanding, but know that you deserve respect. If you both make your expectations clear up front, the process will be smoother for it.

Scheduling Rehearsals

One of the most important steps during pre-production is finalizing the rehearsal calendar. Many theatres work on a semi-set schedule that is adjusted depending on the conflicts and the availability of the performers for a specific production (e.g., rehearsals are always 7:00 pm–10:00 pm, days off are always on Sunday, the company works 36 hours per week, etc.). Often, the basic landmark dates will already be given to you by the producer/production manager (e.g., first rehearsal, tech dates, opening night, closing night). Beyond that, however, the rest of the schedule is commonly left to the discretion of the director and stage manager. This conversation will ideally happen in person, but can also be a phone call or video chat. Avoid written correspondence (e.g., texting, emailing) unless absolutely necessary, as this will slow down the process considerably and is more likely to result in miscommunication.

Conflict Calendar

Once you have collected all conflicts, it can be helpful to maintain a "conflict calendar" to keep track of all of them. Any unexpected conflicts are handled on a case-by-case basis and are usually decided upon by the director, artistic director, and producer as needed. Keep the calendar updated with any subsequent approved conflicts that arise. This calendar should only be shared between the stage management team and the directing team (if they would like access to it). Do not distribute scheduling conflicts to the rest of the company (Figure 6.9).

Creating the Rehearsal Schedule

Creating the rehearsal schedule will be done in collaboration with all directors and choreographers on the project (including music directors, when applicable). Before beginning the process, be sure to have the scene breakdown and some scrap paper handy as well as

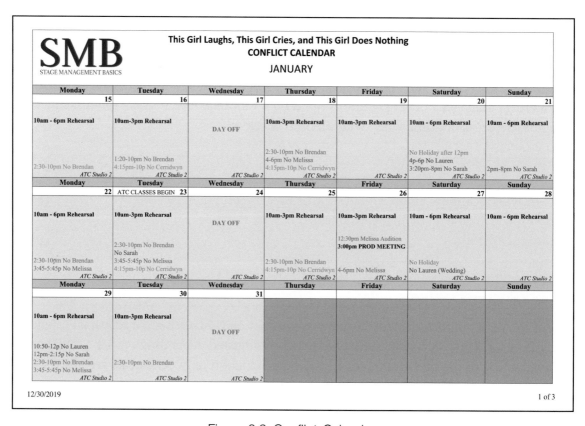

Figure 6.9 Conflict Calendar

any known conflicts to take into account (e.g., don't schedule a run through on a day when two performers are going to be missing). To begin, set the general hours for each day (subject to change, but will mostly remain as indicated). Based on the general timeline, establish basic "goalposts" for the calendar. For a straight play, typically it will be a day or so of table work, then staging/blocking rehearsals, then work throughs of large chunks of the text, followed by **stumble throughs** and run throughs (including a designer run), and then tech. For a musical, you will also need to schedule time for music rehearsals and dance/choreography rehearsals. Be sure to include the music director and choreographer in all scheduling meetings so that everyone gets the time they need.

> Prior to this meeting, determine whether additional rehearsal rooms will be available for use in order to have multiple rehearsals happen simultaneously (commonly, you can double up on music rehearsals and staging/choreography rehearsals so as to get the most out of limited rehearsal hours). Take this into account when scheduling.

Once the general outline for the schedule is made, it is a good idea to discuss some internal goals for the schedule as well (we would like to have all of Act I staged by this date, we'd like the whole show staged by this date, we'd like the cast to be completely off-book by this date, etc.). These types of goals may or may not be shared with the whole company (they may just be goals for you and the directing team to keep an eye on) and may move around during the rehearsal process depending on how quickly the work is progressing. However, by setting them early on, they can serve as reminders of the big picture timeline, which the team can sometimes lose sight of when they are in the thick of rehearsals. They also serve as a good indicator of the pacing in your rehearsal room (perhaps the cast takes a bit more time to learn than expected or, conversely, they are picking things up very quickly and you might be able to work at a faster pace, leaving more buffer time during the last few rehearsals to clean and finesse).

If there are fights or intimacy involved, try to determine which day(s) will be used to learn the fight or intimate moment(s) based on the fight/intimacy director's availability and estimated progress of staging. After the initial staging, there should be at least one additional "cleaning" rehearsal with the fight/intimacy director to check in on how the moment is going and make any necessary adjustments or notes. Fight and intimacy calls should also become a regular part of rehearsals at that point.

> If in an academic setting, remember to take the food service hours into account when scheduling rehearsals. If food is not being provided, all students on the meal plan need to be given at least a 30-minute break during the food services operating hours to eat. In a professional environment, make sure to take any union regulations into account if applicable.

If you and your director are unsure how to begin, here is a basic layout example for a production calendar with 3 weeks of rehearsal, 5 days of tech/dress, and 1 week of performances.

Straight Play (2 acts):

Week 1: Meet and Greet, Table Read, Analysis, 1–2 days of table work, 3 days of staging

Week 2: 6 days of staging (finish staging both Acts)

Week 3: 2 days to work through Act I, 2 days to work through Act II, 2 days of run throughs (including a designer run) and notes

Tech Week: 1 day of spacing (if possible), 2 full days of tech rehearsals, 2 days of dress rehearsals

Performances

Musical:

Week 1: 2–3 days of Music Rehearsals (depending on how much music there is), Meet and Greet, read through/Sing-through, 1–2 days begin staging

Week 2: 6 days of staging/choreography (Finish Act I, start Act II)

Week 3: 4 days of staging/Choreography (Finish Act II), stumble through, Designer Run, **Sitzprobe** (if time)

Tech Week: 1 day of spacing and possibly start tech, 2 days of tech, 2 days of dress (usually this is when the orchestra is added)

Performances

Once the rehearsal calendar is complete, distribute it to all members of the team. It should include rehearsals, designer run, tech rehearsals, dress rehearsals, and performance dates (Figure 6.10).

> **!** It is best practice to include the phrase "Subject to Change" on all calendars and schedules.

Daily and Weekly Calls

On the day prior to each rehearsal, you will distribute the daily rehearsal call (known colloquially as the daily or the call) to the cast. Each call should include the date, the location (particularly if multiple rehearsals are taking place at once), and a detailed breakdown of the day, including what will be rehearsed and who is expected to be in attendance (who is called). It can also be helpful to include a small section that notes any special needs for the day (e.g., dance rehearsal – be sure to bring your character shoes and wear comfortable clothing that you can move in, Music rehearsal – be sure to bring a pencil and a recording device, fittings – wear appropriate undergarments, etc.).

Some directors like to schedule their breaks into the day and include them on the **daily call**, while others prefer to play it by ear in the room. If the rehearsal is long

SMB
STAGE MANAGEMENT BASICS

PROOF
REHEARSAL & PERFORMANCE CALENDAR
Schedule is subject to change with due AEA notice

SUNDAY	MONDAY	TUESDAY	WEDNESDAY	THURSDAY	FRIDAY	SATURDAY
3 (March)	4	5 First Rehearsal 11a Equity Bus. 11:30a Meet & Greet 12p Designer Presentations 12:30p Read Thru 4p EOD/Prod Mtg	6 Rehearsal #2 11a Rehearsal 4p EOD	7 Rehearsal #3 11a Rehearsal 3p Break/Walk to Park 3:15p Press Photos 4:30p EOD	8 Rehearsal #4 11a Rehearsal 4p EOD	9 Rehearsal #5 11a Rehearsal 4p EOD
10 – Daylight Savings Time Starts Equity Day Off	11 Rehearsal #6 11a Rehearsal 4p EOD	12 Rehearsal #7 11a Rehearsal 4p EOD	13 Rehearsal #8 11a Rehearsal 4p EOD	14 Rehearsal #9 11a Rehearsal 4p EOD Fittings tbd	15 Rehearsal #10 11a Rehearsal 4p EOD	16 Equity Day Off
17 Day Off	18 Day Off Set Load In	19 Rehearsal #11 11a Rehearsal 4p EOD	20 Rehearsal #12 11a Rehearsal 4p EOD Designer Run-through	21 Rehearsal #13 11a Rehearsal 4p EOD Load out from Rehearsal Space	22 Rehearsal #14 At Theater 11a Actor Walk-Thru 4p EOD	23 Rehearsal #15 At Theater 11a Spacing Rehearsal 4p EOD
24 Equity Day Off	25 Day Off	26 TECH 12p Actor Call 12:30p Tech Reh 9:30p EOD	27 TECH 12p Actor Call 12:30p Tech Reh 9:30p EOD	28 TECH 1p -5p TBD Reh 5:00p Photo Call 7:30p Half Hour 8:00p Invited Dress	29 Preview #1 7:30p Half Hour 8:00p Curtain	30 Opening Performance 7:30p Half Hour 8:00p Curtain *Reception to Follow

Director: Dan F.
Rehearsal Location: Studio 353; 353 West 48th St., New York, NY 10036, *2nd Floor, Studio 3*
Tech & Performance Location: Whippoorwill Hall Theatre, North Castle Public Library, 19 Whippoorwill Rd. E, Armonk, NY 10504
PSM – Emily Roth: (555) 304 - 5555, smb@smb.com

1 of 2

Figure 6.10 Rehearsal Calendar Excerpt

enough to require a meal break (typically any rehearsal longer than 5 hours) include that in the schedule. Try to adhere to the scheduled time of these longer breaks as much as possible. These may be relied upon by the cast or the directors to take important phone calls, run errands, or have meetings that they may not be able to schedule outside rehearsal hours.

As you are scheduling, confirm who is needed for a given call; sometimes the director will only want to work with some of the performers in a scene or may need more people than are listed in the script as background performers (especially with musicals – confirm whether they want to work just the song, just the dance, the book scene, or the whole thing). Having different performers called at different times is referred to as a staggered call. You may also be scheduling separate vocal work, dance calls, or measurements/fittings. In many cases, these take place simultaneously with the regular rehearsal. The stage manager is often relied on to carefully arrange these rehearsals and fittings such that no performer is accidentally scheduled to be in two places at once. The daily call should be distributed as soon as possible after each day's rehearsal (Figure 6.11). Some directors prefer to schedule on a weekly basis instead of daily. In this case, you would distribute a weekly call at the start of each work week as well as a daily email outlining the next day's schedule and any additional information (Figure 6.12).

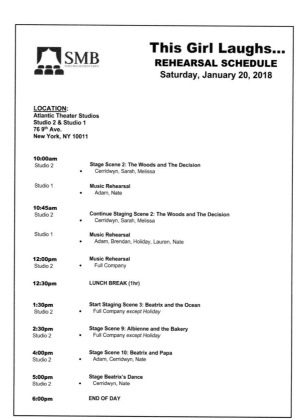

Figure 6.11 Daily Call

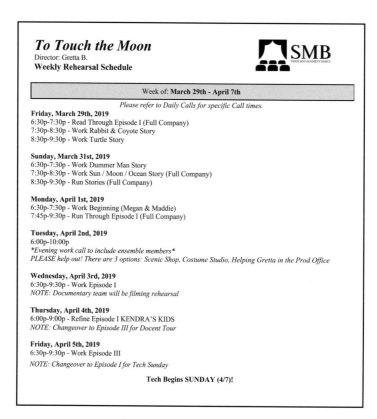

Figure 6.12 Weekly Call

Copies of the calendar and the daily should be posted on the callboard and kept in the promptbook. Remember to keep all these schedules updated throughout the process.

Scheduling Fittings

Often, the stage manager will coordinate between the performers and costume shop to schedule costume fittings prior to or during the rehearsal process. Out of respect for the performers' time, these are commonly scheduled during rehearsal hours. However, they may be scheduled outside of this if the shop's working hours don't align with rehearsals. Discuss this policy with the costume shop manager or PM during prep week so you know what to expect. Determine from the costume designer what days and times they are available to have fittings and how long they need to see each performer.

First Contact with the Cast

Once the schedule for the first day of rehearsal is set, make time to reach out to each cast member to answer any questions, share relevant information, and confirm first rehearsal details.

Prepping the Rehearsal Space

In order to properly prepare the rehearsal space, you should have a solid understanding of what will be happening in each rehearsal. Discuss with the director what their plan is for each rehearsal day (e.g., **table reads, table work, music rehearsal, staging rehearsal, choreography**, etc.). Use this information to determine how to set up the rehearsal room each time. This is also a good time to start asking the director when they would like to start having rehearsal furniture/props, rehearsal costumes, etc. For more on types of rehearsals, see Chapter 9.

Rehearsal Props/Furniture/Costumes

It is often the stage manager's job to pull rehearsal props and rehearsal furniture for the performers to use until the real props and furniture are available. These stand-ins should be about the same size and weight as the real thing so that the performers can become accustomed to working with them. Discuss the protocol of pulling rehearsal pieces with your PM, TD, or props department (depending on who is responsible for overseeing prop/furniture storage).

Having a rehearsal prop that is close to what the final prop will be is ideal; however, it is okay in many cases to use a stand-in. For example, a sanded block of wood of similar size and labeled for easy identification can make a perfect bar of soap or

Figure 6.13 Example Rehearsal Props: A solo cup and a block of 2×4, each labeled for easy identification

a phone (Figure 6.13). Remember that glass items have a strong tendency to break. For glassware and other fragile props, try to use plastic, acrylic, ceramic, or other sturdier materials until nearer to performance time.

It is important to have rehearsal furniture for blocking rehearsals. This furniture, like the props, should be similar in shape and size to the final furniture (e.g., the rehearsal chair should have arms if the final chair will have arms). As much as possible, use the final furniture as it becomes available (and you have been given approval to use it), but it is very likely you will be using mostly stand-ins. Larger furniture can be represented by acting cubes or chairs.

It is important to remind your director that you are using rehearsal pieces. Sometimes they will make staging choices based on the rehearsal pieces that will not be relevant with the real prop or piece of furniture. This is good for you to remember as well, since spike marks will need to be adjusted once the finalized pieces are in.

Rehearsal costume pieces may be needed for the show as well: women may need skirts or corsets, men may need suit jackets or hats. This is especially important with period costumes which might take up more physical space or create acting restrictions that will need to be taken into account when blocking. The performers will need time to adjust to acting in this garb. Shoes can also greatly affect movement and blocking and rehearsal shoes may be employed early on to get performers used to walking and dancing in the style of shoe they will be performing in. Additionally, the costume designer may have performers start wearing their show shoes during rehearsals if they are a brand-new pair (either to break them in and/or to give them a little "wear and tear" so they don't look brand new). Talk to the costume designer or wardrobe supervisor (if one exists) and request rehearsal pieces from them. Some theatres will require a sign-out sheet for items taken to rehearsal. Remember that rehearsal costumes that aren't related to period clothing are a luxury and that, professionally, performers are often expected to provide a few standard pieces (character shoes, dress shoes, slacks, and light sweaters) themselves.

> If there will be a lot of physical activity for a performer, especially down on the floor, it is considerate to provide kneepads in rehearsal. Kneepads may also be necessary in final costumes – keep your costume designer appraised, as this could affect the design and should be discussed in production meetings.

Prop Storage

All props (rehearsal and final) should be kept in a convenient, safe location. Many rehearsal spaces and theatres have dedicated tables or cabinets for this purpose. It is very important to keep the props neat and organized. Labeling the table or shelves of a props cabinet either by piece or scene by scene (usually with masking tape or white gaffers tape) will help performers put things back in the right spot and allow for quick and easy identification when something is missing. Many prop storage locations have locks because props have a habit of growing legs and wandering off. If this is the case, the storage needs to be locked every night, so make sure it is on your post-rehearsal checklist.

Callboard

A key element of any rehearsal room is the callboard. This should be centrally located, clearly labeled, and cleanly organized. The callboard is often a corkboard or fabric board mounted on a wall, but the information can also be taped directly onto a wall if a board is not available. The exact contents will vary depending on your production, but typically include sections for the rehearsal calendar, cast list, daily call, sign-in sheet, and important information. It is courteous to include a pencil/pen on a string near the sign-in sheet. When rehearsals move out of the rehearsal space and into the theatre, the callboard should come with you (Figure 6.14).

Tape Out

Once the groundplan is finalized and before staging rehearsals begin, the set needs to be taped out. This helps the entire team envision the space they'll eventually be working in. Tape out involves laying down tape on the rehearsal room floor outlining the shape of the set. This is to be done at full **scale** using the exact dimensions noted on the groundplan. When working in a space that is not the one you will use for the show's run (i.e., a rehearsal space), it may also be helpful to **tape out** the structural features (proscenium arch, front

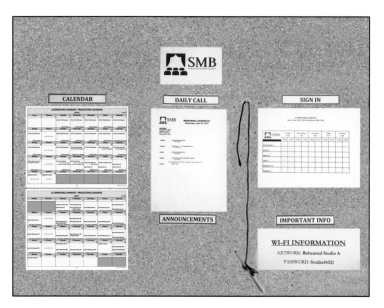

Figure 6.14 Picture of a Callboard

edge of the stage, back wall of the theatre, etc.) of the performance stage. Plan for it to take at least an hour. If it is a large or complex set, anticipate it taking longer (Figure 6.17).

Check in with the director to see if they have a preference about the orientation of the tape out in the rehearsal space. If the rehearsal space isn't large enough to tape out the entire set/theatre, discuss with the director (and choreographer if applicable) what they feel are the most important items to have taped out.

For designs that have moving **wagons** with multiple positions onstage, taping out each and every position can create a giant confusing web of spike tape. Instead, it can be helpful to use a section of carpet, cardboard, or muslin that is cut to match the size and shape of the set piece. Be careful, though – depending on the floor surface and material used, it can become slippery. If you are taping repetitive shapes of the same size, create a cardboard template to use so you don't have to measure the shape every time. Using different colors of tape for each position can help.

Required Tools for Tape Out

1. Broom and dustpan (and a mop, if available)
2. Spike tape (multiple colors)
3. Measuring tapes – two-four reel and two rigid (25 feet or longer). It is possible to do tape out with two tape measures, but having at least four is much easier and more accurate (Figure 6.15).

Figure 6.15 Required Tools for Tape Out

4. Architect's* Scale ruler (used to take measurements off a scaled groundplan; if you don't own one or know how to use one, this is an important investment both in time and equipment – they can be purchased online or at many office supply stores).
5. Scale groundplan – 1/4 or 1/2 inch is the most typically used scales in the United States.
   a. If you received an email with a groundplan, this DOES NOT mean that it is to scale! See the technical director for a printed scale groundplan to work from. If you know how to use Vectorworks or AutoCAD, an updated file will also work. If you do not know how to use a **CAD** program, it is very beneficial to learn the basics.
   b. For faster taping, take time prior to tape out to measure key points on the groundplan (Figure 6.16).
6. A framing square or laser level can be useful for your first few tape outs to help make sure your lines are straight.
7. A buddy (it is useful to have at least one other person to help, especially if you are new to the process).
8. Music and snacks (this can be a lengthy process, so having some tunes and food can make the time go faster!).
   *NOT an Engineer's scale ruler.

When taping the stage or space, use spike tape, as it is specifically designed to rip nicely in a straight line and its adhesive does not leave residue on the floor. Additionally, it is available in a variety of colors, which comes in handy for color coding different scenes or levels onstage. Always use what's needed to create an accurate tape out, but don't waste tape – it is expensive. It is a good idea to spot check and make sure the tape will indeed come off the floor without damaging it. Other sorts of tape should never be used for this purpose.

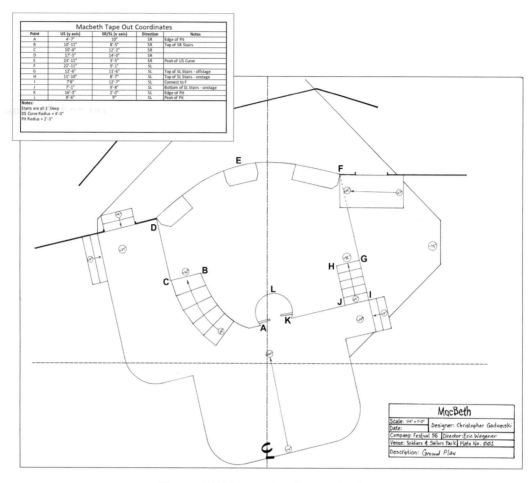

Point	US (y axis)	SR/SL (x axis)	Direction	Notes
A	4'-7"	10"	SR	Edge of Pit
B	10'-11"	8'-5"	SR	Top of SR Stairs
C	10'-0"	12'-2"	SR	
D	17'-5"	14'-0"	SR	
E	23'-11"	3'-5"	SR	Peak of US Curve
F	22'-11"	9'-1"	SL	
G	12'-6"	11'-6"	SL	Top of SL Stairs - offstage
H	11'-10"	8'-7"	SL	Top of SL Stairs - onstage
I	7'8"	12'-7"	SL	Connect to F
J	7'-1"	9'-8"	SL	Bottom of SL Stairs - onstage
K	16'-3"	2'-0"	SL	Edge of Pit
L	8'-6"	9"	SL	Peak of Pit

Macbeth Tape Out Coordinates

Notes:
Stairs are all 1' Deep
DS Curve Radius = 4'-0"
Pit Radius = 2'-3"

Figure 6.16 Example of Coordinates

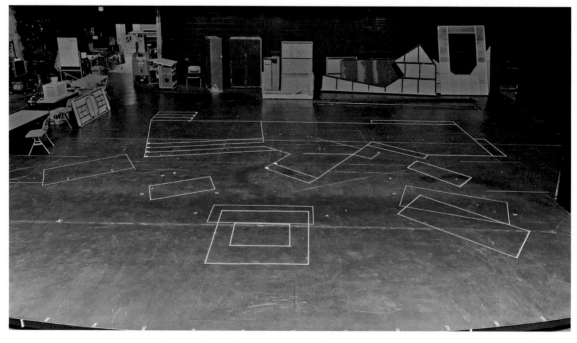

Figure 6.17 Example of a Completed Tape Out

Taping Out

X Y Coordinate

1. Prior to your scheduled tape out, measure the ground plan to find the (x, y) coordinate points for each corner of each piece of scenery. Create a chart to record this information, then you can easily plot them on the floor based off the **centerline (y)** and the **plaster line (x)** and speed up the whole process. Label the points – letters work well.

2. Thoroughly sweep the space prior to any taping. The tape will not stick well on a dusty floor. Mop if possible.

3. Lay out measuring tapes marking the plaster line and the centerline.
   a. Tape down at either end and at the intersection point to keep in place. These will need to remain stationary throughout the tape out process (Figure 6.18).

4. Use the groundplan, your tape measure, and your previously plotted points to mark out key coordinates on the floor.
   a. Go up the centerline (the y axis) to the first coordinate and then measure out stage left or stage right to the other (x) coordinate. Measure from the plaster line (if you are using one) up to make sure the line stays even.

5. At each point place a small piece of spike tape, label it with the appropriate letter.

6. Connect the dots to mark out the groundplan.
   a. Leave gaps to indicate doorways and include a strip of tape, imitating the door itself, to indicate which side the door is hinged on and which direction it opens.
   b. Switch colors to indicate different levels or playing areas.
      i. If objects (e.g., **platforms**) overlap, = you can use a dashed line for one and a solid line for the other.
      ii. As much as possible, make a color-coded plan prior to tape out, taking into account which colors and how much of each are on hand.

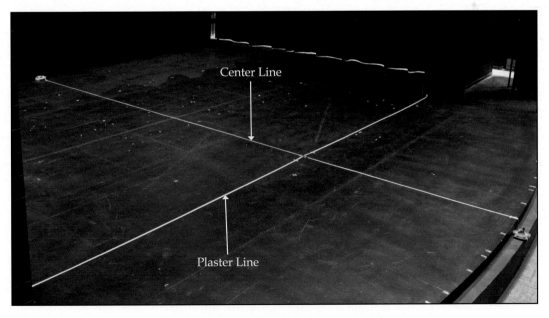

Figure 6.18 Example of XY Coordinate Setup

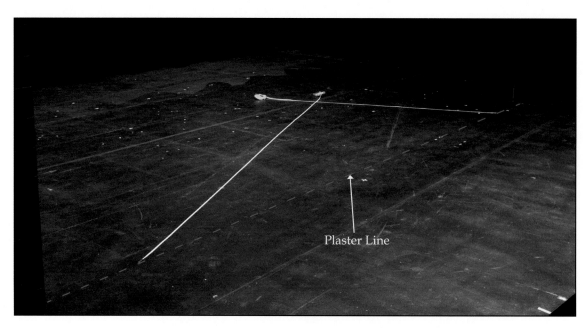

Figure 6.19 Example of Triangulation Setup

Triangulation

1. Prior to your scheduled tape out, choose two fixed points from the ground plan that also exist in the theatre (e.g., 4 feet from center SL and SR on the plaster line).
2. Label the main points of the set and measure their distance from each of your fixed points. Also note which quadrant of the stage the point is in (USL, DSL, USR, or DSR).
3. Thoroughly sweep the space prior to any taping. The tape will not stick well on a dusty floor. Mop if possible.
4. Find and mark the fixed points that you identified in step one. Hold or affix the zero point of a reel tape measure to each point (Figure 6.19).
   a. Screwing them to the floor works well if that is allowed, otherwise have someone hold them at the appropriate spot.
5. Use your ground plan, tape measures, and your measurements to lay out the groundplan.
   a. Find the distance from the fixed SR point to the first labeled point (point A) on your ground plan, hold that mark on the SR reel tape, and then find the distance from the SL fixed point to point A.
   b. Move to the quadrant that the point is in and find the spot where the tape measures cross.
6. Place a small piece of spike tape (labeled "A") under the crossed tape measures.
7. This step is the same as for X Y coordinate taping (connect the dots).

Outdoor

"Taping out" for outdoor rehearsals can be tricky but thankfully many of the same principles apply. Some of the unique considerations for outdoor theatre are how/if you are allowed to alter the ground you are working on (think marking things with paint like a sportsball field), making sure that you haven't created trip hazards, and having something sturdy enough to hold up to the elements and/or repeated use. Some options include rope and tent stakes, spray paint, or streamers/ribbons weighted with rocks.

Taping out is one of many aspects of stage management where practice makes perfect. Tape out can be quite tricky, depending on the complexity of the groundplan and your experience with plotting points, and can be hard to master. But it will get easier with time and practice. Do the best you can and don't be afraid to ask for help if you get stuck!

> Cloth spike tape is more likely to stay in place for longer if it is stretched slightly as it is laid down. Pull tightly and press down firmly so that your marks will last through rehearsal. If you are using a non-cloth spike tape, use scissors when cutting to prevent the tape from curling up.

Dance Numbers

When doing a musical or show with heavy dance/choreography, it is advisable to also tape out **dance numbers** or **quarters**. Check with the choreographer to see if they have a preference. These divide the stage into easily visible equal sections and help the performers and choreographer with spacing.

To make dance numbers, make a mark at the centerline on the far downstage edge of the stage This will serve as the "0" point. From there, make tick marks every two feet and tape out or write numbers (on gaff tape) at each of these marks (the marks two feet out from center should both be numbered "2", the next out will be "4", etc.). Make sure these numbers are large enough and facing in the correct direction for the performers to read from the stage. The choreographer may also want tick marks every foot, so ask for their preference. Depending on the complexity of the show, these numbers may also be required for performances. In that case, repeat this process on the stage after the floor treatment has been completed. These can also be painted on, depending on the floor treatment and the preference of the scenic designer and the director (Figure 6.20).

Quarters are less visually obvious and are most common in dance (Figure 6.21). They divide the stage into quarters and eighths. After splitting the stage in half by marking center, continue to divide the stage into quarter and eighth segment. To do so, mark halfway between center and the proscenium (a quarter), then mark an onstage eighth between

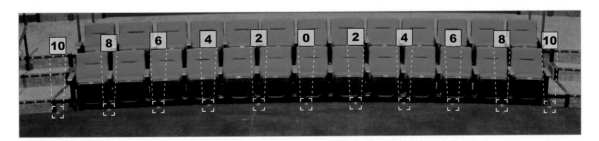

Figure 6.20 Example of Dance Numbers on a Stage

Figure 6.21 Example of Quarters

center and the quarter, and then an offstage eighth between the quarter mark and the proscenium. Typically, center and quarters are marked in one color of spike tape and are slightly larger marks, while the eighths are marked in a contrasting color and are slightly smaller.

Basic Tools and Supplies

There are basic tools and supplies that all stage managers should invest in. Listed below are a few of the more critical ones.

Office Supplies

A good stage manager is never without a full stock of office supplies. From pens, pencils, and highlighters to paper, sticky notes, a hole punch, and a stapler, all will become critical to have on hand. Invest in high-quality supplies for your own use, as well as cheaper extras of everything to provide for your team. Inevitably, the performers will forget a pencil, the director will forget notepaper, and no one will ever have an eraser. Usually, the stage manager can (and should) be reimbursed for shared office supplies, so be sure to keep receipts for these purchases.

> Back-to-school season is a great time to stock up on office supplies. Some good supplies to be on the lookout for are Pilot FriXion pens, highlighters and pens, sticky notes, post-it flags, mechanical pencils, extra scissors, and legal pads.

Tape

Many different types of tape are required for different purposes and jobs. **Gaffers (gaff) tape**, spike tape, **glow tape**, and **marley tape** will be the four most heavily used tapes. These are often available from the venue. If not, they will likely be purchased out of the stage management budget.

It is a good idea to invest a little money into a personal tape stock, but be careful to get reimbursed for the tape you use as it gets expensive quickly. One roll of gaff tape and a couple colors of spike tape are a good starting place; glow tape and Marley tape are good additional items to have around. Be sure to keep your personal tape secure and labeled so it doesn't grow legs and wander off or get used by one of the other crews.

Tools

Similar to office supplies, there are a few standard tools that a stage manager should invest in. These include a high-quality 25- or 30-foot tape measure, a 100-foot flat reel tape measure, screwdrivers (both Phillips and flathead options), a utility knife, a stopwatch, a good flashlight, and an **architect's scale ruler**. Also highly recommended are a multi tool, a hex key set (commonly needed for doors with crash bars), and a power strip.

Stage Management Kit

A **stage management kit** is essentially a toolbox (oftentimes literally) of basic supplies that might be necessary in rehearsal or in performance. Tackle boxes and Pelican cases are great for this. Depending on the theatre, a stage manager may use a personal kit or the theatre may have one for use by the stage manager. If it is a personal kit, sometimes theatres will reimburse the stage manager for items taken from the kit. If it is the theatre's kit, find out who is responsible for supplies and replenishment.

Generic Kit Contents

- Pens/pencils/Sharpies/erasers/highlighters
- Refills of lead and erasers for mechanical pencils
- Notebook paper/notepads
- Hole reinforcers (donut stickers)
- Sticky notes
- Sticky arrows, tabs, flags
- Paperclips
- Rubber bands
- Three-hole punch
- Small stapler
- Scissor
- Spike tape
- Crescent (adjustable) wrench
- Screwdrivers (Phillips head and flat head)
- Flashlight
- Pocket knife
- Multitool
- Extension cord
- Power strip
- Hand sanitizer
- Tissues
- Lotion
- Tide spot cleaner
- Wet wipes
- Feminine hygiene products
- Pain relievers (Ibuprofen and acetaminophen – have both in case of allergies)
- Triple antibiotic ointment
- Burn cream
- Tums/Pepto Bismol tablets
- Non-drowsy allergy pills
- Decongestant tablets
- Glucose tablets or gel
- Band-Aids
- Ace bandage
- Ice packs
- CPR barrier mask
- Cough drops
- Mints/mouth spray (for performers)
- Disposable toothbrush/toothpaste
- Deodorant
- Dental floss
- Disposable razors
- Bobby pins
- Hair ties

- Clear nail polish
- Safety pins
- Mini sewing kit (needles, thread, seam ripper, thimble)
- ~~Deck of cards~~
- Batteries

- USB Powerbank
- Bluetooth Speaker
- Common charging cables
- Stress ball
- Coloring books and crayons/colored pencils (markers are not recommended)

> Depending on the theatre and local laws, the stage manager may not be legally allowed to dispense over-the-counter medications. They can, however, mention that the supplies exist and point folks in the right direction.

Chapter Seven
Promptbook and Paperwork

A critical aspect of a stage manager's job is creating and maintaining both the promptbook and show paperwork. These serve as a way to maintain clear and constant communication between all departments and company members, keep track of the massive amounts of information that the stage manager must be responsible for, and, ultimately, will stand as an archive of the production. The paperwork you will need to produce will vary depending on your company and your production. There are many pieces of paperwork that you will use for every show and some that will be necessary on certain productions, but not others. You may also find that you need to create a brand new type of paperwork, especially for a particular show. There is also no one way to format any particular piece of paperwork, as long as it is easily understandable for anyone reading it. Find or create a style that works best for your needs!

Paperwork

When preparing for a show, it is important to use your prep week to complete, partially complete, or make a template of all the paperwork needed for the production. By doing so, the stage manager can save time and mental energy later in the process that will be needed for other tasks. Some paperwork examples are provided in this book, as well as on the companion website. Additionally, there are many websites and other stage management books with further examples. Try out multiple versions and find or create the templates that work best for you.

After selecting or creating templates for all of the paperwork, the next step is to customize them for the production. Each page should include not only the name of the production, but also a few other consistent pieces of information, including the date, page X of Y, name of the stage manager who created the paperwork, and version (if applicable). Some stage managers also list the director and the name of the production company. In addition to consistent information, paperwork should use only a couple of standard, legible fonts (e.g., Times New Roman, Arial) that are consistent between all documents for each show. Additionally, it can be fun to choose a "show font" for the show title (one that is a bit more whimsical and matches the mood and style of the production). It is also considerate to have consistent formatting across similar pieces of paperwork (rehearsal reports, **performance reports**, meeting notes). This will make them easily identifiable and easy to read,

DOI: 10.4324/9781003133049-8

and will create unity among the paperwork. Some companies may have headers, logos, and/or specific paperwork formats that they would like you to include and/or use.

> Remember over the course of your career you may do shows multiple times, so noting the producing organization and year will help you better keep up with your archive.

It is good practice to include the date in the name of any distributed documents so that everyone is sure to be working from the same document (e.g., Grease Rehearsal Report 9.14.pdf). This is especially important with calendars/schedules, when working off the most updated information is of the utmost importance. If multiple reports are distributed on the same day (e.g., a two-performance day), distinguish these in some way as well (e.g., Sylvia Performance Report 2.2 2pm.pdf and Sylvia Performance Report 2.2 8pm.pdf). If it is the same report with updated or corrected information, include UPDATED or REVISED in the title.

Prep Week Paperwork List

At this point in the process, check in again with your prep week checklist to make sure you complete all necessary paperwork prior to the start of rehearsals. If you have the time, it is beneficial to prep more paperwork than you think you might need for the show; that way you have it ready just in case it becomes necessary. Here are the essential pieces that should be created:

Paperwork to Complete During Prep Week

Contact Sheet

Get initial contact information from the producing company and reach out to all members of the company (cast, crew, creative, production, etc.) to confirm/fill in any missing information. Before distributing to the full company, confirm with each person what information they are comfortable having distributed beyond the stage management team and edit the document for distribution accordingly (Figure 7.1). This can be a good place to note people's pronouns as well.

Emergency Medical Forms

This is a basic form that should be filled out by everyone who will be present in the rehearsal room on a regular basis. It will provide you with each person's emergency contact information as well as dietary restrictions, allergy information, pre-existing injuries, etc. It should be noted (both in person and on the form) that this is confidential and for stage management only and that all provided information is voluntary. Be sure to have more blank forms available during load-in or the first day of tech for any technicians or backstage crew members to fill out as well. Shred these documents as soon as the show has closed (Figure 7.2).

- Allergies should be taken into account for any edible props or company meals, but additionally can be relevant to the wardrobe and makeup departments and even the sound department (if there are any allergies to certain mic tape adhesives).

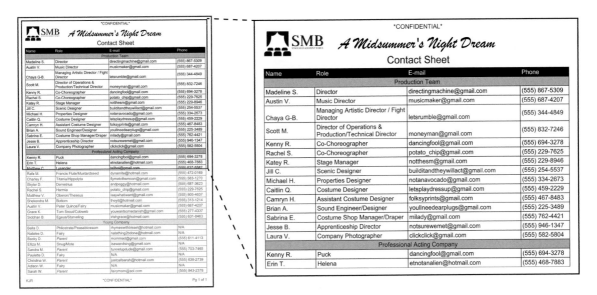

Figure 7.1 Contact Sheet

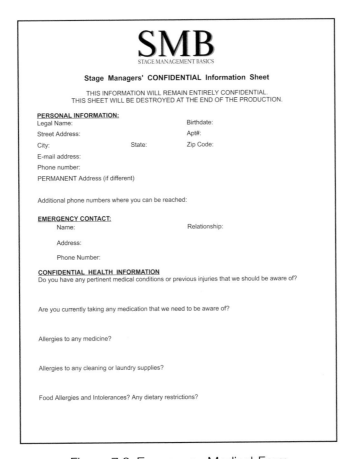

Figure 7.2 Emergency Medical Form

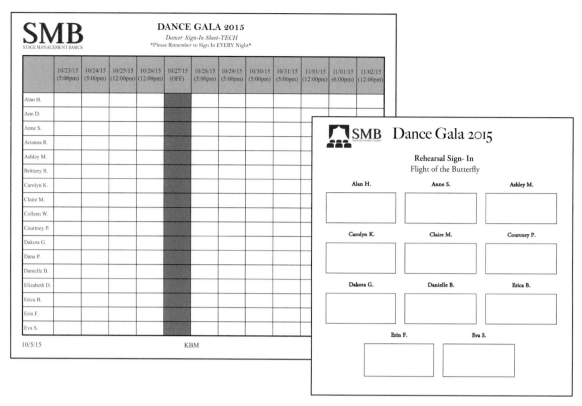

Figure 7.3 Sign-in Sheet(s)

Sign-in Sheets

These can be very useful on large productions or shows with lots of staggered calls. These can be made either weekly (if you need a running record of attendance) or a single reusable version (laminated or in a plastic page protector that can be erased each day). Even on a small show, sign-in sheets will be useful once you get into tech and performances, when it can be less obvious when everyone has arrived (Figure 7.3).

Running Order

This is optional, but can be a very useful piece of paperwork for the performers once you start running the show. It is a very bare-bones list of all the scenes in order. If there aren't scenes, create your own breakdown either by French scenes or by large definable sections. Post these around the rehearsal room and/or backstage at common entrances/exits and by **prop tables** for cast and crew to reference as a reminder of what is coming up next (Figure 7.4).

Blocking Symbol Shorthand Key

This is primarily for yourself and for anyone who might need to read your promptbook. Create a basic key of all the symbols/shorthand you will use for blocking on this particular

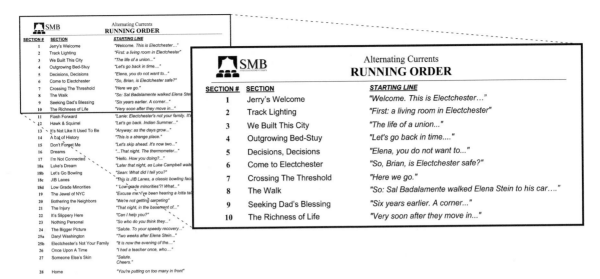

Figure 7.4 Running Order Excerpt

production (including character shorthands, set/furniture shorthands, etc.). This list will likely evolve throughout the rehearsal process. See Chapter 9 for more information about blocking.

> When taking blocking notes (and also in notes for reports), it is good practice to use character names rather than performer names. This will clear up confusion if there are performers playing multiple characters or if there are understudies or replacement performers. Designers are also much more likely to be familiar with character names.

Templates to Create During Prep Week

Rehearsal Report

This is a report generated at the end of each rehearsal that outlines information about what was accomplished that day, any notes or questions for designers or production areas, and any other important notes. While exact layout and content will vary depending on the production and company, your report should also always include the show title, venue/location of the rehearsal, date and time of the rehearsal, the preparer's name (yours), sections calling out any absences or lateness, and any injuries or illness (Figure 7.5).

Meeting Notes

Similar to the rehearsal report, these are an organized record of the things discussed at any meetings (we will go into more details on this in the next chapter), commonly divided up by department for ease of comprehension. These typically include time and date of the

Written by David Auburn
Directed by Dan F.

Proof
Rehearsal Report # 1
Prepared by Emily Roth

Tuesday, March 5th, 2019

Location:	**REHEARSAL ACCOMPLISHED:**
Studio 353, 2nd Floor, Studio 3	11:00am Equity Business
353 West 48th Street, New York, NY 10036	11:25am Design Presentations (Scenic, Costumes, Sound)
	11:50am Break / Costume Measurements
START: 11:00am	12:24pm Read-Thru (Act I)
END: 4:00pm	1:13pm Break (Intermission)
TOTAL: 5.0 hours	1:23pm Read-Thru (Act II)
	2:08pm End read / initial responses
LATE: N/A	2:12pm Break
ABSENT/EXCUSED: N/A	2:24pm Table Work
INJURIES/ILLNESS: N/A	3:40pm END OF DAY

GENERAL NOTES:
1. A great first day of rehearsal! We started the day with some quick equity business before our designers arrived for presentations. Dan gave an overview of the set for us, then we heard from Leslie and Garrett. We were running ahead of schedule, so we took an extended break while Leslie checked in with the actors individually for measurements and to discuss Thursday's photo shoot. We had a lovely read-through, followed by a good hour of table work.
2. We discovered during the read-through that we have two different versions of the script in the room! Over the next couple days, we're going to look at the few minor discrepancies and decide which version we are using.
3. **Read-Through Run Time:**
    Act I: 47min 31sec
    Act II: 41min 31sec
    Total: 1hr 29min 26sec

SCENIC:
1. No notes today, thank you!

PROPS:
1. Thank you for stopping by rehearsal today!
2. As discussed, we would love for the drawer key to be on a chain with another charm or something already on it – as though Catherine added the key to something she already owned. Perhaps something her mother gave her?

COSTUMES:
1. Thank you for stopping by rehearsal today!
2. Thank you for the rehearsal jackets and shoes!

LIGHTING:
1. No notes today, thank you!

SOUND:
1. Thank you for stopping by rehearsal today!

FIGHT CHOREOGRAPHY:
1. No notes today, thank you!

PRODUCTION MANAGEMENT:
1. No notes today, thank you!

COMPANY / GENERAL MANAGEMENT:
1. Thank you for stopping by rehearsal today!

1 of 1

Figure 7.5 Rehearsal Report

meeting, a list of all attendees, and a distribution list, in addition to the notes themselves (Figure 7.6).

Performance Report

This is a report generated at the end of each performance summarizing the performance for company members that were not present. It includes information such as time/date, performance number, run time(s), house count, any notes or concerns regarding design

The Heiress
Production Meeting Notes
Monday, July 1st ~ 10:30pm

SCENIC:
- ❖ Catherine will be sitting in the window seat with a hurricane lantern in Act II, scene 2. We need to make sure that the curtains will not catch on fire (either flame retardant material or placement onstage)
- ❖ The mayor will be lending us the chair set for the Sloper chairs!
- ❖ The window seat will be 24" tall. There needs to be a discussion between Jonathan and Evie about details on how this will look.
- ❖ The baseboards will be made out of 2" foam.
- ❖ The front door will not be seen (for shadow and sound only). So, we'd like a solid door, but it doesn't have to look any particular way.
- ❖ Completed set pieces will be moved into the wings of the Grace for Evie to start cartooning
- ❖ We will be using Chris' white Writing Desk from Lend Me A Tenor

COSTUMES:
- ❖ Catherine will have a bonnet and gloves to put on in Act II, scene 2
  - o We would like to make a reticule for Catherine that will match her dress in II.2.
- ❖ We would like a rehearsal jacket for Dr. Sloper.
  - o His jacket is very similar to a blazer. We will ask Bob if he has one he can bring in to start working with. If not, Costumes can have one for us by Sunday.
- ❖ Please stretch Dr. Sloper's's shoes as soon as possible so we can start rehearsing with them.
- ❖ We would like hoops and corsets fitted for rehearsal by Saturday.

LIGHTING:
- ❖ We will be having a sound meeting at 12pm on Sunday, July 7th.
- ❖ Hurricane Lanterns are in the Prouty, Jen will take some time to work with them and see how much light they throw.

SOUND:
- ❖ We will be having a sound meeting at 12pm on Sunday, July 7th.
- ❖ Rather than getting a doorbell, we would just like a door knocker and we will adjust the line that refers to a doorbell.

PROPS:
- ❖ To obscure the clock face, we will try to find an ornate Victorian clock face and remove the hands.
  - o If this doesn't work, we can just fog the glass with soap.
- ❖ The brandy glasses need to be more ornate.
- ❖ For the hurricane lanterns, we will want one that flares up or is a straight cylinder (these are the safest).
- ❖ The final prop add date is Sunday, July 7th.
- ❖ All of the chairs should be armless (the only exception being Dr. Sloper's chair).

1 of 2

Figure 7.6 Meeting Notes Excerpt

elements (broken props, costume repairs, a light that looks out of place), and typically a quick summary of how the performance went (including audience engagement and any notable occurrences in the performance) (Figure 7.7).

Preset Lists

This is a checklist that you will eventually use before each performance to set the props, costumes, and set pieces in the appropriate spots to run the show as efficiently as possible.

PETER & THE STARCATCHER
Performance Report

Performance #5
Time: 2:00pm

Wednesday, July 25th, 2018

Act I	Intermission	Act 2
2:06pm-3:03pm; 56min 16sec	3:03pm-3:18pm; 14min	3:18pm-4:14pm; 56min 02sec

Total Run Time: 1hr 52min 19sec

House Open: 1:40pm
House Count: 78

ACCIDENTS/INJURY:
1. Andrew scraped his finger sometime during Act II before his uke song. He doesn't know exactly when or how it happened. He got a bandaid backstage.

LATE / ABSENT:
1. N/A

PERFORMANCE NOTES:
1. Good performance today! We had a typically quiet matinee audience, which was definitely a bit of an adjustment after yesterday's house. The cast was also a bit on the tired side today, so we lost a bit of the preciseness we usually have throughout the show. In particular, we ran into some traffic issues during the end of Act I throughout all of Hurricano. No one was injured, but we had a few minor collisions and unusual traffic patterns. Act II ran much more smoothly. The running scene in particular was really on point! The audience also warmed up more for Act II and we had a rousing round of applause at curtain call, along with a full standing ovation.

TECHNICAL NOTES:
1. **SCENIC:** The dock posts seem to be coming loose. Could these please get re-tacked down before tomorrow evening's performance?
2. **SCENIC:** The new sliders on the Act I ship are working great. Thank you so much!
3. **PROPS:** A slider came off one of the trunks during fight call today. We re-glued it and it didn't give us any more issues throughout the show.
4. **COSTUMES:** Black Stache has ripped a hole in his left pants knee again. Could this please be repaired and reinforced before our next performance?

1 of 1

Figure 7.7 Performance Report

At this point in the process, you will not be able to fill in any information on this sheet. However, by putting together a template, you will be able to fill it in as rehearsals go along, thus saving time later (Figure 7.8).

Incident Report

This template should include a place to document the incident type, who was involved, a description of the incident, if and what type of medical treatment was administered, and

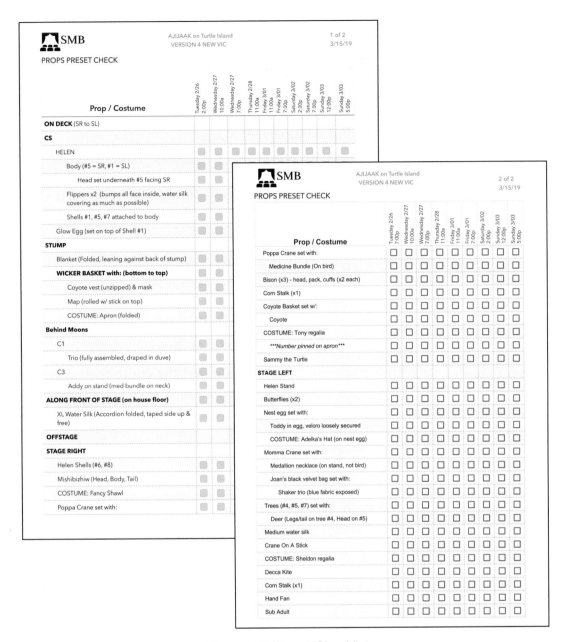

Figure 7.8 Preset Checklist

a place for any witness information. Incident reports may be provided by the company or workers compensation insurance company (see Figure 5.2, p. 40).

Run Sheet

This paperwork will serve as the backstage "task" list during the run of the show. It outlines every action that happens backstage to make the show happen (transitions/scene changes, costume quick changes, prop handoffs or catches, curtain **pages**, etc.). There should be sections that answer the questions *who* is doing *what*, *where*, and *when* along with a section for additional notes. These sometimes include limited pre-show duties, such as

SMB

Urinetown

SMB Productions

WHO:	TASK:	WHAT:	WHERE:	WHEN:	NOTES:
TOP OF SHOW					
	Sweep	Deck		Prior to House Open	
	Damp Mop	Deck		Prior to House Open	
	Set	Props SL, SR, Onstage		Prior to House Open	
DURING I.1					
INTO I.2 TO UGC - "*Mr. Cladwell*" - Shift Red					
DURING I.2					
INTO I.3 TO THE STREET - Shift Blue					
INTO I.4 TO THE AMENITY - Shift Violet					
INTO I.5 TO UGC - Shift Pink					
INTO I.6 TO THE AMENITY - Shift Navy					
INTERMISSION					

Updated: 7/28/14 KBM 1 of 6

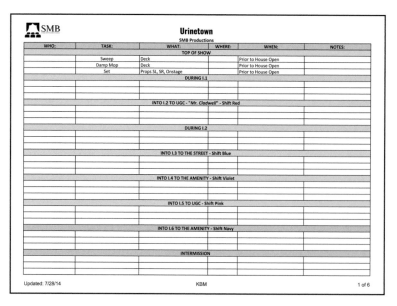

Figure 7.9 Preliminary Run Sheet Excerpt

sweeping, mopping, presetting props (as a note to do it, not the entire prop preset list), and checking top of show presets for scenery. Prep sections for each scene and the transitions between scenes. This can be a lot of information and will likely become your most extensive piece of paperwork (Figure 7.9).

Entrance/Exit Plot (Ent/Ext Plot)

This is very similar to a French Scene Breakdown, but goes into further detail about exactly when and where each character comes on and off stage. It can also include information about props and costumes. You will be filling this in during rehearsal as the staging is set (Figure 7.10).

String of Pearls

Entrance/Exit Sheet

Pg	Character	Actor	Ent	Ex	Line	Prop	Costume
9	Hallie	Becca F.		DSL	"What?"		
9	Roberta	Maggie H.		DSR	"What?"		
9	Beth	Amanda W.		DSL	"I'll call him."		
10	Beth	Amanda W.	DSL		"...on our work and on each other."		
10	Amy	Kimberly H.		DSR	"And the dress."		
10	Beth	Amanda W.		DSL	"..throw in the towel and elope."		
10	Amy	Kimberly H.	USR		"..throw in the towel and elope."	Stack of wedding photos	
10	Beth	Amanda W.	DSL		"White, shiny, round as marbles."		
12	Amy	Kimberly H.		USR	"She was thirty-nine. August 1969."	--Stack of wedding photos	Beth removes housecoat
Scene 2 - Beth Gets the Pearls from Ethan (1969)							
13	Saleswoman	Jessica P	DSL		"I went to Bonwit Teller"		Red Dress
13	Saleswoman	Jessica P		DSL	*after the dress is on Amanda*		
14	Beverly	Alisha S.	DSR		"...and dragged me over to the bar."		
14	Beverly	Alisha S.		DSL	"Besides, you look like you could use it."		
16	Beverly	Alisha S.	USR		"...and whispers "String of Pearls"		
17	Beverly	Alisha S.		USR	"Too much work."		

1/5/21 KBM 1 of 1

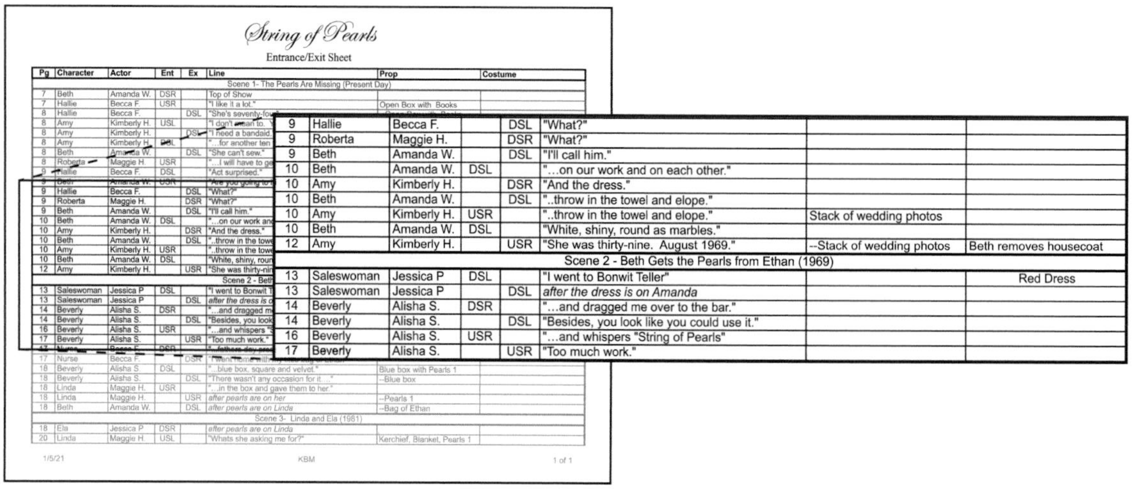

Figure 7.10 Entrance/Exit Plot Excerpt

Often, it can be useful to combine the ent/ext plot and the run sheets into a single document during rehearsals. From the ent/ext plot, you will be able to better predict the best times/places for prop handoffs, quick changes, speedy crossovers, etc.

Blocking Pages or Slip Sheets

These pages are typically printed on the back of each script page or slipped between the pages of the script (hence the name "**slip sheet**") and are used to notate blocking. These are very much an individual preference in terms of layout, but typically include a mini image of the groundplan and lines or space for staging notes. Some stage managers also like to include boxes or sections for notes such as prop and costume tracking or scenic notes (Figure 7.11).

Line Notes

Create a template for distributing line notes to the performers. There are a variety of ways you can do this depending on if you are writing notes by hand in rehearsal or typing them up later to distribute via email. Find the method that works best for you and your team (Figure 7.12).

Optional and Additional Paperwork to Create

Welcome Packets

Depending on your theatre, you might make a welcome packet for your cast and creatives. These are especially common on shows working with anyone from out of town. Usually, they will have a welcome letter from stage management, including information about the

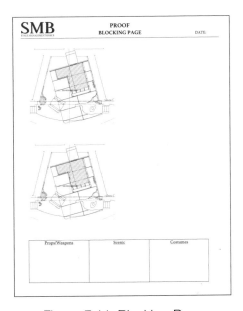

Figure 7.11 Blocking Page

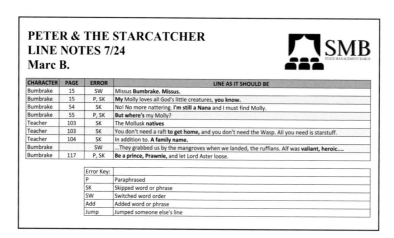

PETER & THE STARCATCHER
LINE NOTES 7/24
Marc B.

CHARACTER	PAGE	ERROR	LINE AS IT SHOULD BE
Bumbrake	15	SW	Missus **Bumbrake. Missus.**
Bumbrake	15	P, SK	**My** Molly loves all God's little creatures, **you know.**
Bumbrake	54	SK	No! No more nattering. **I'm still a Nana** and I must find Molly.
Bumbrake	55	P, SK	**But where's** my Molly?
Teacher	103	SK	The Mollusk **natives**
Teacher	103	SK	You don't need a raft **to get home,** and you don't need the Wasp. All you need is starstuff.
Teacher	104	SK	In addition to. **A family name.**
Bumbrake		SW	...They grabbed us by the mangroves when we landed, the ruffians. Alf was **valiant, heroic....**
Bumbrake	117	P, SK	**Be a prince, Prawnie,** and let Lord Aster loose.

Error Key:	
P	Paraphrased
SK	Skipped word or phrase
SW	Switched word order
Add	Added word or phrase
Jump	Jumped someone else's line

Figure 7.12 Line Notes

rehearsal/performance spaces, Wi-Fi info, company policies, etc. Sometimes the producer, AD, or **company manager** will also provide you with a letter, which may include information on tickets/comps, parking, etc. For out-of-towners or those new to the area, it is common to include information on local restaurants, amenities (laundromats, grocery stores, gyms, tech repair shops) as well as locations of hospitals and urgent care centers. If you are handing out welcome packets, these will also be where you put things like the rehearsal schedule, scene breakdowns, blank emergency medical forms, copies of the company handbook (if one exists), etc. (Figure 7.13).

Script Cover Pages

If you are distributing script binders or welcome packets to your cast, it can be a nice touch to make a cover sheet for each individual that includes the show title (typically in the form of a show logo), the producing company or theatre, and the individual's name and role/

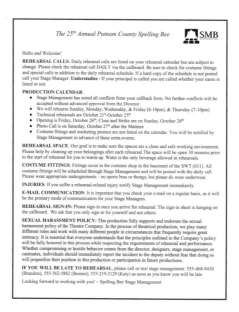

Figure 7.13 Welcome Letter

Figure 7.14 Binder Cover Page by Lauren Fitzgerald Veit

position. These are helpful for quickly distinguishing scripts and add a little personalization for each team member (Figure 7.14).

Script Changes Tracking Sheet

For any new works, the stage management team is often in charge of tracking script changes throughout the process. Create a master document for keeping track of all of these changes. It should include page numbers, the type of change being made, the text of the change, and the date the change was made (Figure 7.15).

Reminder of Paperwork Previously Introduced

- Production Analysis (see Figure 6.5, p. 50)
- Prop List (see Figure 6.6, p. 53)

PG	CHANGE	LINE	DATE
3	LINE ASSIGNMENT	MARIA: SHELDON: Lend us a smile!	5/2/19
4	CHANGE	EEL: I hear it's so sparkly, even the Shimmerfish had to wear shades when she saw it. just to look at it.	5/2/19
4	CHANGE	POUT-POUT: Saw Look at what??	5/2/19
6	CHANGE	MS. CLAM: Splendid. But here's a bit pearl of advice, Pout-Pout. Happy. Smile.	5/2/19
6	LINE ASSIGNMENT / CHANGE	MS CLAM + MARIA + ANA: THE PEARL, THE PEARL, MS CLAM + MARIA + ANA: MY PEARL.	5/2/19
7	CUT	POUT-POUT: Happy. Smile. Cherry cheeries. Sounds... Let's show em what ya got.	5/2/19
7	LINE ASSIGNMENT/ADD	ANASTASIA: POUT-POUT: Happy! Angry! Surprised! Confused! Scared! Silly! Bored! Stunned!!?? This is impossible.	5/2/19
7	CHANGE	POUT-POUT: Confused! Disgusted! Silly! Scared! Stunned!!?? This is impossible.	5/2/19
9	CHANGE	POUT-POUT: THEY'RE GONNA WISH THEY HAD A FACE LIKE MINE	5/2/19
10	CHANGE	BULLY SHARK: It's just not worth it anymore...I've been dreaming up... I'm not in the mood	5/2/19
14	CHANGE	ANASTASIA: And as Pout-Pout blubbed his final blub...he let out the biggest dreary-weary ever. exited his mouth.	5/2/19
20	ADD	POUT-POUT: C'mon, my reef is in danger. I need that pearl. Have a heart! OCTOPUS: I've got three.	5/2/19
20	CUT	OCTOPUS: You're the one giving me that sour look. Try asking a little nicer.	5/2/19

The Pout-Pout Fish
Script Changes
as of 5/7/19

E. Roth   1 of 8

Figure 7.15 Script Changes Tracking Sheet Excerpt

- Scene Breakdowns (Standard and French, if needed) (see Figure 6.7–6.8, p. 54, 55)
- Conflict Calendars (see Figure 6.9, p. 58)
- Rehearsal Schedules (see Figure 6.10, p. 61)
- Daily and Weekly Calls (see Figures 6.11 and 6.12, p. 62, 63)

GENERAL NOTE ABOUT PAPERWORK

Whenever you distribute any paperwork electronically, it is good practice to send it in PDF form. This helps prevent any format changes or accidental editing on the part of the recipient. Only send editable versions of things when you intend them to be edited. Additionally, for reports and schedules, it is helpful to copy and paste the contents into the body of your email as well as attaching a PDF version. Your co-workers are more likely to read it if they don't have to open an attachment and there is less possibility of faulty documents impeding the process. Always double-check formatting and accuracy of information before distributing.

The Promptbook

One of the most important items for a stage manager (and any production) is the promptbook. The promptbook, sometimes called the "Show Bible" or "The Book," is a binder (or binders) containing any and all important information pertaining to the show. This binder is put together and maintained by the stage manager. Prep week is when you should begin putting together the preliminary elements of the binder, which will then be added to and updated throughout the rehearsal and performance process.

Typically, this will require a rather large binder (anywhere from 2 to 5 inches depending on the show). It is best to use a view binder (the kind with a plastic sleeve around the outside), so a cover page and spine label can be used to easily identify it as the show promptbook. Use binder tabs or dividers to separate the major sections (e.g., Cast Information, Script, Rehearsal Reports, etc.).

If your show has a stage management team (more than one person), each member will typically have their own book to take notes in and maintain throughout the process. However, it will be the Production Stage Manager or lead stage manager whose book will ultimately become the official promptbook for the production, using information compiled from all team members.

Promptbooks will vary from production to production, but an archive-ready promptbook will usually include the following information:

Preparing the Promptbook Script

Another important step in promptbook preparation is prepping the blocking script. Just as with the paperwork you have created ahead of time, you will save yourself a ton of time and anxiety later in the process if you take the time to organize and prepare the script ahead of rehearsals.

- Inserting blocking pages/slip sheets – Decide which method of blocking you would like to use (see Chapter 9 for more details). If using the groundplan and numbering method, you can either insert your slip sheets between script pages or print them on the reverse side of your script pages.
- Hole-punching your script – Decide which side of the binder you would like your script pages to be on vs. your blocking notes (if you are not writing your blocking in the text). This is very much dependent on your personal preferences and even possibly on the particular production. Try different layouts and see which works best for you! Punching on the right hand side of the page can make it easier to write, especially for leftys (think about where your hand will be writing in relation to the rings in the binder).
- Tabbing your script (mark each act and scene or however else you and the director plan on splitting up the script if acts/scenes aren't defined). This is to save time in rehearsal from having to flip needlessly through every page in the script trying to find sections. It can be useful to tab acts across the top of a page and scenes down the side. Be sure to label the tabs for easy identification (printable tabs will make your final product look more polished).
- Note sound effects – Depending on the sound designer and the rehearsal room setup, you may be running sound cues during rehearsals or you may just need to call them out so the performers can react to them (e.g., phone ringing, door knock, thunder crash, etc.)
- **Libretto**/Score page references – When working on a musical, it can be highly beneficial to take the time to cross-reference page numbers between the libretto (script pages) and the score (music pages) and note them on your script.
- Music tracks – If you are using tracked music during the rehearsal process (rather than a live accompanist), take the time during prep week to sit down with your script and the music tracks and note timestamps in your script at each new stanza or musical phrase. Be sure to also note any dance breaks or long instrumental sections that aren't indicated in the text. This will be critical for saving time in rehearsal so everyone isn't waiting on you to find the right section in the music each time. It can be helpful to have a short discussion with the music director about how they will need/want to utilize the tracks during rehearsal (Figures 7.16 and 7.17).

When first starting a new production, especially when working with a new company or new individuals, it can be difficult keeping everyone's names/roles straight. Keep a small cheat sheet on the bottom left inside corner of the promptbook that lists all performers (full name) and the characters they play. One can also list all the members of the production team. This way, there is an easy reference that can be seen at all times, no matter which page it is opened to, and there is no need to keep flipping back to the contact sheet to remember who is playing Malvolio.

Page 4 of 55

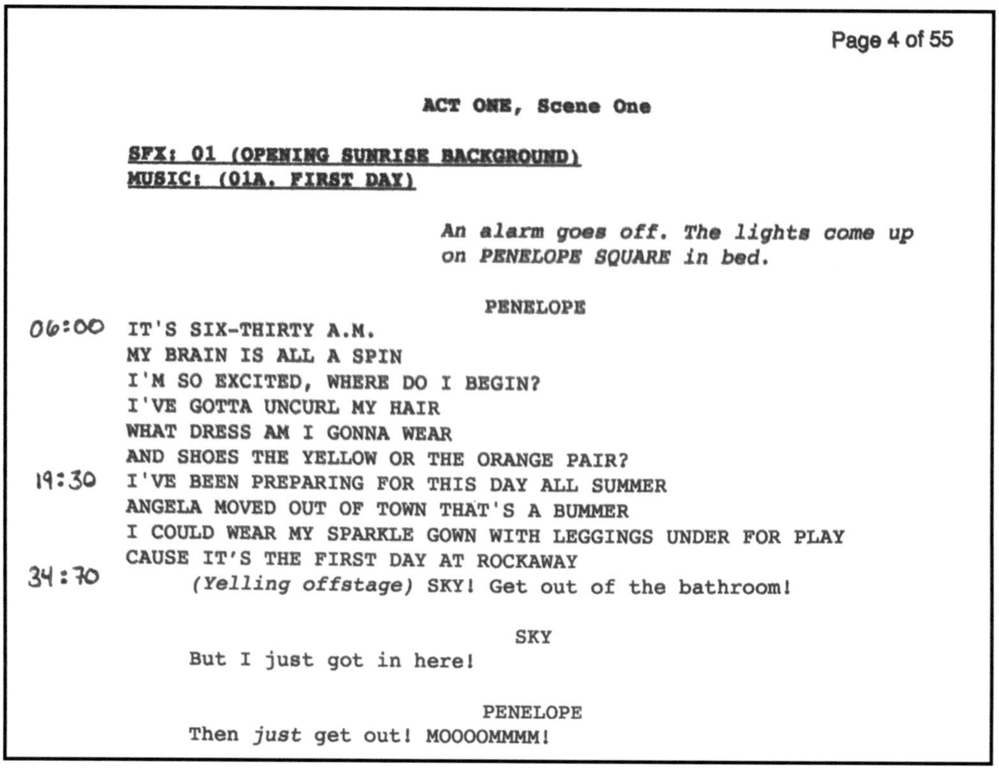

ACT ONE, Scene One

SFX: 01 (OPENING SUNRISE BACKGROUND)
MUSIC: (01A. FIRST DAY)

An alarm goes off. The lights come up on PENELOPE SQUARE in bed.

PENELOPE

06:00 IT'S SIX-THIRTY A.M.
MY BRAIN IS ALL A SPIN
I'M SO EXCITED, WHERE DO I BEGIN?
I'VE GOTTA UNCURL MY HAIR
WHAT DRESS AM I GONNA WEAR
AND SHOES THE YELLOW OR THE ORANGE PAIR?
19:30 I'VE BEEN PREPARING FOR THIS DAY ALL SUMMER
ANGELA MOVED OUT OF TOWN THAT'S A BUMMER
I COULD WEAR MY SPARKLE GOWN WITH LEGGINGS UNDER FOR PLAY
CAUSE IT'S THE FIRST DAY AT ROCKAWAY
34:70 *(Yelling offstage)* SKY! Get out of the bathroom!

SKY

But I just got in here!

PENELOPE

Then *just* get out! MOOOOMMMM!

Figure 7.16 Timestamps in a Promptbook

Promptbook Checklist

1. Cast Information
   a. Cast/production team contact sheet
   b. The original or copies of the audition forms (*optional*)
   c. Script sign-out sheet
   d. Emergency contact forms (for everyone in the rehearsal room)
   e. A copy of the company handbook, if one exists
   f. Copies of any research/dramaturgical materials handed out to the cast throughout the production

SMB POLKADOTS Timestamp Cheatsheet

SONG TITLE: FIRST DAY
SCRIPT PG(S): 4 - 6
SCORE PG(S): 1 - 8
CHARACTERS: Penelope, Sky, Mrs. Square, Lily

TIMESTAMP	MEASURE (mm)	LYRIC / MUSICAL DESCRIPTION	SCRIPT PG	SCORE PG
00:00.00	mm. 1	Top of song	4	1
00:06.00	mm. 5	IT'S SIX-THIRTY A.M.	4	1
00:19.30	pickup to mm. 13	I'VE BEEN PREPARING FOR THIS	4	1
00:34.70	mm. 22	First music interlude	4	2
00:41.45	mm. 26	WHY IS SHE ALWAYS SO LOUD	4	2
00:53.89	pickup to mm. 34	I HAVE NOT BEEN WAITING FOR	4	3
01:09.20	mm. 43	Second music interlude	5	4
01:15.71	mm. 47	MY LITTLE ONES	5	4
01:44.10	mm. 64	Third music interlude	5	6

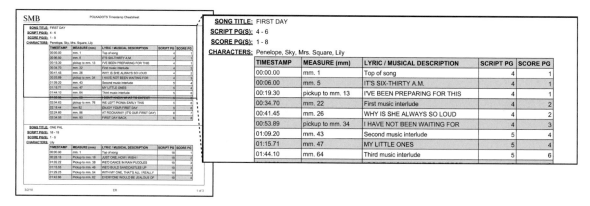

Figure 7.17 Timestamp Cheat Sheet

2. Schedules and Calendars
   a. Production calendar
   b. Rehearsal schedule (either daily or weekly calls, depending on the production)
   c. A conflict calendar
3. Script
   a. Entrance and exit plot
   b. Scene/character breakdown and/or French scene breakdown
   c. Production analysis
   d. Blocking symbol/shorthand key
   e. Blocking script, including all blocking notes
   f. Calling script – a clean copy of the script with cues written in the margins (might be the same as the blocking script)
   g. Music score (if show is a musical or has any songs)
4. Props Information
   a. Complete prop list
   b. Prop preset
   c. Run sheet
5. Scenic Information
   a. Groundplan – clean copy, to scale
   b. Furniture list
   c. Any sketches or renderings that may be relevant to a rehearsal
6. Lighting Information (this should be provided to you by the lighting designer)
   a. Light cue list
   b. Light plot
   c. Channel hook-up
   d. Color lists
   e. Instrument schedule
7. Sound Information (this should be provided to you by the sound designer)
   a. Sound cue list
   b. Mic plot (if mics are used) – this lists which performer has which mic and tracks if mics are swapped during the run of the show
   c. Speaker plot – this shows the location of all speakers and monitors in the production and relevant information for troubleshooting purposes
8. Costume Information (this should be provided to you by the costume designer)
   a. Costume plots/piece list – breakdown of characters by scene and each item that is worn
   b. Costume sketches, if available
   c. Any special instructions regarding cleaning/maintenance
9. Rehearsal Reports
   a. Print hard copies of all rehearsal reports
10. Performance Reports
    a. Print hard copies of all performance reports
11. Production Meeting Agendas and Notes
    a. Print hard copies of all production meeting agendas and reports

During prep week and the rehearsal process, you may need to keep the promptbook with you outside of rehearsals (for reference or to work on paperwork). If you do choose to leave it in the rehearsal space, make sure it is in a secure location where it can't walk off. However, once performances begin, the promptbook should never leave the theatre. In case of an unfortunate event where the stage manager cannot attend a performance (e.g., catastrophic injury, illness, etc.), the promptbook needs to be available and organized for the replacement.

Chapter Eight
Meetings and Communication

As the hub of communication for a production, the stage manager will spend a lot of time in meetings. Often, the stage manager will schedule and run the meetings, but even if they don't, they will always take detailed notes and send out reports that are a record of what happened in the meeting. The most common type of meeting is a production meeting. Production meetings serve as a regularly scheduled (typically weekly) check-in with all members of the production team. They will involve the sharing of sketches, renderings, drawings, progress reports, delays, challenges, problems, etc. This is also the stage manager's chance to follow up on anything that has not been addressed from rehearsal reports. The stage manager's attendance is mandatory.

Scheduling Meetings

Coordinating meetings typically falls to the stage manager. If an initial meeting hasn't already been set up by the company, email the production staff asking for their weekly availability (it can be helpful to use a scheduling app rather than an excessively long email chain). Compile their responses, find a mutually agreeable time, and assign the determined time as your weekly production meeting time. Announce this time to your production staff as soon as possible. If the first meeting has been predetermined by the company but isn't established as the regularly scheduled meeting time, then establish a weekly meeting time during the first meeting. In the event a regular meeting time cannot be set, do your best to schedule a meeting once every 6–10 days as schedules allow. Production meetings are frequently scheduled for an hour, though this can vary by company, so be sure to find out what is typically expected.

Next, determine exactly who will need to attend the meetings. This usually includes the producer, artistic director, director, production manager, designers (scenic, costumes, lights, sound, media), the props person, and the technical director (and stage management, of course!). For shows that have a music director and choreographer, they should also be included. Depending on the company, the scenic charge, shop foreman, and/or the head electrician may also be present. Associates and assistants need not be present at meetings unless the primary expresses a desire for their attendance (assistant stage managers should attend and take notes if they are contracted for the duration of the production).

DOI: 10.4324/9781003133049-9

> Schedule a time that works for the people in the primary team, then invite all others (associates, assistants, shop managers, etc.) to join the meeting if they are interested/available.

Sometimes, you will have to leave one or more people out due to conflicts. Determine this on a case-by-case basis. In these cases, find out if it is possible to include missing team members virtually or by phone. Make sure to plan what method and technology will be used to do this and always test it before meeting time. Technology is fickle; don't expect it to always function properly. If they are unable to participate at all, request that they send you any discussion topics regarding their department prior to the meeting. During the meeting, bring up their topics for discussion and carefully record the conversation and any other information pertinent to them as well as any questions that need their immediate attention. (This is one of the reasons why taking detailed notes is so important.) It can be useful to audio record the meeting as long as none of the attendees objects.

When initially reaching out to the production team about their schedules, also request their preferred contact information. If you already have their contact information, confirm that it is correct. You will want to have a contact sheet put together before your first **concept**/production meeting so it can be distributed. Additionally, make a point to input all contact information into your phone or other readily available location. As the communication center of the production, you will frequently be called upon to contact the other members of the team, so having this information easily accessible is a must.

> If you are not using a university email system, set up a "work" or "professional" email account (something other than ilovepandas@pandapower.com) to ensure communication stays flowing. Always remember to check and keep up with your inbox.

Prior to Meetings

Create an agenda for each meeting. These should have a section for each department (including stage management) and include discussion points and questions. If you don't have anything specific for a department, you should still give them a chance to voice questions and/or concerns. When compiling the agenda, look back at previous rehearsal and production meeting reports for any unanswered questions that may have come up or items or discussion points that were tabled from previous meetings. Either distribute the meeting agenda electronically prior to the meeting or have copies of the agenda on hand for all involved parties, including yourself (Figure 8.1).

Send out an email reminder 24 hours prior to the meeting, including the time (including time zone), date, and location of the meeting. If folks are joining remotely, be sure to include any information needed to get them connected. Many calendar programs allow for invites to be sent to all parties, which will add the event to their calendars and push reminders to those who have push notifications on.

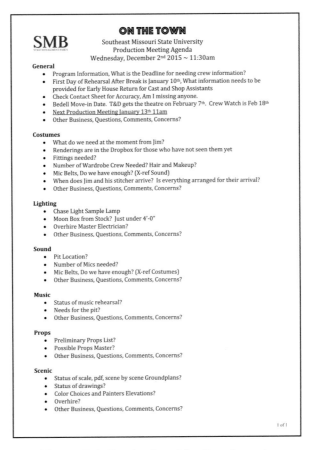

SMB
STAGE MANAGEMENT BASICS

ON THE TOWN

Southeast Missouri State University
Production Meeting Agenda
Wednesday, December 2nd 2015 ~ 11:30am

General
- Program Information, What is the Deadline for needing crew information?
- First Day of Rehearsal After Break is January 10th, What information needs to be provided for Early House Return for Cast and Shop Assistants
- Check Contact Sheet for Accuracy, Am I missing anyone.
- Bedell Move-in Date. T&D gets the theatre on February 7th. Crew Watch is Feb 18th
- Next Production Meeting January 13th 11am
- Other Business, Questions, Comments, Concerns?

Costumes
- What do we need at the moment from Jim?
- Renderings are in the Dropbox for those who have not seen them yet
- Fittings needed?
- Number of Wardrobe Crew Needed? Hair and Makeup?
- Mic Belts, Do we have enough? (X-ref Sound)
- When does Jim and his stitcher arrive? Is everything arranged for their arrival?
- Other Business, Questions, Comments, Concerns?

Lighting
- Chase Light Sample Lamp
- Moon Box from Stock? Just under 4'-0"
- Overhire Master Electrician?
- Other Business, Questions, Comments, Concerns?

Sound
- Pit Location?
- Number of Mics needed?
- Mic Belts, Do we have enough? (X-ref Costumes)
- Other Business, Questions, Comments, Concerns?

Music
- Status of music rehearsal?
- Needs for the pit?
- Other Business, Questions, Comments, Concerns?

Props
- Preliminary Props List?
- Possible Props Master?
- Other Business, Questions, Comments, Concerns?

Scenic
- Status of scale, pdf, scene by scene Groundplans?
- Status of drawings?
- Color Choices and Painters Elevations?
- Overhire?
- Other Business, Questions, Comments, Concerns?

1 of 1

Figure 8.1 Production Meeting Agenda

Running a Meeting

If you are running the meeting, arrive at least 10 minutes early to allow time to set up both the space and any needed technology and to get everyone assembled. If this is your first meeting or time in the space, plan extra time to set up. If any team members are missing or late, the stage manager should call them and find out their ETA (Estimated Time of Arrival). Begin the meeting on time and start by asking the director if they have any general comments or questions to bring to the table. Go department by department and give them time to talk and ask questions. Follow the agenda; it is a great tool to keep meetings on track and on time. If people begin to go off topic, it is your job to gently guide the conversation back on track. At the end of each department's discussion, make sure that all agenda items have been answered (or at least addressed and, if necessary, tabled for later discussion) and ask if there is anything else for that department. If everything has been discussed, move promptly on to the next department.

It is a nice gesture to rotate the order from meeting to meeting, so the same department isn't always waiting their turn and potentially being short-changed each meeting by coming at the end when everyone is ready to go or time is cut short.

At the end of the meeting, ask once more if there are any other items of business that need to be addressed (particularly in areas that may not have representatives, i.e., front of house). End the meeting with a reminder of the time, date, and location of the next meeting. Immediately following the meeting can be a great time to encourage breakout sessions or one-on-one meetings between departments. These quick discussions are a convenient and efficient way to address items that were tabled during the full production meeting without having to schedule a future meeting and prolong the decision. If the item will still need a longer discussion, use the breakout session to schedule a meeting with all relevant parties.

Occasionally, it will be beneficial and/or necessary to hold a department-specific or other additional meeting (e.g., props meeting, costume check-in, set dressing discussion). Typically, stage management will also coordinate these. Depending on the nature of the meeting, the stage manager's presence may or may not be required. Check with everyone involved to see if they would like the stage manager there and schedule the meeting accordingly.

> **!** In terms of additional meetings, attend if you are able and come prepared to take notes, even if you are told the meeting is optional for you. Many people claim to take good notes and that they will distribute them, but it is often more reliable if they come from a centralized person, namely the stage manager.

Meeting Notes and Reports

As soon as possible after the meeting, send out production meeting notes (use the template you created during prep week). These should go out within 24 hours. The sooner, the better, especially if any departments were unable to attend.

Information to Include in Every Report

Every report should contain basic identifiers, including the show title, producing organization, name of stage manager, time and date of meeting, meeting duration, time and date of next meeting, people present and absent, and a distribution list. The body of the report should contain detailed notes on anything and everything discussed. The notes need to be comprehensible, clear, and formatted for easy reading. They will be referenced throughout the production process as a reminder of what and how decisions were made, which decisions were tabled as well as to inform anyone not present at the meeting of what was discussed. Separate notes by department (e.g., scenic notes under a scenic section, props under props, etc.). Include notes that affect multiple departments in each of those sections (this should also be a practice used when writing rehearsal reports), e.g., a note about a cane or hat may fall under costumes and props. If a department or field does not have a note or any information, it is important to place text in that field to the effect of "There are no notes at this time" to show that the field was not accidently left blank.

Be precise and concise in the distributed report. Write in complete sentences and if you don't know what something means, seek clarification rather than including a vague note. The notes that are sent to the team should make sense to someone who wasn't there. It can be helpful to take more elaborate notes for yourself during the meeting and then distill them down for the distributed report. Keep a copy of your original notes for reference. It is to your advantage to take notes on all items discussed, even ideas that are decided against. Should a problem arise with the decision, there is a record of the other ideas that were thrown around so you don't have to re-brainstorm. When in doubt, write it down!

Communication

Communication is one of the primary aspects of stage managing. There are a variety of ways to communicate information and each method has pros and cons, so it is important to choose the appropriate method of communication depending on the information being conveyed and the intended tone of the message. Information can be posted on a physical or digital callboard, it may be emailed, texted, or relayed face-to-face. Relaying the next day's rehearsal schedule can happen via email, whereas a sensitive discussion about personnel should happen face-to-face.

Callboards

Physical callboards are a traditional method of communication for a theatre company. They are convenient for folks in the building and they are a great place to gather important information. Posting notices, calendars, daily calls, sign-in sheets, and other correspondence are great uses for a callboard, but you should never post confidential information (like the contact sheet). Digital callboards are becoming more common and can serve a lot of the same purposes as a traditional callboard. They have the added bonus of being easily accessible even when you aren't in the building, as long as there is internet access. One advantage to digital callboards is that you can post digital content like videos and links to resources. Some online callboards will even let you set passwords or have restricted areas so you could post a contact sheet that could only be accessed by the company. If a callboard is being utilized, the stage management team should keep the information accurate and up-to-date; the cast is responsible for checking the callboard regularly (daily) to make sure they have the most recent information.

Email

Corresponding via email is probably the most common form of workplace communication now. It is great for disseminating detailed and important information to large groups at once. However, there is an art to effective email composition. Overloading an email with too much information or presenting it in a disorganized fashion can lead to confusion and important information getting lost or overlooked. Utilizing formatting (such as bullet points, bold/italic/underline, highlighting, etc.) and concise language are incredibly valuable in composing clear emails that everyone will read and understand. The biggest downside to email is that it can be hard to discern tone.

There will be times that longer emails are appropriate, but best practice is that emails should be limited to about five sentences. The email should answer the questions: who are you? What do you want? Why are you asking me? Why should I do what you are asking? And, what is the next step? Spelling, grammar, punctuation, and word choice count. Writing in full coherent sentences and including enough information to convey your message are also important elements in a professional email. Even if you are sending a short note or reply, be aware of tone and professionalism. Make sure the subject line concisely describes the email contents and specifies the show it relates to. Show titles and venues are often abbreviated (Into the Woods = ITW, University of Stage Management = USM); using these as tags can help make emails more findable (e.g., Subject:[USM] [ITW] Production Meeting Report 6-6-2066). If multiple topics need to be addressed, multiple emails can be sent; however, information can be lost if you overwhelm someone's inbox with an influx of emails. There is a delicate balance to sending emails; too many emails and people start to ignore them, but one very long email can often contain too much information for people to digest.

Be cognizant of timing; address the most pressing matters, and either wait to send additional emails or connect via a different means of communication. Shop managers and office staff are most likely to check email first thing in the morning, so sending them an urgent request at 4:00 pm may not be the best way to get information. Throughout the process, we advocate for sending notes out prior to the start of the next work day so that you have the highest possibility that information will be seen.

> There will be people who are upset by being included in an email they don't really need to be on, but it's better that they have the information and not need it than not have the information and need it.

Text Messaging

Texting is by far the most informal way to communicate and, as such, should be used sparingly, unless it is someone's preferred mode of communication. It can be particularly helpful though if the stage management team is short staffed or have their hands full during rehearsal. It is a quick and quiet way to communicate with an ASM before you are in a space with headsets and you can also text a cast member to see if they are on their way without having to leave the rehearsal space to make a phone call. Texting is another place where tone and intent can be hard to convey and it is easy to make mistakes if you are working quickly (curse you, autocorrect).

It can be useful to have the cast save your phone number in their contacts sometime during the first day of rehearsal (you should also have their numbers saved in your contacts). One very efficient way to do this, particularly with a large cast, is to ask them to text you their name after they have saved your information. This serves the dual purpose of getting you their name and number as well as letting you know that "I didn't have your phone number" should never be an excuse for not contacting you.

Perhaps the most important piece of advice to remember about texting is: be certain you are texting the person that you think you are. It can be hard to recover from an inappropriate text. You want to have a strong relationship with the director, but in most cases calling them pookie and wishing them good night probably isn't what either of you had in mind. Worse yet, you don't want to send some venting frustration text to the person you are venting about instead of your best friend.

Phone Call

Making phone calls has gone out of fashion, but sometimes it is important to speak to someone rather than communicating via the written word. It can also help to build connections and show a genuine desire to support and provide information. Calling each cast member during prep week before rehearsals have begun to ensure that they know when and where the first rehearsal is happening, and answering any questions they might have can really go a long way toward establishing trust and instilling a sense that they are important to you. One of the other times you may find yourself making a phone call rather than emailing or texting is when someone is late or not where they are supposed to be. It is important in these instances to be aware of your tone and language. "Where are you?" Or "Are you planning to join us?" can sound pretty aggressive, and while you may be frustrated that they are late, it is always better to start from a place of concern. "Hi this is the stage manager, we were expecting you at rehearsal at ___time and hadn't seen you yet so I wanted to make sure that everything is okay" will go a lot farther toward building mutual respect. "You are called for rehearsal this evening, are you on your way?" can also work if asked in a cheerful rather than an accusatory tone. One of the cons of phone calls is that sometimes people won't pick up, but if they have your contact information saved (which they should), they should know it is you and not some random number. Phone calls are also the best way to communicate information in case of an emergency. While a text can be a starting point, "I'm at the hospital" should be followed up with a phone call.

Face-to-Face

Face-to-face conversations give you the highest odds of having your tone and intention be clearly understood. It is also the best way to have difficult or in-depth conversations. It is a good idea to practice important conversations ahead of time to make sure you are clear on what you need to say and why you need to say it. This can help you stay cool and collected if things get tense because you already know what you want to say and have practiced saying it. Another pro to in-person conversations is that you can watch a person's body language to see how things are landing and have a better idea about when to push and when to ease back. It is important to also be aware of your body language as you are talking to someone. A downside to face-to-face conversations is that they can be challenging to schedule and, if it is going to be a difficult conversation, face-to-face can be scary.

> **!** If you discussed things that may be important to the production or the rest of the team in a face-to-face meeting, send a follow-up email recapping the conversation or highlighting the pertinent points.

Chapter Nine
Rehearsals

Rehearsals are the time when the director's vision starts to be realized. The cast brings the characters to life and the performative element of the production comes together.

The rehearsal period can be extremely short (two weeks), very long (9–10 weeks or longer), or anywhere in between. It will depend a lot on the environment of the theatre. In an academic environment, labor and personnel budgets are not typically a factor, so the rehearsal process can be longer but the production may only run for a weekend or two. Conversely, if the theatre is paying production staff and performers, then typically the rehearsal process will be shortened with a longer performance run to keep costs to a minimum while maximizing revenue.

Types of Rehearsals

Read Through

Typically, the very first rehearsal for a play will consist of a **read through** (sometimes referred to as a table read), in which the whole cast sits around a table and reads through the entire script out loud, each reading their role. The stage manager may be asked to read the stage directions aloud and/or call out sound effects. The director or an associate may do this instead – determine this before the rehearsal begins. Be sure to time all read throughs of the script. This will give a frame of reference for approximately how long the play will be once it is in performance. Typically, designers are invited to this rehearsal. This is a great time for them to meet the cast, get to hear the script out loud, and give a brief presentation to the cast on their preliminary design ideas.

> **!** First rehearsal is when scripts are given out, if they have not already been distributed. This is also when you traditionally hand out the welcome packets and go over the paperwork contained therein. Finally, be sure to pass around a copy of the contact sheet for people to double-check and give permission for their info to be shared. Update it before the next rehearsal for distribution. Remind the company that contact information should not be shared publicly.

DOI: 10.4324/9781003133049-10

Table Work

Another type of rehearsal that may take place in the first week or two is called **table work**. Similar to a read through, these rehearsals also take place seated around the table. The goal is typically to work slowly through the script, stopping to talk about character, pacing, story background, etc. These rehearsals are common, especially on new works, where intention and character traits are still being sussed out by the playwright, and in academia, where character work is part of the educational process. For any table work rehearsals (including the table read), it is courteous to come prepared with plenty of pencils, pens, highlighters, and pencil sharpeners. It is also helpful to have tissues and hand sanitizer.

Blocking

Once table work has been completed, the performers will get on their feet. Sometimes, they will jump directly into blocking/staging (these terms are used interchangeably), typically starting at the top (beginning) of the show. Other times, there may be a day of movement in which the director and choreographer (if there is one) will run through some exercises to see how the performers move and interact together. This is typical for shows with dance or choreography, or in highly stylized pieces. For blocking rehearsals, be sure all previously agreed upon rehearsal furniture, props, and costumes (if applicable) are available and set up, and that the floor is taped out. For movement or choreography rehearsals, an open floor plan might be more appropriate. Check with your choreographer before setting up for the day. Rehearsals may not always take place in the same location; if you are using an alternate rehearsal space, inquire what will be needed in that space (props, costumes, a tape out, etc.).

Blocking rehearsals may take many forms depending on the director. Blocking is any action given to the performers by the director or taken naturally by the performers and approved by the director. During blocking rehearsals, the director and the cast determine when and how people move around the stage. The stage manager creates a record of the movements in the prompt book (more about recording blocking later). The director may have a very specific plan or may take a more organic approach, letting the cast shape the scenes initially and then fine-tuning things later. Some directors will try several variants of a scene one after another and others will work all the way through the show before revisiting a scene again.

Stumble Through/Run Through

Later in the process, you will have rehearsals where you start putting together large chunks of the show. This could be a group of scenes, an entire act, or the whole show. A general term for this is a stumble through. It is assumed that things will move slowly and that there will be hiccups (or major train wrecks) along the way. Once things start to get solidified, you will move from stumble throughs to **run throughs**. During these rehearsals, the stage manager should be checking that the performers are maintaining the blocking set in blocking rehearsals and making sure the run flows as smoothly as possible.

> **!** Two other types of rehearsal are technical (tech) rehearsals and dress rehearsals. They come later in the process and we discuss them in depth in Chapter 11. Once a show is up and running, brush-up rehearsals and put-in rehearsals may also come up. We discuss those in Chapter 12.

Musicals

For musicals, there will be some additional types of rehearsals.

Sing Through

If you are working on a musical, your first rehearsal may be a sing through. If not on the first day, this will most likely happen sometime during the first week. This is much like a read through, but with music. For this rehearsal, a piano or keyboard, and the rehearsal accompanist will be necessary, so prepare accordingly (e.g., make sure that the piano has been tuned or that you have the appropriate cables/amps/speakers/stand to set up the keyboard). If they are available, music stands can be very helpful so that performers can group around the piano or keyboard and still have a place for their materials.

Music Rehearsals

For music rehearsals, a piano or keyboard will need to be available as well as chairs and music stands for the performers. Consult with the MD about their preferred room set-up. This is the time for the music director to work on notes, style, and technique with the performers. In these rehearsals, the stage manager is there to monitor breaks, keep track of time, and lend a hand when help is required. This is a good time to get familiar with the music (including the music director's instructions to the cast) to help you with calling and maintaining the show later in the process. You should be actively noting any cuts or changes and who is singing during any group sections. Sometimes, music rehearsals will take place simultaneously with staging or choreography rehearsals in order to increase the efficiency of rehearsal time. In these cases, a separate room will need to be reserved. Ideally, there should be a member of stage management present in each rehearsal room. However, music rehearsals tend to be very self-sufficient. If you are working on a show solo and have simultaneous music and staging rehearsals, always attend the staging rehearsal.

Working without an Accompanist

If a rehearsal pianist is unavailable or if there is not the budget for it, you will need to have rehearsal tracks. If tracks haven't been purchased as part of the production, coordinate with the music director to record all musical numbers. Ideally, they will be recorded prior to rehearsals. However, if that is not possible, prioritize individual tracks according to the rehearsal schedule. If the official recording matches the score, you can work from the cast album. Either a recording or a pianist MUST be available at the time the number is rehearsed. When using rehearsal tracks, be sure to have speakers or access to the sound system so that tracks will be loud enough to be heard by all while singing in full voice.

Running a Rehearsal

Before Rehearsal

Prior to rehearsal each day there is a certain amount of preparation that stage management must complete. The specifics of this preparation are, of course, dependent on the company, the director, the space, and the type of rehearsal taking place, but the basics remain the same.

Check-in with the Shops

Before the end of the shops' working hours, stage management should check-in with costumes, scenic, and props. In terms of scenery, this is particularly important if rehearsals and scenic construction are happening in the same space; find out what has changed and if anything needs to be avoided or treated in a particular way. Determine if props have been added to the prop storage area or if anything has been modified. Different costume shops will have different policies, but this check-in can be a time to pick-up any rehearsal garments and find out about any fittings that need to be scheduled. Prior to sending out fitting notices to cast members, be sure to confirm the fitting location with the costume designer (or shop supervisor, as appropriate) and if the performer needs to wear or bring anything in particular to the fitting with them (character shoes, specific undergarments, dance belt, etc.). From there, coordinate a fitting based on the performer's call schedule for rehearsal. Depending on where the fitting takes place, be sure to take into account any travel time to and from rehearsal. Typically, each performer will have one to two fittings during the process.

Always ask permission before utilizing any new items in rehearsal. Additionally, if you need something specific for rehearsal, make sure to coordinate and communicate early and often so that the shops have time to make accommodations, if possible.

> **!** It is a luxury to be able to work with scenic elements, final props, and rehearsal garments throughout the rehearsal process. Treat these items with respect and care and don't take them for granted.

Arrive at every rehearsal with the promptbook, stage management kit, stopwatch, something to take notes on (electronic or paper), your phone, and a positive attitude.

Unlock and Turn On

The stage manager is almost always the first person in the space. Arrive at least 45 minutes prior to rehearsal to allow time for preparation. First, unlock doors as needed and turn on lights and sound systems (if applicable). Update the callboard. This is also a good time to check supplies in the bathrooms and first aid kits. While you won't necessarily be accountable for replacing these items, you should contact the space coordinator if supplies are running low.

If you have assistant stage managers, they should arrive at this time as well. If applicable, have them set up **hospitality**. Take a couple of minutes to talk through the schedule for the rehearsal and assign responsibilities for the day (who is taking blocking notes, who is monitoring performer arrivals, who is tracking props, etc.).

Clean and Prep the Rehearsal Space

For safety and out of consideration for the performers, do a thorough sweep of the space before each rehearsal. A good sweeping is especially necessary if rehearsal takes place on the stage where scenery is in the process of being built (common for academic productions), as wood splinters, stray screws, and other potential safety hazards can remain after a day of shop work. It is good practice to mop the space as well, particularly if performers will be barefoot or on the floor.

Discuss with the director ahead of time what will be happening during each rehearsal so proper setup can be planned. Set up chairs and tables if table work or a read through is planned. If blocking is planned, make sure the space is properly taped out, all rehearsal furniture and props that are needed for the first scene you are working are set, and all other pieces are easily accessible. Set up chairs outside the playing area for the performers to set their belongings on and to sit when they aren't on stage. Double-check that none of your spikes have moved or peeled up, pick up any trash, and generally tidy up. A clean, welcoming room will foster better productivity, creativity, and positivity.

> **!** If a scene is being worked on that has new rehearsal props or costumes, be sure to communicate this with the performers prior to beginning the scene work so they are not startled or distracted by new things in the heat of the moment.

Prep Your Workstation

Set up a table facing the playing area, ideally close to the door. This will be for stage management and the director, as well as any visiting designers, choreographers, etc. who may be sitting in on rehearsal. Run a power strip to the table. The stage manager (or ASM) is up and down constantly throughout rehearsal, so settle in a place where you can easily get in and out without being disruptive. The director should also be able to move between the table and the rehearsal space easily. Include a cup with extra pencils (sharpened), pens, and highlighters for people to borrow. It is also a good idea to keep a box of tissues and a bottle of hand sanitizer on the table.

> If your computer is open during rehearsal, make sure it is set at an angle to you. It may seem trivial, but if you place it directly in front of you it acts as a virtual barrier between the cast and you, and that is not something you want to create. You'll also want to be able to see past it to take blocking.

Review the rehearsal schedule for the day and keep a copy next to your promptbook for easy reference. Open your promptbook to the first section being worked on, prep a blank sheet of paper or document for notes, and have your favorite pen, pencil(s), and eraser ready. Keep your stage manager's kit nearby and pull out commonly used items for quick access (for rehearsals, these would be spike tape, gaff tape, sticky notes/tabs, stapler, and spare paper).

Check Attendance

Five minutes before rehearsal is scheduled to begin, check the sign-in sheet to see which performers have arrived. Start calling those who haven't yet checked in to confirm they are on their way. Establish early on that being on time for rehearsal is critical, as any delay can impact the entire rehearsal call. Encourage all of the company members to maintain open communication with you and to always contact you if they're going to be late. It still isn't good for them to be late, but if you know ahead of time, you and the director can adjust the rehearsal plan accordingly. Note any tardiness or absences in your daily report.

> A dual purpose can be served by using cell phones as a way of signing in. Labeling the pockets on a clear multi-pocket shoe rack with each cast member's name and asking them to put their cell phone in the pocket to indicate that they are present gives you a quick visual way to see who is present, as well as minimizing digital distractions in the rehearsal room. Be sure that the shoe rack is in a secure location and easily visible to protect phones from theft or loss.

Starting Rehearsal

When it is time for rehearsal to begin, close the door to the space (if possible) and post a "Quiet please, rehearsal in progress" sign on the outside. Call the company to attention, announce the start of rehearsal, and give a quick reminder about the plan for the day. If the director wants to jump right in, have the performers get in place for the scene being worked on. If they want to speak with the company first, pass the attention to the director.

> **!** When working in academia, you will often find yourself working with a faculty director and it can be tricky navigating the space between being a co-worker and being a student. As a student, confronting a professor may not be in your best interest, but keeping the cast safe is just as important. Don't be afraid to reach out to your advisors or mentors for advice or assistance in tricky scenarios.

During Rehearsal

Take Notes

So much happens during rehearsal that the only way to keep track of it all is to write it down. Never assume you will be able to remember something. There is no reason to allow something to be overlooked or forgotten about because you relied on your memory rather than jotting down a quick note.

Rehearsal Reports

One of the stage manager's responsibilities during rehearsal is to create a rehearsal report (see Figure 7.5, p. 80). This will lay out anything important that occurs in rehearsal as well as any notes or questions that need to be passed on to the various departments. This includes any added props, repairs that need to be addressed, blocking notes that could impact costumes, lighting, etc., and script changes (including cuts/additions). A section should be provided that includes the original rehearsal plan and a summary of what was actually worked, as well as start, end, and break times. Any injuries (especially any requiring first aid), late arrivals, unexcused absences, or unusual circumstances should also be noted in these reports.

> **!** Keep note of any and all things the director says in regards to anything technical. This particular task can be tough for first-time stage managers and is a skill that definitely develops over time and with experience. It requires strong focus, multitasking skills, and detailed note-taking. Don't get too frustrated if you aren't able to get everything down. Write what you can and take note of the items you need to follow up on.

Prep a new report at the start of each rehearsal and add notes as they come up. It will be easier than trying to remember everything at the end and that way nothing will be left out accidentally.

Personal Notes

Take note of any action items for yourself. This may be a reminder to send out the new fitting schedule, to look up the correct pronunciation of a foreign word in the script, to buy more sticky notes, etc. Things may come up in rehearsal that are worth noting or remembering but that don't belong in a rehearsal report; include these in your personal notes.

Track Script Changes

Generally, for artistic integrity and copyright purposes, no changes should be made to the script. However, if you are working on a new piece or directly with a playwright, it is possible that script changes will be made during the rehearsal process. In these cases, it may fall to the stage manager to keep track of the changes. No matter the situation, note all changes in the script, make announcements of all permanent changes to everyone (including the production team, as script changes can affect them as well), and keep a running document noting the change and the date the change was made. Be sure to keep this document updated and available for perusal in case anyone has questions or missed a change (see Figure 7.15, p. 87).

> If gender pronouns are changed due to casting, be sure to track these changes through the full script and pass them along to the whole team.

> If you are working on a very new work, there may be large changes. It can be helpful to copy each set of changes on a different color of paper – that way you can easily make sure everyone is always using the same version. Additionally, always include the date and a version number in the header or footer of the changed pages. As small changes occur, you should date those on the page as well.

Take Blocking

Stage managers take blocking so that there is a record of the movement for each scene. This is important for a variety of reasons, among them, encouraging consistency between performances, training understudies, and communicating with the design team. The key to taking blocking is to find a system in which one can write quickly and concisely while still capturing as much of the movement as possible. Be precise. If you didn't create one during prep week, you will need to create a **blocking key**, including character abbreviations, movement symbols, and stage directions (Figure 9.1). It can also be useful to create shorthand for all furniture pieces, moving scenery as well as any entrance/exit locations.

> Prior to the start of blocking rehearsals, print out a copy of the groundplan and split the stage into sections: USL, USC, USR, SL, CS, SR, DSL, DSC, and DSR (depending on the set, one can choose to split the groundplan into greater or fewer sections). Use this as a reference while taking blocking notes in order to be as precise as possible.

Macbeth Blocking Key:

Cast:	Entrances:	MISC:
MB – Macbeth	SL-A – Stage Left Around the masking wall	@ - At
LB – Lady Macbeth		& - And
BQ – Banquo	SL-D – Stage Left through the Doorway	↓ - Sit
FL – Fleance		↑ - Stand
ML – Malcolm	SR-A – Stage Right Around Masking Wall	→ - Then/Next
DB – Donalbain		X – Cross
DN - Duncan	SR-D – Stage Right through Doorway	EXT – Exit
MD – Macduff		ENT – Entrance
LD – Lady Macduff	CAL – Enter from the Cauldron Center	£ – Lights Up
LN – Lennox		B/O – Black Out
RS – Ross	SL-H – Stage Left House/apron	
AG – Angus	SR-H – Stage Right House/apron	
SI – Siward	DH – Down House through the Audience Aisle	
PR – Porter		
W1 – Witch 1	UCL – Up Center Left – Between Standing Stones	
W2 – Witch 2		
W3 - Witch 3	UCR – Up Center Right – Between Standing Stones	

Figure 9.1 Blocking Key

All notes taken in the script should be written in pencil. Come to every rehearsal with multiple pencils, some large erasers (white Pentel hi-polymer or Staedtler Plastic erasers work very well), extra paper, and some patience. The blocking *will* change and there will be a lot of erasing and updating as progress is made. Never write blocking in pen.

As you are recording blocking, remember to also keep track of where props come on and go off. This will make your preset list and prop tracking easier throughout the run of the show.

Margin Notation Method

One method of recording blocking is to write it directly in the margins of the script (Figure 9.2). Next to the line where the performer moved, write down in shorthand their path and where they end up. You may also utilize a small version of the ground plan on the back of the previous script page to diagram complicated movements and clarify your notes. This method tends to take up a large amount of space in the margins, which can make it difficult to also use that same script as the calling script. However, if blocking or cues are minimal or a second separate "calling" script is created, margin notation is a commonly used notation option. It is also a good method to use when first becoming acclimated to taking blocking, as it involves the fewest steps.

Groundplan and Numbering Method

Another method of recording blocking is to use a groundplan and numbers to track the cast's movements. With this method, print a small groundplan on the back of each script page or a slip sheet and include space to write down blocking and other notes (Figure 9.3).

Figure 9.2 Margin Notation Method

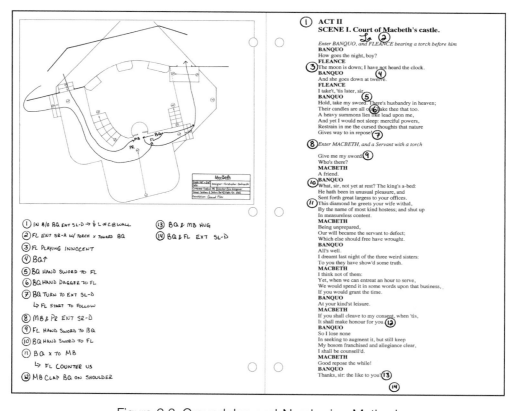

Figure 9.3 Groundplan and Numbering Method

Write a number next to the word in the script where the performer moved and, on the opposite page, write the number and their movement using your blocking shorthand. Use the groundplan to diagram particularly complicated sets of movement or a strange path followed. The groundplan is also very useful to keep track of lots of characters in large group scenes.

> **!** Taking blocking notes is something that will improve with time and practice. Use these guidelines as a starting place and then find a method that works best for you. What is important is that it is legible and can be deciphered by anyone who picks up the promptbook.

Choreography

Dance

In some productions, there is an additional element that needs to be tracked and recorded: choreography. Choreography is the sequence of steps and movements in a dance; it is essentially dance blocking, though it is never referred to as such. Often dances involve a large number of people, this is where the groundplan on the blocking page comes in handy. Many dances will have a series of formations or tableaus with movements in between. Often the most important thing to record from choreography is where everyone is standing in each formation. That said, ultimately there needs to be a record of the entire dance. Much like regular blocking, notating choreography has a number of uses: it will allow you to follow along even if there are no words (during a dance break), communicate useful information to designers and will come in handy when you get to calling a show.

When writing out choreography, listen to the language that the choreographer is using and copy it, even if the words aren't familiar or meaningful at the time. Having a common vocabulary with the choreographer and the cast will help with communication throughout the process. For example, if there is a part of the dance that the choreographer calls the jeté (which means jump) section, the dancers can be directed to "start from the jeté section" rather than saying "start at the jumping part." You may also have choreographers that use terms that are descriptive of the movement or the music.

> If the terms used by the choreographer are unfamiliar, the stage manager should find ways to describe the movement for themselves that will help them follow along and connect to the unfamiliar terms (e.g., "jump" = "jeté").

Often choreography will happen in tandem with the lyrics of a song and can be recorded as such (e.g., clap on the word "down"). When there are no lyrics or choreography is happening on specific beats in the music, it can be helpful to either work from the score or use **Dance 8s.**

To use dance 8s, first figure out how the music is being counted. Assuming the dance phrases are 8 counts, write out the numbers 1 through 8, giving yourself plenty of space around each number. Then, either above or below the number, write what happens on each count (Figure 9.4). It can be helpful to start this process on extra paper outside of the prompt book because choreography isn't always learned in sequence and the different sections may need to be reorganized.

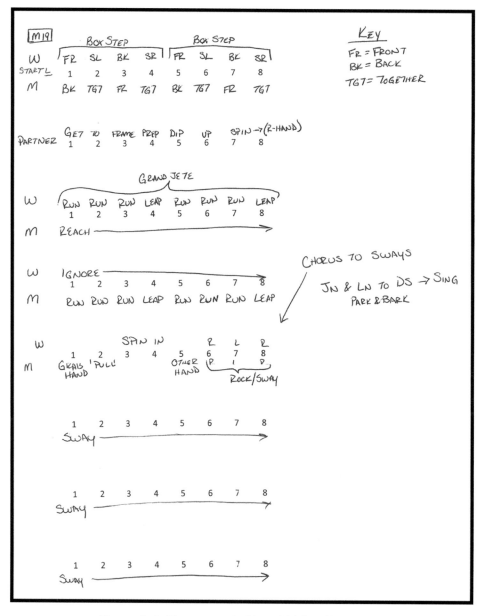

Figure 9.4 Choreograph Noted Using Dance 8s

DANCE "8S"

Typically, dancers work in phrases of 8 counts, but this depends on the music. For example, in a waltz, they tend to work in 3s so you would use dance 3s. Likewise, you might find a song that is in 6s – listen to the choreographer and it should become apparent how they are counting/teaching.

FIGHT

Similar to dance, fight choreography comes with specific terminology and it becomes exceedingly important to build a common vocabulary with the fight director and the cast. Since stage violence is very different from actual violence (specifically because in stage violence, no one should get hurt and there is minimal actual contact), understanding the safety measures used in the choreography is of utmost importance. Any production that includes fights, scuffles, slaps, or any other physical altercations should be using a certified fight director to choreograph and will require a fight captain (a cast member chosen by the fight director) to maintain safety. As violence is being blocked, take note of everything. Often a fight is blocked in phrases or short sections that can be worked independently until they are up to speed. Positioning for violence is very precise because the performers need to be a safe distance apart but placed so that it looks like they could actually be making contact. Even slight variations can, at best, make things look fake and, at worst, cause injury. Eye contact and focus are also very important for the fighters and it is crucial that when violence is being rehearsed, distractions are limited.

Most elements of violence will have three parts: the aggressor will give a cue, usually by doing a larger-than-life prep for a movement (e.g., drawing the fist back to indicate an impending punch), the victim will start to react to the prep acknowledging that they are ready to proceed, and then the aggressor will follow through with the action. This is sometimes called the Cue, Reaction, Action Principle (CRAP). The stage manager should note each of these pieces for every element of a fight and also be aware of the target for each attack (e.g., the aggressor's right hand should be in the same plane as the defenders bicep, etc.). Additionally, in most hand-to-hand combat situations, there will be a **knap** (sound) associated with an action. There are a variety of ways that a knap can be done. Make sure to include that information in your notes. It can be useful to track each individual's movements rather than writing out a running narrative of the fight. Break large fight scenes down into their smaller components – a full company brawl can be overwhelming but the individual fights within it are manageable.

Once fights are staged, it is important to continue working them. All violence is worked in a "**fight call**," a time set aside specifically to run through the fight sequence independent of the surrounding action. This allows the performers to remind themselves and their bodies of the action in a safe, clinical fashion before putting it into the context of an (usually) emotion-filled scene. If possible, all fights should be reviewed daily. Even if the schedule won't allow for a full fight call, always review any fights that will be in the material being worked that day before you get to them. Working with the fight captain, have the cast run

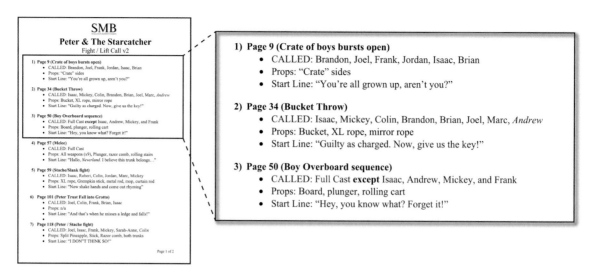

Figure 9.5 Fight/Lift Call Excerpt

through all fights as set by the fight director, making sure everything runs safely and smoothly. For safety, there should be silence apart from any noise from the fighting performers during the fight call. Fights are typically run at half speed for the first run through. If everyone involved feels comfortable, then the speed can be ramped up to three-quarter speed, which is usually the fastest you will ever run a fight, even in a performance.

A specific call can also be given to complicated dance choreography and lifts for review before runs as needed (Figure 9.5).

> **!** Performers (especially dancers and singers) may "mark" during rehearsals when they are required to run a sequence many times. This means that they may not use their full voice or do their full blocking/choreography in order to avoid strain or injuries. This may take place for only a small portion of the song or choreography (e.g., high notes or lifts) or an entire rehearsal.
>
> It is important to let the director and relevant designers know if someone in the cast is marking, especially during tech.

Pictures and Video Recording Blocking

When working on a musical or other large production, it can be difficult to keep track of blocking/choreography/fights (there is only one of you and so many of them!). A helpful trick is to take a video of the rehearsal: record the large group numbers, complicated choreography, and fight rehearsals. These can be used to help accurately check blocking and they can be distributed to the cast and choreographer to review outside of rehearsal. These should be updated whenever the blocking changes, just as with your normal blocking notes. Sometimes it is useful to take pictures of large group scenes where it will take too much time to write down everyone's names – in rehearsal, mark where bodies are and then go back and look at the images after rehearsal to update your script with specific names. Photos can also be your best friend for presets – take pictures of complicated or intricate prop set-ups for visual reference later.

Before recording any rehearsals, check with your director and/or producer. If you are working with union performers or in a union house (Actors' Equity Association or otherwise), it is strictly against the rulebook to video or audio record ANY rehearsals. You also need to be cautious about distribution of the videos, to avoid any issues with copyright infringement. Any recorded material should be distributed only to the performers and the production team.

> Learning the basics of video software will allow you to size down the videos so they do not take up as much space. Another good way to save space and ease sharing is to create a private link on the video hosting, social media, or cloud storage site of your choice (e.g., YouTube, Google Drive, Facebook group, etc.) and post all videos there. Make sure you have permission from your director and choreographer before posting and always restrict access to only those who need it.

Keep Rehearsal on Time and Monitor Breaks

Much like production meetings, the stage manager keeps track of the time and keeps the rehearsal as close to schedule as possible. Give gentle reminders to the director when you are nearing a break or the scheduled time to move on to a new scene or task. Agree on the best way to do this prior to the start of rehearsals (sometimes it is verbal, sometimes with hand signals, or a passed note). Avoid giving these reminders in the middle of a scene or during a speech from the director. For many directors, this will take them out of the moment or derail their train of thought, which is frustrating. This is another skill that you will develop over time and will vary (sometimes dramatically) from director to director.

The director will also look to you to keep the rehearsal focused. Help keep side conversations and noise to a minimum and rein in the focus onstage if the action derails. Rehearsals should be fun, but also productive. Jokes and hilarious line flubs can and will happen. It is fine (and important) to allow the company to enjoy these moments. However, don't be afraid to step in with a gentle "Focus, please" after they've had a moment of fun to keep the rehearsal moving forward.

Breaks

It is important to take breaks. AEA rules state that breaks must be taken according to the following breakdown: a 5-minute break after every 55 minutes of rehearsal or a 10-minute break after every 80 minutes. Many companies follow these guidelines, whether they are Equity or not, but discuss this with the director and the producer (if applicable) prior to the start of rehearsals. Even in non-Equity situations, it is important to take breaks and be respectful of the company's time and energy. Keep an eye on the time so that breaks occur as required and set a timer so rehearsal can start again as efficiently as possible.

> Sometimes a director's preference for break times will vary depending on what they are working. In dance rehearsals, it is often best to use the 5 after 55 rule to keep the dancers fresh, but if they are doing in-depth character work or blocking a large scene, it may make more sense to work for 80 minutes and then take a longer break.

Monitor Staggered Performer Calls

In the instance of staggered performer calls, check in several minutes before the performers' call time to make sure they have arrived or are on their way. Also, keep open communication with the director about releasing performers early who will not be needed for the full rehearsal. Never release a performer without the permission of the director. Similarly, no performer should ever leave the rehearsal without being released by the stage manager. Make this point clear at the first rehearsal.

Spike Marks

Once furniture is set in place on the stage, stage management should spike each piece with spike tape. This will allow for easy and accurate placement of furniture as it moves from scene to scene and for when it needs to be placed for rehearsal. Spike furniture at the end of rehearsal before striking it for the evening or within the rehearsal once the director is happy with the placement.

> Before rehearsals begin, it's important to communicate with the scenic designer about their feelings on furniture placement. Some designers want to be intimately involved in the specific placement and angle of furniture, others give the director free reign to adjust as needed. When something moves or needs to move make sure to note it in the **rehearsal report** in a way that is appropriate to how the designer would like to be involved/not involved.

To spike, rip or cut two small pieces (approx. 1.5 inch each) of spike tape and stick them together to make a right angle. Use these to frame the upstage corners of the furniture/set piece (chair legs, platform corners, etc.). For most chairs and tables, marking the two upstage legs will be enough. For smaller chairs and tables, especially those where the angle of the furniture piece doesn't matter, sometimes it is better to mark an "X" directly at the

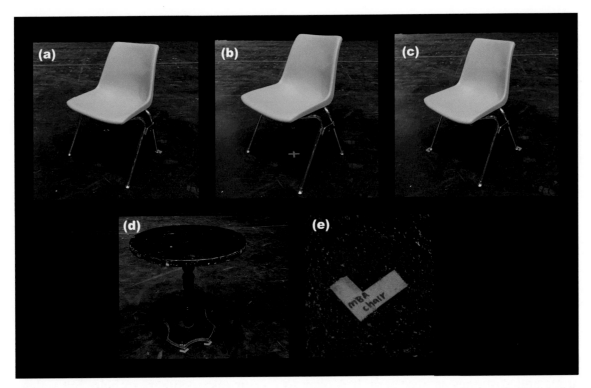

Figure 9.6 (a) Upstage Spike Marks, (b) Centered Spike Mark, (c) Alternate Corner Spike Marks, (d) Unusual Shaped Piece Spike, and (e) Labeled Spike

center of its placement rather than marking legs. For unusual-shaped pieces, you might need to get creative on how it is spiked (Figure 9.6).

If furniture placement changes, move the spikes or make new ones. Be sure to remove all old spike marks in order to avoid confusion. Sometimes it is helpful to label each spike directly on the tape. Use a Sharpie or another thick pen so that you can read it.

> In the UK, spike tape is typically a vinyl tape similar to electrical tape; it is very important to use scissors to cut this type of tape to prevent the ends from curling up.

It is a good idea to use a different color of spike tape for each of the different scenic locations (as much as possible) and keep a record of which color is for which scene. If color options are limited, they can be mixed or marked to create more options. Pick these colors carefully, according to their purpose. For rehearsals, bright, bold colors are best (yellow, pink, orange, light blue) or, if the rehearsal space has light-colored floors, dark colors for contrast. For most shows, it is preferable not to see the spike marks onstage during performances, so you should stick to darker colors and ones that can blend into the floor color (but not so much that you can't find the mark), especially in raked houses where the floor can more easily be seen by the audience. For scene changes that occur in darkness, it is better to use brighter colors that will be easier to find (blues and light greens are nice for this). You may even use glow tape to mark these, if finding the spike mark in the dark is too difficult.

> It is not uncommon to work with performers/crew members who are colorblind. Determine this early on so that you can choose spike colors accordingly.

Execute Scene Changes

Have a discussion with the director about who will be doing scene changes (performers or crew members or both). Depending on the aesthetic the director is going for, they may want the performers to execute all of the transitions or not be a part of them at all. This information will also need to be discussed at a production meeting so that the correct number of crew are brought onboard for the show.

During rehearsals, stage management is responsible for executing any scene changes not assigned to the cast. Execute these as quickly and as accurately as possible, including props and costumes as necessary. It is okay to recruit cast members to help; but unless the director is actively using the cast to complete changes as part of the show, stage management should be up and active in all transitions. Make sure to dress appropriately for rehearsal to be able to quickly and safely accomplish the changes. As you start doing transitions in rehearsal, start filling in the run sheet (see Figure 7.9, p. 84) that you created during prep week.

If a single scene is being run multiple times, you may end up resetting rather than transitioning to the next scene. Knowing when things enter, move, and exit throughout the scene will enable you to reset quickly, accurately, and efficiently.

> Throughout the rehearsal process, it can be helpful to keep a post-it note on the first blocking page of each scene. As each scene is worked in rehearsal, jot down all set pieces and props needed for the scene and any props/set pieces that are in the previous scene that need to be struck. Once runs or scene change blocking begin, this can easily be referenced to make sure everything is accounted for.

After Rehearsal

Performer Dismissal

Thank everyone for their work, make any announcements, and give a quick reminder about the time/location of the next rehearsal as well as a reminder to check the daily call for specifics.

Director Check-in

Once the performers are dismissed, check in with the director and any other relevant staff (music director, choreographer, etc.) to confirm the schedule for the next rehearsal. Clarify any questions from your personal notes and give any reminders. Review the rehearsal report with the director and see if they have any additions or clarifications. Thank them for a good rehearsal.

> **!** Learning how to avoid being a naysayer when ideas are pitched in the rehearsal room is an ability you will need to develop. It is not your place to determine whether or not a design or choice is possible. Instead, use phrases like "I'm not sure, but let me look into that" or "we can ask!". Try not to shoot down ideas until they have been run by the team in order to come up with creative solutions. If you are concerned about safety, you should always speak up and share that concern with the larger decision-making team.

Complete and Distribute the Rehearsal Report

Before sending the report, be sure that all of the notes make sense to someone who was not present in the rehearsal and are written in complete sentences. Tone is important. The report must convey the necessary information without stepping on anyone's toes. Generally speaking, notes should take one of four forms:

1. Asking a question – "Does Susan's costume have pockets? If not, would it be possible to add one?"
2. Presenting a problem and seeking a solution – "The safety rail is loose, is there a way to reinforce it?"
3. Stating a desire – "We would like to discuss using area mics."
4. Statements of fact – "In scene 3, Juliette enters through the house."

While stage managers are adroit problem solvers, it is up to each department to solve problems as they see fit. The stage manager may have a great idea about how to reinforce the safety rail, but it isn't their place to tell the shop how to do its job and the TD may have an even better solution. This is why we ask questions and present challenges rather than dictate solutions. There is sometimes room to include a suggestion, especially if the director has a specific idea about something (e.g., "Alice's necklace will be ripped off in scene 4, the director suggested a magnet clasp" or "…, perhaps a magnet clasp?"), and it is great to offer ideas when asked but avoid unsolicited advice in reports.

There are many ways to say the same thing. A good rehearsal report note has adequate information, allows room for discussion, and is clearly written. Figure 9.7 includes some examples of good and bad notes.

BAD NOTES		
N1	*The director hates Sally's act 2 dress*	While it may be true, it isn't tactful
N2a	*Fix the door*	Not Enough Information. Demanding
N2b	*When Steve came through the door in scene 7 for the "I love you I hate you monologue" something wonky happened with the door*	Both too vague and too much extraneous information
N3	*We need flowers for act 2*	Not enough information
GOOD NOTES		
N1	*We would like to discuss Sally's act 2 look at our next meeting*	This lets costumes know that there may be an issue and allows for face-to-face discussion for clearer communication
N2	*The screws came out of the top hinge of the DSL door when it was thrown open this evening.*	The shop knows which door, what the problem is, and the action that caused the problem. There is sometimes the urge to add "Can this be fixed?" But it is clear to most TD's that this needs to be dealt with
N3	*Please ADD a bouquet of flowers that coordinates with Sally's costume for the wedding scene (Act 2 scene 2)*	Gives information about what sort of flowers are needed and what scene they are for

Figure 9.7 Examples of Good and Bad Notes

Double-check that all of your information, including headings, is accurate and up-to-date. There shouldn't be any empty sections in the report; if there is nothing to report, say so (e.g., "There are no notes at this time" or "None, thank you," etc.). As with all distributed documents, always send it as a PDF to avoid any formatting issues or accidental changes to the document and include the information in the body of the email. Rehearsal reports are distributed to all members of the production team, but not the cast. Be sure to send them out before the start of the next work day (immediately following rehearsal is preferable).

> **!** Use your best judgment when choosing what should be included in the rehearsal report. Many times performers will come up to you with questions about what they will be wearing or what their prop will be; unless this is a question from the director as well, do not include it in the rehearsal report. You can ask the director the question and if they don't know and/or want to know, then it can be added to the report.

Distribute Daily Call

Email the cast the daily call. This should include a reminder of the time, location, and summary of the planned work for the next rehearsal as well as any fittings and any other important notices/reminders.

Clean Up and Close Down the Space

Put away all props and rehearsal furniture. Clean up your table. Leave the space the way you found it, especially if it is a borrowed, rented, or shared space. If the rehearsal space will be used exclusively by your company during the run of your production, speak with the technical director or space coordinator about how much must be struck (put away) each night. In some cases, the table and some furniture can remain in the space, making for a simpler rehearsal setup each night.

Shut off lights and sound systems, take down rehearsal signs, and lock the doors (as applicable).

As Rehearsals Progress

First Rehearsal Off-Book

In the days prior to any off-book rehearsal, remind the cast (through both verbal and written reminders) of the upcoming off-book date and that they need to have all of their lines memorized by this time. Performers may be required to be off-book all at once or in sections (one act or a couple of scenes at a time). In professional productions, scenes are typically expected to be off-book the second time they are worked in the rehearsal room.

Prompting

Once a scene is off-book, a new job for the stage management team is to be "**on-book**." This means that someone is following along word by word in the script, ready to give the next line to a performer if they become lost. This is called **prompting**. As trivial as this may seem, it is a big responsibility – the longer a performer has to wait for their line to be delivered, the more "out of the moment" the cast becomes and the less productive the rehearsal is. It is crucial to follow the text vigilantly and jump in immediately with the line if someone calls for it. Even if it seems as though the performers know all of their lines for a scene, stick closely with the script; the moment you look away will inevitably be the moment someone forgets a line. Eliminate nearby distractions (phones, computer, etc.) to avoid becoming drawn away from the text. Work with your team to establish a plan for implementing prompting before starting rehearsal. If there are multiple members of the stage management team, decide who will be on-book for each rehearsal and stick with the same person to avoid confusion. Inform the performers of who will be on-book so they know who's voice to expect. If that person needs to step away for any reason, reassign the job until they return. Most importantly, don't have multiple people on-book simultaneously because hearing multiple voices respond is counterproductive.

As the cast starts to work off-book, make it clear that you will only feed a line to a performer when they call "Line." When prompting, speak clearly and loudly. Enunciate. Read the first few words and continue the line until they begin to speak or pick it up. This will become more natural with practice.

> Sometimes a performer will take a dramatic pause within or before certain lines as part of their character choice. It can be helpful to note these times in your script so as to avoid accidentally giving an unnecessary prompt and interrupting a theatrical moment.

Line Notes

Once performers are off-book, you will also need to start giving them line notes, so they know exactly which lines they need to work on. There are many different ways to take line notes, so experiment until you find a method that works best for you. Follow along closely in the script and take note of any and all mistakes that the performer makes. In addition to places that the performers called line, line notes can also include skipped words or phrases, paraphrasing, adding words or phrases, jumping ahead or backwards in the text, and any other errors the performers may make. As with blocking, this is a fast-paced process; so using shorthand is to your advantage. It makes the most sense to take line notes when you are running big chunks; it is, generally, unnecessary to take line notes while you are just working through scenes multiple times (Figure 9.8).

> To keep your script in a clean condition, put each page in a page protector and take line notes with dry or wet erase markers (wet erase markers require water to wipe off, but tend to smear less than dry erase markers). These can be easily erased at the end of every night, so that the script is clean and ready for the next run through.

At the end of the rehearsal, line notes will need to be distributed to the performers. Some stage managers handwrite their line notes and distribute them before the performers leave for the day. Others type up the notes and distribute via email. If you are using a digital script, you might be able to highlight, copy, and paste. Like rehearsal reports, line notes should be issued as soon as possible after rehearsal so the performers can work on correcting errors before the next rehearsal.

Figure 9.8 Line Notes Shorthand

If there are not any assistant stage managers, you will be responsible for both being on-book and for taking line notes. On-book responsibilities always take higher precedence than line notes. Mark as much as you can using your shorthand as you go along, but don't fret if you miss some line mistakes. Like all aspects of stage management, this is a skill that will become easier with time and practice, as will balancing these tasks along with your other duties.

Maintaining Blocking

Once the blocking has been set, the stage manager is responsible for helping maintain consistency. Be prepared to prompt the performers as to where their next move is if they get lost or to gently remind them of the correct blocking if they wander too far astray. This is another reason why clean and accurate blocking notation is important. For many directors, the blocking will not be set completely in stone until dress rehearsals or even opening night (with minor tweaks being made to account for spacing or lighting or the set). With this in mind, treat all blocking reminders as just that – a reminder of what was written down last time, with the knowledge that the director may prefer what the performer did instead and that the blocking may change from what is in your book.

Discuss protocol with your director before rehearsals begin. Have a plan on how and when you should make comments on the blocking. (Should you interrupt the scene or let it play out and address the change when the scene is complete? Should variations be discussed with the full group or privately with the director?)

Putting It Together

About half to two-thirds of the way through the rehearsal process, you will reach a point when the cast is ready to put together large chunks of the show and you will start doing stumble throughs. The intent is to start building continuity and get a feel for the show as a whole. Blocking will be clunky, props and transitions will be missed, lines will be a mess, and character intricacies are often forgotten. Often the goal is to keep pushing forward as much as possible and give notes at the end. However, it is okay to stop and fix as needed, especially if there are any safety concerns. Depending on the show and the length of the rehearsal period, the stumble through may be a small chunk of scenes, a single act, or the whole show.

After stumble through rehearsals, you will have at least one run through rehearsal. Like the stumble through, this may happen a single act at a time or the whole show at once (again, usually dependent on the show and on your rehearsal period). By this point, the cast should have an idea of the continuity. Now, the intent is to reintegrate all the things they discovered in rehearsals with character as well as to have another chance to get technical things correct (blocking, lines, prop tracking, and transitions). Unlike stumble throughs, run throughs should not stop unless absolutely necessary.

> Whenever a large part of the show is being run, it is nice to inform or remind the production team so they can attend if they desire.

Be sure to get timings of any stumble throughs or run throughs. If possible, get timings not only for the whole show, but also for individual acts and scenes. At this point in the process, the specificity of scene timings will assist the director in determining which scenes need to be tightened up. Include timings in your rehearsal report as this can be useful information for the production team. Some departments may need additional, specific timings (e.g., timings for costume changes, length of transitions, etc.). The front of house staff will also need timing information.

One of the run through rehearsals (or the run through, if there is only one) should be scheduled as the designer run. This will be a chance for designers to see a run of the show before tech starts. Get this rehearsal on the calendar as soon as possible and send reminders about it. Make sure there is enough seating for all designers. This is also a good time to get your crew in to see the show if possible. It may be the only chance they have to see a full run.

As with all points in the process, the more prepared you are for these rehearsals, the smoother they will run and the less stressful it will be for all parties. Carefully track props, have a plan for all transitions (any that are not accomplished by performers will be taken care of by stage management) and be glued to the promptbook. Quick prompting will be critical here as line errors will be the first thing to slow down a run. These rehearsals will be a major test of your multitasking abilities. It will be stressful and things will go wrong, but this is why we rehearse. You are not expected to have all the correct answers yet, or else the show would be in performances. Answer questions as best you can, take note of things that need to be solved, and remember to breathe.

Post Designer Run Meeting

Following the designer run (often right after the rehearsal), there is usually a short production meeting held to allow the production team to ask any questions they have about the run and also to discuss the upcoming tech process. This can be a good time to lay out basic goals for each day of tech as well as how tech will be conducted (as a cue-to-cue, a start & stop, etc.; these terms are discussed more in Chapter 11). Consideration can also be given to when and how furniture will get spiked, how the team wants to handle complex transitions, and when complicated wigs and costumes will be added to the process. In academia, the designer run may be held much earlier in the rehearsal process, so the logistics of tech conversation may happen later on, closer to the start of tech.

Balancing Safety and Diplomacy

The stage manager's primary job is to support the production by running a safe, efficient, smooth, and productive rehearsal to accomplish the work planned for the day. The stage manager's relationship with the director and cast will develop over time as you grow accustomed to your working relationship. You should always treat people with respect, but you must also protect the cast from unsafe situations. If a team member is endangering the cast or asking them to break company rules, it is part of your job to remedy the situation, which might mean talking to the artistic director or producer if the team member is unwilling to adjust. If issues arise, avoid getting into an argument or a major disagreement in front of the rest of the company. Speak to the person after rehearsal (or during a break) to work out any issues privately.

Publicity Events

Throughout the rehearsal process, there may be opportunities to create buzz for the show by participating in publicity events. These can include a variety of things like staging publicity photos, recording radio or television interviews and ads, performing a short section of the show in public, or helping distribute show posters. Stage management's involvement will vary from situation to situation. Most often, they will be called on to help with scheduling and coordination. Below we will discuss two of the most common publicity events you are likely to encounter.

Publicity Photos

A publicity photo will sometimes be taken before tech begins to help sell tickets. The date and desired shot should be chosen in coordination with the production team. As soon as possible, communicate this time and date to cast members involved in the shot. If the location is not at the theatre, make sure that it has been scheduled and/or reserved and the performers have transportation to and from that location. Be sure to schedule enough time for the performers to get into costume, hair, and makeup before the photographer arrives.

Interviews

The production company or publicist may set up interviews with the cast, designers, or director to help promote the show. The stage manager may be asked to help coordinate these interviews to best fit within the rehearsal schedule and the company members' availability. Additionally, with many companies the stage manager may be required to arrange transit.

Chapter Ten
Prior to Tech

Prior to technical rehearsals you will need to update several pieces of paperwork that you created during prep week and partially filled in throughout rehearsals. During load-in you should familiarize yourself with the venue and prepare the space for the cast. This is also when you will start adding cues to your calling script.

Pre-Show Checklist

During performances, the stage manager will have a number of tasks to accomplish from the time they arrive until they settle in to call the first cue of the show. This list is often extensive and certain tasks will need to happen at or by a specific time, so having them in an organized checklist will ensure nothing is overlooked. Some of these tasks may be handled by other departments or staff during the tech process, but it can be helpful to create this list early regardless and add to it as needed. This can include things like unlocking the booth, opening dressing rooms, checking attendance, making time calls to the cast (we'll address this in greater detail in Chapter 11), checking in with the front of house, as well as any other pre-show duties (Figure 10.1).

Post-Show Checklist

Along with the pre-show checklist, there should also be a post-show checklist. This lists everything that has to happen before the last person leaves for the night. Make sure it is clear that these items are just as important to get done as the preset items and that no one on the stage management team should leave the building until the list is complete. This list could include tasks such as locking up weapons, cleaning up food or fake blood, getting furniture out of the way if there is a day crew, etc. (Figure 10.2).

Preset Checklist

One of the tasks that should be completed during rehearsals prior to tech is to compile a preset list. This is different from a pre-show checklist. This should include all set pieces and props that need to be set onstage/backstage prior to the start of the show. It should

DOI: 10.4324/9781003133049-11

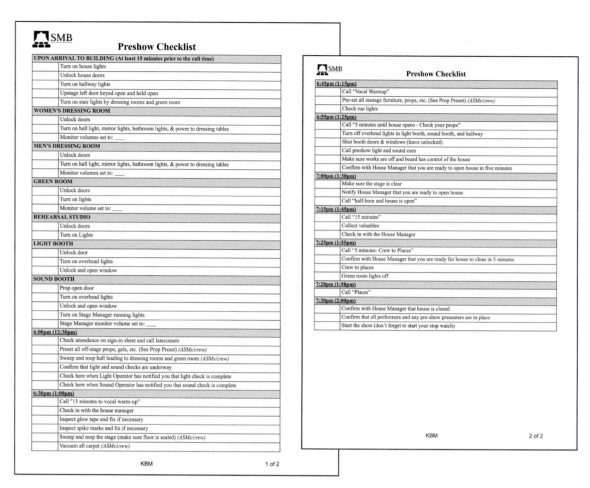

Figure 10.1 Pre-Show Checklist

Post-Show Checklist — SMB

HANNAH

	STRIKE props to road box	Lock after mugs are washed
	STRIKE gloves to actor boxes	*Do a once-around the theatre after house is clear*
	STRIKE harnesses to road box	
	TURN OFF blue touch lights	INCLUDING aisle/operator lights
	PICK UP dressing room *(if needed)*	
	STRIKE trash cans to DSL hallway	
	RESET SL "Comfort Inn" rooms	Make beds - Check state of rooms - Accordion fold curtains
	PRESET SL masking curtains	
	TURN OFF all backstage worklights	
	PUT OUT and plug in ghost light	

TRAVIS

	STRIKE props to road box	Lock after mugs are washed
	STRIKE gloves to actor boxes	*Do a once-around the theatre after house is clear*
	STRIKE harnesses to road box	
	SET "Comfort Inn" desks (ONLY practical lamps)	PLUG IN
	TURN OFF blue touch lights	INCLUDING aisle/operator lights
	RESET SR "Comfort Inn" rooms	Make beds- Check state of rooms - Accordion fold curtains
	PRESET SR masking curtains	
	CHECK flying points	Make sure all put back into resting positions
	EMPTY water stations	
	TURN OFF and return comms to SM office	All batteries on chargers, headsets hung
	LOCK dressing room, booth, and road box	Keys returned to SM office

1 of 1   Updated 4/3/18

Figure 10.2 Post-Show Checklist

also include any costumes that need to be preset backstage or onstage (this usually falls to the wardrobe crew, but you should check that they are there). It can be helpful to create diagrams or insert photos of complicated or super-specific presets. If there is an ASM on the project, they should be in charge of creating and maintaining this list. A copy of the preset list should be posted near each prop location backstage and a copy should be kept in the promptbook. It can be helpful to have a column for each dress rehearsal and performance next to each item on the list, so they can be checked off before each run. The list will evolve throughout tech week, but coming in with a preliminary one will make tech run more smoothly (see Figure 7.8, p. 83).

Run Sheet

As previously discussed, the run sheet details all the transitions that happen in the show. Go through your script scene by scene, updating the run sheet as you go, and double check all prop tracking, scenery moves, and costume quick changes you noted in rehearsal. When these are not assigned to specific performers, assign crew members to them.

Print multiple copies. Post copies in multiple places backstage (ideally near a light source that will be on during the show). Have physical copies for each crew member as well (including any ASMs). This way, they can take personal notes on their specific jobs. It is a good idea to keep electronic versions of all paperwork. Keep a copy on a personal computer as well as additional backup copies in multiple locations (flash drives, cloud-based storage, etc.).

Take time before the first tech rehearsal to go over the run sheet with everyone who has an assignment. Make sure they know what they are moving, when they move it, how it moves, and where they are expected to move it (this may happen during crew training) (Figure 10.3).

The run sheet is a living document up until opening. It is very important to keep the run sheet updated as things change throughout the tech process. Ask the crew to make notes on either the posted copies or their personal ones, collect them at the end of rehearsals, make the changes, and print new copies before the next rehearsal. Accuracy is important; should any member of the crew call in sick, their job should be documented well enough that the show can be run seamlessly by a stand-in.

Tech/Performance Schedule

The tech schedule may be predetermined by the company or it may be a discussion with the production team about what is needed. In either case, the stage manager is frequently responsible for hammering out the details of the schedule and distributing it to the cast, crew, and production team. Creating the tech schedule can be complex and takes time and communication. There are some industry standards that can help guide the process, but at the time of this printing, there is also a push to make the industry standards more equitable so this information may be out-of-date. Commonly, tech consists of longer rehearsal days

SMB				Urinetown	
			SMB Productions		
WHO:	**TASK:**	**WHAT:**	**WHERE:**	**WHEN:**	**NOTES**
			TOP OF SHOW		
	Sweep	Deck		Prior to house open	
	Mop	Deck		Prior to house open	
	Set	Props	SL, SR, Onstage	Prior to house open	
	Places / Cue	SL - Gretchen, Josh, Gabby, Andrew, Anna, Spencer, Jeff			
	Places / Cue	SR - Abby, Gabrielle, Deanna, Amelia, Will, Michelle, Jack, Vallen, Devann, Cassandra, Emma, Micah, Lorina, Casey			
	Places / Cue	HL - Ben, Sam, Moriah, Olivia, Arielle			
			DURING I.1		
	Catch	Broom	SL		
	Handoff	Mop	SL		
		INTO I.2 TO UGC - "Mr. Cladwell" - Shift Red			
	Fly Out	Amenity Wall	Line 10	S.M. GO	Speed?
	Fly Out	Amenity Masking	Line 11	"	Speed?
	Fly In	UGC Sign	Line 8	"	Yellow Spike
Josh & Will	Strike	Amenity Table	>SL	B/O	
Anna	Strike	Amenity Chair	>SL	"	
Deanna	Strike	Cleaning Supplies	>SL	"	Dead
Andrew & Jeff	Set	UGC Desk	< SR	Able	
Micah	Set	UGC Chair	< SR	"	
			DURING I.2		
	Quick Change	Vallen Poor to Rich		Upon Exit	Timing?
	Quick Change	Amelia Poor to Rich		"	Timing?
		INTO I.3 TO THE STREET - Shift Blue			
	Fly Out	UCG Sign	Line 8	S.M. GO	
Spencer & Andrew	Strike	UGC Desk	> SR	B/O	
Micah	Strike	UGC Chair	> SR	"	
		INTO I.4 TO THE AMENITY - Shift Violet			
	Fly In	Amenity Wall	Line 10	S.M. GO	Spike Color?
	Fly In	Amenity Masking	Line 11	"	Spike Color?
	Set	Amenity Table	< SL	Able	w/ Ledger, pen, and Cash Box
Gretchen	Set	Amenity Chair	< SL	"	
		INTO I.5 TO UGC - Shift Pink			
	Fly Out	Amenity Wall	Line 10	S.M. GO	Speed?
	Fly Out	Amenity Masking	Line 11	"	Speed?
	Fly In	UGC Sign	Line 8	"	Yellow Spike
	Strike	Amenity Table		B/O	
	Strike	Amenity Chair		"	

Updated: 7/28/14 — KBM — 1 of 6

Figure 10.3 Run Sheet Excerpt

which are often 10 out of 12's (10/12), meaning the company works for 10 hours out of a 12-hour time span with 2 hours of extended break time (e.g., 10 am–3 pm and 5 pm–10 pm). These 2 hours are exclusive of the normal 5- or 10-minute breaks. There are other variations like the 8 out of 10 or 7 out of 9, which follow the same basic principle. It will vary from company to company, but sometimes dedicated rehearsal hours apply to the cast but not the crew, production team, or stage management. In other instances, the stated span of day is for the entire company. In academia, tech rehearsals during the week tend to happen in the evening with longer days on the weekend. Once you know the hours allotted for tech, you will need to determine when cast and crew will be called. Establish the desired time to begin working with performers on stage and then work backwards to determine the crew calls.

Below, we will outline how one might create a tech schedule where the performers are called for an 8 out of 10 starting at 12 pm and the theatre is open from 9 am to midnight. In this case, 9 am–12 pm can be used as crew prep time, the "rehearsal day" is considered

12 pm–10 pm, and any remaining crew notes/shutdown duties must be completed between 10 pm and midnight.

Cast Calls

During tech, the cast will always be called at the top of the rehearsal day, although the start time for work onstage will vary. For a simple tech rehearsal, performers will be called at noon with the expectation that tech will start eminently. If full costumes are being worn, the cast is usually allotted a minimum of 30 minutes to get into costume prior to starting work onstage (in this case, a 12 pm call for a 12:30 pm start). The first time the cast is getting into costume, it is helpful to plan for a little bit of extra time.

For performances, cast call times will be based on the sum of pre-show activities that must take place before curtain (e.g., getting into costume, getting into mic and doing mic check, any fight/lift/intimacy calls, vocal or physical warmups, etc.). Usually, this equates to anywhere from 30 minutes to 90 minutes prior to curtain.

> **! HALF HOUR**
>
> In most theatres, the house opens 30 minutes prior to curtain time. In AEA, this is also the latest time that performers can arrive at the theatre (barring any fight calls, etc. that must happen prior to the house opening or other elaborate hair/makeup, etc. as established above) and is colloquially referred to as **Half Hour**.

Crew Calls

Once you have a good grasp on the **pre-show** checklist (discussed a bit later) and the amount of preparation the crew will need to do each day, you can calculate call times. Some companies have set call times and IATSE (the stagehands union; more details can be found in Chapter 13) has specific rules about when you can be in the venue. Determine the earliest and latest times that people can be called (talk to whoever is in charge of scheduling). Work with the department heads to figure out how much time the crews and cast will need to get prepared for rehearsal and then put those pieces together.

If there isn't a standard or mandatory call, a good starting place is to call the deck crew 1 hour before half hour (90 minutes before curtain/start time – in our scenario 11:00 am). Of course, if the prop list is 20 pages long it might take them a bit longer to check, so make your best estimate and adjust as you go.

Depending on the complexity of the light plot (and accessibility to the lights if there is a problem), the person doing channel/dimmer/rig check should be in 30 minutes before the deck crew (2 hours before curtain – in this scenario 10:30 am). This gives them time to troubleshoot if anything isn't working correctly.

The sound operator will need time to prep and check all of the mics and speakers and to troubleshoot things if necessary. If you are responsible for determining their call time, start them at the same time as the electrics crew.

For dress rehearsals, you will need to add wardrobe crew calls to the schedule. Thirty minutes before the performers are called is a good starting place (in our scenario 11:30 am). Wardrobe calls tend to vary widely, so talk to the wardrobe supervisor to determine how much time is needed. For productions with lots of costume changes or very specific costume needs, costumes might be added at the top of tech rather than waiting until dress rehearsals (Figure 10.4).

In a scenario where the span of day ends at the same time for the cast and the crew (say in our scenario, the building actually closes up at 10 pm), all onstage rehearsal must end with enough time for the crew to shut down prior to the end of day. Usually, 30 minutes are allotted for this, depending on the venue.

Once the initial schedule is established, share it with the relevant parties (cast, crew, designers, etc.). You can't expect the crew to show up on time if you never told them what time to show up.

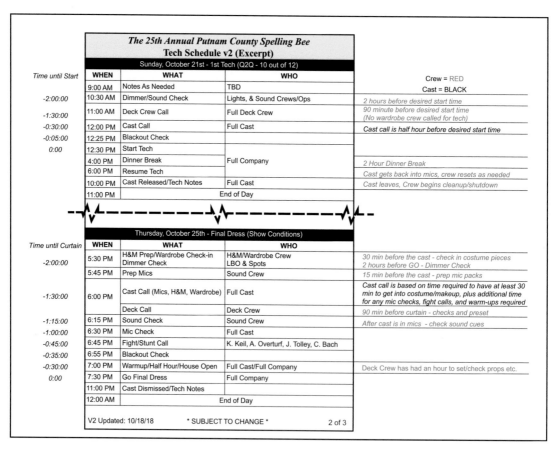

Figure 10.4 Tech Schedule and Crew Call Excerpt

Once the crew has a strong understanding of their daily tasks, call times may change. If, for example, you realize that the pre-show set only takes 20 minutes, there is no need to call the crew an hour early, or if the preset isn't getting done in time, you may need to call them earlier. As you adjust calls, be sure to leave time for troubleshooting. Additionally, you may need to adjust calls once you reach performances since, generally speaking, everything that needs to happen on stage must be completed before the house opens at half hour.

As you create the schedule, it is important to be humane, especially when everyone involved is a student and balancing class work, projects, outside jobs, self-care, and rehearsals.

Tech Requests

A tech request is a written list of items needed for tech that will need to be coordinated between departments. It needs to be created early enough in the process that there is time to implement the requests. It may include items such as the locations of tech tables and quick change booths, the number and type of headsets needed and their locations, cue light placements, prop table needs, **run light** requests, a **god mic**, and even tech table light and power needs. Even if an official request isn't created, all of these elements need to be considered and discussed prior to tech.

> **!** A God mic is a microphone dedicated to the stage manager to allow them to communicate with the cast and crew, call holds, and give instructions. Make sure to ask the technical director or sound engineer about the possibility of having a God mic; it will save your voice over a long tech period. If possible, request for it to go through the green room and dressing room monitors as well.

Who's on Headset

During Tech/Dress

Below is a list of people who may be on headset with you during tech. This will vary based on equipment and channel availability.

- Stage Manager
- ASM(s)
- Deck Manager
- Head **Flyrail**
- Automation Operator
- Console Operator(s)

- Deck Crew (as needed)
- Programmers (as needed)
- Spot Operator(s)
- Lighting Designer
- Media Designer
- Sound Designer

Headsets may come from sound, electrics, or production management – find out who is responsible well in advance of tech.

During Performances

- Stage Manager
- ASM(s)
- Deck Manager
- Head **Flyrail**

- Automation Operator
- Console Operator(s)
- Deck Crew (as needed)
- Spot Operator(s)

Load-In

If the production hasn't been rehearsing in the performance space already, load-in is the first time that all of the tech elements will be brought into the theatre. This typically takes place a couple of days before the first tech rehearsal. It will be your chance to prepare the space for the performers.

If your rehearsal space is in a different building from the theatre, you may need to help coordinate the transfer of items (props, costumes, furniture, stage management kits, etc.) from one location to the other. Speak with the production manager (or your production's equivalent) to iron out logistics.

During load-in, take the time to become very familiar with the space; find all bathrooms, water fountains, and the callboard (or a good central place to put a makeshift callboard), familiarize yourself with the place you'll be stationed to call cues, and find good locations for prop tables backstage. Explore all paths through the theatre. Try to get lost or locked out (if you can, others are bound to), and if you do, figure out how to get back. Start planning out where you are going to need run lights (for safe passage, seeing prop tables, and for quick changes); identify what might be a safety hazard and which doors lock automatically (these will need to be taped or roped open during the performance if they are being used), including doors that will be accessed during breaks.

Once you are familiar with the space, get to work on organizing the backstage in the best arrangement for the show's needs.

Prepping the Stage and Backstage

Signage

In many theatres, it can be easy to get lost, especially for performers who are new to the space and particularly when they have just been dancing around in circles onstage. As a helping hand to everyone on the production, post directional signage in strategic locations backstage ("this way to stage left," "this way to dressing rooms," "this way to bathrooms," etc.).

Spike Marks

When it is time to move from the rehearsal space to the performance space, plot out the locations of any spike marks for furniture or moving scenery that were not originally on

Figure 10.5 Masking Spike Tape

the groundplan or that have been modified during rehearsal. Measure from a feature that can be replicated/found in the theatre (e.g., the plaster line) and record these measurements as coordinates (sometimes referred to as a **spike map**), so they can be easily taped out on the stage.

If rehearsals are taking place on the performance stage or if spike marks are transferred before the floor treatment has been completed, be sure to take precautions before any paint covers up the marks. Keep open communication with the scenic designer and TD about when the floor treatment will be happening and schedule time prior to that to cover up the spike marks. One-inch masking or blue painter's tape works very well for this. Tape over your spike marks, being careful to cover your full mark but as little of the stage as possible. Leave a little "flag" in the painter's tape (a small folded-over section that makes the tape easier to grasp and pull up). After painting is complete, simply go back through and peel up the masking tape, leaving your spike mark (and its color) intact (Figure 10.5).

Spike masking should be pulled prior to the next rehearsal call but finding the flags/spikes can be time consuming, so plan accordingly.

Once spike marks are final (they have been transferred onto the performance stage, spacing has been finalized, and all floor treatments are complete), it is a good idea to cover them with clear vinyl (Marley) tape. This type of tape is manufactured to seam dance floors, but can come in handy to help secure spike marks and dance numbers. This will prevent the tape from pulling up over the course of performances. If Marley tape is not available, clear packing tape works as well, although it is not as durable or long-lasting.

Sightlines

Sightlines delineate the areas of the stage/backstage that can be seen from the house. Often they are the areas between masking curtains. They can be marked to help keep the cast

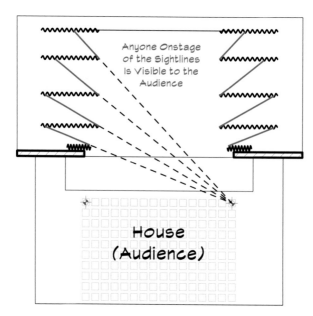

Figure 10.6 Sightlines Diagram

and crew out of the audiences' line of sight. To mark a sightline, place tape along the line at the edge of the area between where the audience can see backstage and where they cannot (Figure 10.6).

Risk Assessment

Assessing the risks that may be present in the space and on the set is important. Hopefully, most of the risky elements will be dealt with by the production team much earlier in the process. However, once the set is loaded in, it should also be assessed by stage management for safety. There are several types of risk to look out for. They include (but are not limited to): injury due to falling, slipping or tripping, spillage, falling objects, unstable surfaces, fire, electrical hazards, impact, weapons, unusual use of objects or equipment, pyrotechnics, and sensory impairment.

At its simplest, risk assessment is acknowledging the risks and finding solutions that balance safety and aesthetics. Many risk assessment forms use a grading system to determine how risky something is and have a ranking system that spans from things that must be dealt with immediately to things that should be observed regularly. A typical assessment might ask how likely it is that something will happen with a range from inevitable to highly unlikely and how severe the consequence would be if it happened with a range from deadly to minor. Something that is deadly and highly likely to happen will need to be addressed immediately, whereas something that is unlikely and will cause only minor damage could be observed or addressed as needed. Just because the risks have been assessed doesn't mean that they will go away. Part of the assessment process is finding ways to mitigate the risk and make things as safe as possible, not necessarily eliminating all risk entirely. Having a railing on a tall platform certainly makes it safer, but dancing eight feet in the air will always have an element of risk to it. Knowing that the champagne flutes that the dancers

Legacy of Light
Risk Assessment

Location: ____Strayer-Wood Theatre____ Date: ____04/13/19____ Assessed By: _____K. McGlaughlin_____

No.	Hazard	Associated Risk	Individual(s) at Risk	Preventative Measures Taken	Preventative Measures Required
1	Loose cable Backstage Left	Trip Hazard	Cast/Crew	Taped cable down and covered with carpet	N/A
2	Chicken wire on tree poking out	Cuts, Punctures, Abrasions	Callie, Jacob, Quinn, Crew	Temporarily Taped over protrusions	Remove, Grind, Fold, or otherwise dull wire
3	Character exits wearing a mask	Sensory Impairment (Vision)	Sam	Ensured Eyeholes were large enough to see through, marked floor with exit path	N/A
4	Uneven steps between levels	Injury Due to Falling/Trip Hazard	Cast/Crew	Performers/Crew given time to familiarize themselves Glow/Caution tape on edges when possible	N/A
5	Swords (Used in Duel)	Weapons Injury	Sam & Jacob	Performers/Crew trained in safe handling	Nightly fight call

Page 1 of 3

Figure 10.7 Risk Assessment Grid

are carrying might spill or break, create a plan for someone to clean up the spill or broken glass in character, if needed.

In terms of fall hazards, this may mean checking that all the appropriate railings have been installed and are secure. Slipping and tripping may mean confirming that the floor surface is even and free from unexpected variations in height or texture and not so smooth that the cast will feel like they are ice skating when they're in their character shoes. Unstable surfaces may be standing on a couch or tap dancing on a suitcase. If the production is using matches, fireworks, candles, etc., there should be a plan in place to deal with those items safely. Impairment could come from a character in a blindfold or with their head covered by a scarf or a bandage, or maybe someone is in handcuffs.

Finding, noting, and mitigating these risks isn't the sole responsibility of the stage manager, but it is something that the stage manager should be aware of as they move into a space. The term "risk assessment" and associated paperwork are much more commonly found in UK and Australian theatre companies than in the USA, but assessment should take place regardless of the formality (Figure 10.7).

Run Lights

Run lights are colored light bulbs or dark-gelled lights (traditionally blue) used to help ease navigation backstage in the dark during performances. They should illuminate backstage paths and prop table areas without causing too much light bleed on stage. Depending on where quick changes are taking place, run lights may also need to be added so the wardrobe crew can see to complete the change. Run lights are typically either clip lights plugged into the wall or lights controlled by the lighting **console**. Occasionally they will be permanent fixtures in the theatre. The lights are usually provided and hung by the electrics department (with input from stage management for locations). Add turning them on and off to the pre-show/post-show checklists (if not console controlled).

Safety Tape

One important step that should be taken to help ensure safety before and during tech rehearsals is to lay down safety tape in any areas of the stage (either onstage or backstage) where performers or crew will be moving that may pose a safety threat (e.g., stairs, ledges, masking flats). Sometimes white or neon colored gaff tape is all that is needed, while other times glow tape may be required. White gaff tape works better in very low light situations, while glow tape works best in total darkness. Never waste tape, but be generous when taping backstage; it is dark and often there is a lot happening in a small space. Contrarily, when taping onstage, use sparingly; depending on the house, the audience may be able to see the floor and excessive bright tape can be distracting. Confer with the scenic and lighting designers to ensure that the safety tape is minimally intrusive to the design, though safety always comes first (Figure 10.8).

Glow Tape

Glow tape is specialized tape coated with photo-luminescent pigments that absorb and store energy from ambient light. In a blackout, the tape glows, allowing people to see without needing to wait for their eyes to fully adjust. Glow tape is a great tool but it is expensive, so use thoughtfully; a small amount can go a long way. Ultimately, it is important that the performers are safe no matter the cost of tape, so take the necessary precautions to ensure their safety. Ask the performers if there are any particular trouble areas that they

Figure 10.8 Example of Safety Taped Steps

would like to have glow taped. If performers are going to need to exit in a blackout, a dotted path of glow tape may need to be created for them. Again, coordinate with the designers to balance safety and aesthetic. Depending on the show, some spike marks may also need glow tape in order to be found in the dark.

It is a good idea to keep at least one flashlight backstage, both for emergency safety reasons and to "charge" any glow tape that doesn't get light exposure during the run of the show. Charging glow tape is a good task to include on the pre-show checklist or run sheet. If there is a lot of glow tape that isn't exposed to light naturally, it may be worth trying something else like white or neon tape that won't need to be charged or perhaps an additional run light if possible.

Clearing Backstage Pathways

Another step in ensuring safety backstage is to maintain clear pathways to all areas onstage and offstage where people must travel. Areas should be swept or vacuumed where possible (especially quick change areas where performers may be in bare feet) and be free of any trip hazards. Any cables crossing these paths must be either taped down or covered with a cable ramp or piece of carpet (this is usually addressed by the electricians, but it never hurts to keep an extra eye out for stray cables). Any screws or other metal snags sticking out of walls or floors should be removed or covered with tape to avoid scrapes or ripped costumes. Wherever possible, pathways should also be lit with run lights. If budgets allow, it can be helpful to outline paths with white gaff or spike tape.

Cue Lights

Cue lights are a way to communicate when verbal communication is not possible/efficient. They can range from homemade systems using regular light bulbs and hand-wired switches to high-tech console-based systems. In their simplest form, the stage manager turns on a switch wherever they are calling and somewhere else in the building a light turns on (typically somewhere backstage to cue an entrance or scene change/automation). The person that sees the light knows that they are on standby (ready and waiting to execute their action). Then, at the appropriate moment (when the G-O would be called verbally), the stage manager turns off the switch, the light goes off, and the cast/crew member does whatever it is that they are supposed to do. If cue lights are needed, they should be discussed well in advance of tech to determine what is available/possible.

Cue lights are often used to cue flying scenery because they eliminate the risk of headset cables getting tangled in pull ropes. They can also be used to cue entrances when the offstage cast member can't see or hear the onstage action (this comes up in a lot of farces). Another use might be if a cue is being executed in a location that can't be reached by headset. Frequently, if the show is using microphones and the person mixing sound is also responsible for executing sound cues, they will be cued via cue light so that they don't have to have their ears covered with a headset.

During load-in, the stage manager should check that any cue lights that have been discussed are set up in the right places and that they are in good working order. The department responsible for cue lights (often the electrics department) may wait for the stage manager to finalize the locations before installing them. Checking the cue lights should be a regular part of either the pre-show checklist or the dimmer check.

Prop Tables

A critical element of a seamless performance is strategic organization and layout of props backstage. Acquire or designate a table/flat surface as the prop table (you may want one for each side of the stage or a few strategically placed near the various entrances to the stage, depending on the theatre and the production). Each prop table should have its own run light so no one has to fumble around in the dark searching for their prop. A good way to organize props is to tape out and label a specific area for each prop that starts on the table. This way, props can be easily found and one can also quickly identify if anything is missing. This same effect can also be achieved with butcher paper and a marker (Figures 10.9a and 10.9b). This method can be beneficial if the prop table ever needs to be repurposed or struck – the paper can simply be removed and replaced as needed, without having to re-tape each time.

Another thing to consider is where props land once they come offstage. It can be helpful to tape off a "prop drop" area of your table or have a laundry basket nearby

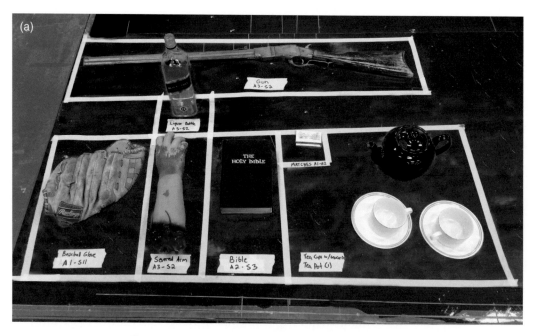

Figure 10.9 (a) Props Table Labeled with Tape

Figure 10.9 (b) Props Table Labeled with Marker

where performers and crew can quickly drop props that have come off in a different location than their original prop table. If your company utilizes prop cabinets, they can also be used for the run if there is enough room for the props to be moved in and out easily and they have ample light.

It's useful to print a complete and finalized prop list and keep it near either the props table or prop storage for quick reference.

Changing Areas (Quick Change Booths)

If there are quick changes (typically any change that happens in less than a minute – more on this in Chapter 11) or any other costume and/or makeup changes that need to happen backstage rather than in the dressing rooms, a specific area should be set aside and outfitted for that purpose. Stage management may be responsible for determining where these areas are and/or setting them up; this responsibility should be determined well in advance of tech. This can be as simple as a chair near a lighted area or as elaborate as a custom-built booth complete with a hoist to hold larger costumes out of the way until they are needed. Depending on the needs of the production, it can be useful to have hooks or a small rack, a chair, a light, and a mirror. Quick change booths are also often carpeted to help protect bare or stockinged feet. If changes are happening without benefit of an actual booth for privacy, then it is important to make sure that these areas are not in the audience's sightline, nor in the middle of busy backstage pathways.

Paper Tech and Dry Tech

Prior to the first full technical rehearsal, you may have a **paper tech** and/or a **dry tech**. These are an opportunity to focus on specific technical areas without the full company present. Both paper tech and dry tech can be very useful for the stage manager.

Paper Tech

For many productions, only a paper tech is necessary. Paper techs are held as a meeting rather than a rehearsal, and cues are talked through rather than fully presented. The stage manager is in charge of running this meeting. By paper tech, each designer should give the stage manager a complete list of their cues detailing the cue name, when the cue is called, and what the cue does. This includes the scenic designer if there are complicated scene shifts or shifts that need to be coordinated with lights and/or sound. If you receive these lists prior to paper tech, you should endeavor to put cues in your book before you meet with the designers.

Talk through the script in order and confirm cue names, placement, and intent. Ideally, the lighting designer will give a basic description of each look so the stage manager and the director know what to expect to see. The sound designer should also talk through each cue and, if possible, play each one for the director to hear. Also talk through how large scene changes, including flies, will take place (go over your run sheet). Paper tech can run the gamut from quick and dirty to thorough and in depth. Either way, by the end of paper tech the stage manager should have all of the preliminary cues in their prompt book, the designers should have an idea about how their different elements are working together, and the director should have a rough idea what the show will look and sound like.

Dry Tech

On technically heavy shows, a dry tech may be necessary. This is a rehearsal in which the production team, except the costume designer, sits in the performance space and goes through the show cue by cue and (if necessary) scene shift by scene shift. This gives the director a chance to look at and listen to each cue. It also allows the stage manager to become familiar with the cues and where they will be called. It can be helpful to have the ASMs and/or crew available to walk the performer paths and move things as needed (performers are not present for this rehearsal).

Sitzprobe or Wandelprobe

When working on a musical, the terms Sitzprobe and Wandelprobe may become part of the conversation about the schedule leading up to tech. These are German terms borrowed from the world of opera. Sitzprobe means seated rehearsal. It is traditionally the first time that the orchestra and the singers rehearse together and the focus is on integrating the two groups. The written scenes are typically skipped and little to no blocking or choreography is incorporated. It can be beneficial to have a Sitzprobe in the performance space, but they can also happen in other locations since all that is needed is space for the orchestra to play and the performers to sit and sing. A Wandelprobe, meaning wandering rehearsal, is similar but also incorporates the blocking and choreography. This is best done in the performance space so that the cast and orchestra get a feel for the actual setup. Book scenes are often still forgone.

Prepping the Calling Script

Regardless of whether you've had a paper tech, you should have cue lists from each designer before the start of tech rehearsals. If one hasn't been provided, request one. Keep a copy of each cue list in the promptbook. Upon receiving the lists, add all cues to the calling script. *Write in pencil.* Draw a line in the margin next to the text or the section of the script where the cue will be called. Write on the line what type of cue it is and the cue number (e.g., light cue number 42 would be written LQ42 or LX42; sound cues are often written with the shorthand FX or SQ and named using letters). Also on this line (or under the line), include a brief description of the cue to serve as a reminder of their purpose (e.g., "daytime look," "doorbell," "transition music," "blackout"). Indicate in the script exactly where the cue should be called, as well. Underline, box, or otherwise mark the cue word/line. If the cue is taken off a visual or an audio cue, specify the action or sound (e.g., on the slap, John crosses to DSL) in a consistent location near the listed cue.

If you haven't already, add the scene shifts from the run sheet into the calling script. The two things that need to be noted are: (a) what signals the start of the scene shift (light cue, sound cue, stage manager-called cue, or performer-driven cue) and (b) what signals that the shift is complete and that the following scene can begin (a **visual cue** or a confirmation from the deck crew/ASM over headset). Be sure to get confirmation of any offstage shifts that may impact the transition (quick costume changes, mic swaps, etc.).

> Giving descriptive names to the scene shifts can help differentiate between them, allowing the crew to quickly identify their tasks even if they don't know the specific scenes in the show. If you do name them, choose things that are brief, easy to say, and don't sound like "lights," "sound," or "go" (e.g., shift green, shift pterodactyl).

The final step is to add **standbys.** About half a page prior to a cue, a standby will need to be called to the console operators and crew members. Write these standbys in your calling script so that you remember to call them. These will be beneficial to avoid being surprised by a cue and to make sure everyone is prepared for the cue, change, or shift. When multiple cues occur in close succession, a single standby can be given as prep (e.g., "Standby lights 9 thru 11 and sound D"). Depending on the skill and experience of the console operators and crew, standbys may be unnecessary. On Broadway, standbys are not always used, but in academia or with novice crew members, they are very helpful. Preceding the standby for a scene shift, a **warning** may be given to the crew a few pages early to give them enough time to get to their assigned positions for the shift in case they aren't already on deck (Figure 10.10).

Take the time to make the calling script as neat, precise, and detailed as possible. The clearer your notes are, the easier it will be to work during tech rehearsals. That said, know that this is not the final layout of your calling script; cues will evolve and change during tech, so be prepared to adjust and adapt.

> Be sure that anything written is large and legible enough to be seen clearly and easily. Feel free to color code as long as your colors will not be adversely affected by run lights (colored run lights will change the way colors appear on the page). Be cautious using stickers, flags, and sticky notes, as they can fall off, move, or tear your pages, especially during long-running productions. If you are creating a digital version, make sure it is easily legible, that the fonts are easily distinguishable, and it is backed up to multiple locations.

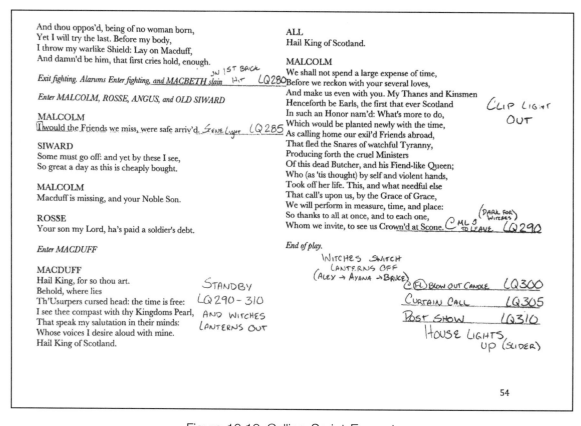

Figure 10.10 Calling Script Excerpt

First Day Onstage

The first time the performers move into the theatre, set time aside at the start of rehearsal to give a tour of the space. Some theatres, particularly in academia, rehearse in the same space in which they perform, in which case this will happen on the first day of rehearsal with additional information shared as scenic construction progresses (if the set is also being built in the space). Professionally, the first day onstage is often the first day of tech. On this tour, point out bathrooms, dressing rooms, the green room, and pathways backstage. Now is the time to fill the cast in on any important information about the theatre (potential safety hazards, food/drink rules, quirky theatre features, etc.). Determine if the designers or technical director need to be present to help familiarize the cast and crew with any technical elements.

If the cast has never rehearsed on the stage before, a spacing rehearsal may be scheduled. This rehearsal is a time to walk through the blocking/choreography, and allow the director to see it in the actual performance space and make adjustments as needed. Depending on the timeline, this spacing rehearsal may cover the entire show or only potentially problematic scenes (scenes with particularly complex blocking, large group scenes, or scenes where exact placement of the performers is essential).

Last Rehearsal before Tech

At the end of your last rehearsal before tech, take a moment to let the performers know what to expect in the upcoming rehearsals.

- Remind the cast not to wear white or bright clothing (unless their costumes are white) to tech rehearsals for lighting purposes. The lighting designer may even request that performers wear colors similar to their costumes. Check with them prior to this discussion so as to give the cast accurate instructions.
- Let them know that things are still being finalized. They should let you know if something is missing, broken, or problematic, but they shouldn't expect it to appear or be fixed right away, unless it is an imminent safety concern.
- Remind them to get plenty of rest and drink lots of water.
- It is also a good time to gently remind them that tech will be less focused on them than the preceding rehearsal process.

If you haven't already, you should also have a moment with your director about their expectations regarding tech. It can be helpful to set goals about what you'd like to accomplish each day of tech.

Crew Training

There is some basic information and training that every crew needs to receive and it is important to go over even with a more seasoned crew. Some of this information may be covered by the PM or TD and it will vary from production to production and venue to venue. Typically you will meet your crew for the first time at first tech, but if it is possible to work with or meet them beforehand, do so.

- Introductions
  - Contact Information
- Review Safety Protocols and Policies
- Expectations of the Crew
  - Clothing requirements such as black clothing
  - Call times and schedule
  - Signing in (be sure to add the crew to the sign-in sheet!)
  - Headset etiquette (discussed below)
- Structure of the specific production
  - Go over pre-show and preset lists, run sheet, and post-show list
- Tour of the Space
- Show-specific training with appropriate parties (e.g., Automation, Pyro, or Special Effects)

Headsets

In many theatres, **headsets** (sometimes referred to as **comms**) are used to communicate between the stage manager and the crew/operators during tech rehearsals and performances. The type of headset will depend greatly on the theatre. It is important to familiarize yourself with how the system functions. If it is a wired system (cords connect the units to the wall), make sure that the crew will be able to perform their duties or reach the locations they need to reach while on headset or indicate to you when they are off headset for a shift. If headsets are unavailable, determine how communication between the booth and backstage will take place. In some theatres, different communication systems may exist for front of house and backstage (e.g., walkie-talkies for front of house and headsets for backstage).

Headset Etiquette

Headset etiquette should be discussed during crew training:

- Keep non-show chatter to a minimum (so as not to miss cues or take up the communication line in case of an emergency).
- Never talk during a standby or calling sequence.
- Be conscientious of the topics discussed as well; some green rooms or box offices have a monitor station and can hear anything said over headset.
- No one besides the calling SM should say "GO" or anything sounding like it with their channel open during the run of the show
- Let them know your preferences for the following:

- How would you like them to respond to a standby (standing by, copy, "name of assignment," etc.)?
- Do you want them to respond to the standby in a specific order?
- Do you want them to let you know they are on headset when they first put it on?

Make sure they know how to use the headset and won't inadvertently leave their channel open, thus causing unnecessary noise or a block in communication. If you are using wireless headsets, make sure that they know how to prep and strike them each day (or charge the walkie-talkies, etc.). If for some reason they need to get "off headset," they should let you know when they leave and when they return, but they should make sure you aren't in the middle of a standby or calling sequence. Let them know that if you say "Quiet on headset" it means stop talking immediately and wait until you are finished; you can also use "You're clear" to let them know they are okay to talk (avoid saying "Go ahead").

Proper Attire

Early in the process, be sure to mention that all backstage and visible crew (including assistant stage managers) will be required to wear all black for all dress rehearsals and performances. This entails long black pants with pockets and belt loops (NOT leggings or tights under shorts), a long- and/or short-sleeved shirt (depending on the production), and black closed-toe shoes. Sturdy clothing helps protect the crew as they are working. Real pants hold up a headset beltpack much better than leggings and pockets provide a place to keep the run sheet and a writing utensil. For some productions, any crew that appears onstage will be costumed to fit into the world of the play. In this case, you may need to help facilitate fittings.

Just as backstage crew must dress appropriately, it is equally important for the stage manager to wear rehearsal and performance-appropriate outfits. Be prepared to have a situation come up where you may need to paint something, use a power tool, carry heavy objects throughout the building, climb around in the **grid** or on a ladder, or anything else imaginable that may need to be resolved at the last moment. Functionality is top priority. In terms of colors, this varies from theatre to theatre and event to event. Black may not be necessary, especially if you are never seen by the audience, but typically dark tones are preferable.

Chapter Eleven
Technical and Dress Rehearsals

Technical Rehearsals

Once a production goes into technical rehearsals, focus shifts from blocking and character building to the design and technical elements of the show. Because of their knowledge about each department's needs (acquired throughout the rehearsal process), the stage manager often takes the helm and leads these rehearsals, helping coordinate between all departments to ensure everyone gets the time and focus they need.

Begin the first tech rehearsal by talking with the cast and crew and explaining the tech process (there are different types of tech rehearsals and it is important to let the cast and crew know what to expect when you call "hold" or when you reach the end of each scene). This information can come from either the director or directly from management (the technical director or production manager may run this discussion – touch base with them and find out). Make sure that it is clear that stage management is running the rehearsal; it streamlines the process when everything flows to and from stage management. Remind the cast (and the director) that this is a rehearsal for the technical elements. Tech rehearsals are not time to work on acting moments, unless they directly impact technical elements and/or timing.

Make it clear to the performers that they should be watching out for their safety during these rehearsals (getting used to being on the set, working with the lights and sound, etc.). Have them keep an eye out for locations onstage and backstage that need more safety tape, glow tape, or a run light. Let the cast and crew know that if at any time during the rehearsal they feel like they are in immediate danger, they should call "Hold!" so the problem can be addressed and resolved. If they feel unsafe but it is not an immediate safety concern, ask them to notify stage management at the next break.

Remind the cast and crew that during technical rehearsals they should stay close to the stage after they exit in case you need to hold and reset; having to find cast and crew members who have left the area takes up valuable time. Remind everyone to remain quiet during holds so necessary conversations can take place. Finally, thank them in advance for their patience and cooperation. Tech rehearsals can be stressful and confusing and can also be dull for the performers. The more cooperation you can get from them, the faster and more efficient the whole process will be.

DOI: 10.4324/9781003133049-12

ASM/Deck Manager

The person who is running and coordinating things from backstage is either an ASM or the Deck Manager. Having an organized and efficient backstage ensures the process flows smoothly. The ASM/Deck Manager coordinates all of the pieces and parts for anything that happens backstage. If there are multiple ASMs, typically one will work from SR and one from SL. They coordinate how the scenery and props live backstage, putting them in whatever arrangement makes the most sense for the flow and needs of the show. This includes making sure that the scenic pieces that need to be accessible for a shift are so and that they land in the right place for the change. The ASM will update the backstage portion of the run sheet as they are most familiar with everything going on backstage. A good ASM takes a lot of pressure off of the stage manager and lets you focus on all of the other things that you need to focus on and not worry about the minutiae of where the dining room table goes when it's not on stage.

The ASM/deck manager will be the conduit for the stage manager when information needs to be passed backstage, and will be the person who receives the G-O for a shift. There are times when the ASM cannot be on comm at the top of a shift because they are part of the crew that is doing the shift. In these instances, the ASM may cue the scene change based on a line or action, but this is in close coordination with the stage manager.

ASMs are also the eyes and ears of the stage manager backstage. If, during a blackout, the stage manager can't see when someone has entered or exited, they may ask for a notification from the ASM that people are in position. If there is an effect that requires any sort of spotting or safety precautions (trap doors, flying), the ASM will give the all clear to the stage manager if the operator isn't on comm to be communicated with directly.

Types of Tech Rehearsals

The first tech rehearsal is typically run one of two ways: a **cue-to-cue** or **stop-and-start**. Discuss this with the production team prior to tech rehearsal. If the first tech rehearsal is also the first rehearsal on stage, it will often serve as a spacing rehearsal as well. Spacing rehearsals are discussed in the First Day Onstage, p. 145.

Cue-to-Cue

In a cue-to-cue rehearsal, the show is run through in order, skipping (just as the name suggests) from cue to cue. These rehearsals are more common in straight plays and shows with minimal cues. Cues from all areas (lights, sound, media, scene shifts, etc.) should be addressed during a cue-to-cue, unless previously discussed.

The best way to run a cue-to-cue is to have the performers begin a few lines before the cue so that a standby can be given, run through the cue, and then slightly beyond the completion of the cue. This allows the director and designers a chance to look at or hear the correctly timed cue sequence and for the stage manager to make sure the cue was called correctly (for details on how to call cues, see Calling Cues, p. 152). Once the cue or cue sequence is complete, call "Hold, please!" (note that sometimes, fades are lengthy and need 20–30 seconds or longer to complete, so always ensure the cue fade has completed before calling hold). If the cue or sequence of cues needs to be run again, have everyone reset and start from the same spot. If everything went smoothly and the director and design team are happy with how the sequence was executed, find the next cue in the script and tell the cast, "We will be skipping ahead to …" Remind both the cast and crew to wait for a specific "G-O" from the stage manager before beginning the new section. This allows the stage manager to communicate with all necessary parties before beginning, including the ASM who should let the stage manager know when the cast and crew are set backstage.

If there are multiple cues in close proximity or if the next upcoming cue is less than a page from the previous one, have the performers continue to run the scene through the next cue rather than stopping and skipping ahead. When trying to decide if it is time to skip ahead, the stage manager should use their best judgment of how much time it takes to reset versus just continuing to play the scene. It takes a lot longer than you think to stop, give instructions, get set, and restart. This is a skill that will become more instinctual with time and experience.

Start and Stop Rehearsal

A start-and-stop rehearsal is similar to a cue-to-cue in that it is meant to acquaint everyone with the technical elements of the show and allow the stage manager time to learn the correct placement of all the cues. These are typical for shows that are heavily cued, like musicals, rather than skipping from cue to cue, you run through the majority of the show – starting, stopping, resetting, and rerunning as necessary until everyone understands each sequence. If there is a large section of text without any cues, it may be skipped over.

Remember that tech rehearsals are the time to make sure everyone feels confident in what they are doing and that all of the technical elements and cues are rehearsed and sequences have begun to solidify. If you do not feel comfortable with the call of a sequence and want to run it again, that is okay. Learning the cue sequence and calling is an important part of the process and the time should be taken to get it right (just make sure to keep within the allotted rehearsal time slot(s)). It may not always be perfect the first time; that is what rehearsals are for. If there is a particularly tricky sequence, it can be helpful to talk it through with the designers to make sure you understand the intent of the cues in the sequence. Knowing why a cue is happening at that specific moment and what the cue is accomplishing can help you and the designer determine the best place to call the cue. Similarly, if the ASM needs more time to coordinate backstage traffic or if scene changes need more rehearsal, they should also feel empowered to request another run through. However, if something was only slightly off and you can make the adjustment for next time without running the sequence again, keep moving.

Full Tech Run

Once a cue-to-cue or start-and-stop has been completed, a full tech run may take place. This is a full run through of the show in which all of the technical elements (sans costumes) are integrated. The goal is typically to try to do a full run without stopping. However, it is absolutely okay to call "Hold!" and go back to fix or rerun a cue if necessary. This is the time to work out kinks and figure out timing so that once you reach dress rehearsals, a full run can take place without stopping for technical issues.

Calling Hold

When to hold? That is the question. Hold anytime you need to stop what is happening on stage to address something. Holds can be for safety concerns, a rough cue sequence, a poorly executed transition, or to allow instructions to be issued. Not every miscalled cue or minor mistake requires a hold. If everyone knows what went wrong and feels that it can be executed correctly the next time, a hold is not necessary. This is a good discussion to have with the directors and designers prior to tech. Ask them if they are ok moving along if you are confident the mistake will not happen again or has already been corrected.

The stage manager should be the only person to call hold to ensure continuity of information and process (unless there is an imminent safety concern, then those with that imminent concern should call hold). It is helpful to politely request/remind the director that if they would like to hold to let you know so you can make the call. This allows for instructions to come from one person and allows you to make sure that it is an appropriate time to hold. Sometimes you might be in the middle of a scene shift that needs specific timing and calling hold in the middle will create a bigger problem than letting it complete. As the stage manager, you know all the bits and pieces going on and can make the hold call with the least adverse consequences.

Holds should be called loudly and clearly over the god mic and, if needed, over comm. Make sure that everyone hears you. During loud moments, you may need to be extra loud to be heard, or have an ASM also pass along the information to backstage. Immediately after calling the hold, it is helpful to inform the cast to either hold their positions (e.g., if a lighting look is being worked on), to relax but stay quiet (e.g., if a sound effect is being worked), to reset, or to turn their attention to a particular party (e.g., the ASM is about to instruct them on a transition).

Calling Cues

Calling cues is one of a stage manager's main responsibilities when a show is running. The satisfaction of calling a complex cue sequence correctly is exhilarating. In technical rehearsal, you are typically calling from a table in the house near the design team (commonly referred to as a tech table). For the dress rehearsals and performances, you will be at the calling station calling cues as you watch the performance.

Cue calling typically has four parts to it: warning, standby, windup, and go. Make sure before tech rehearsal begins, you have all of your cues, warnings, and standbys written into your prompt book in pencil or erasable pen. Cues, warnings, and standbys will inevitably change during the tech process so do not use something permanent (e.g., pens, and highlighters).

The warning is called 1–2 minutes before the cue will be called. It gets the attention of the crew member(s) who will be part of the cue sequence, ensures that they are paying attention, and have time to get to the proper location to execute their role if they aren't there already. Using a warning allows you to know that everyone is ready and you are good to proceed. If a crew member does not respond, this gives you a short amount of time to assess the situation, attempt to get in contact with that crew member, and prepare for any contingency you may need to put in place. It is up to you if you would like a verbal acknowledgement from the crew members (e.g., "lights," "sound"). Putting the word "warning" at the beginning of the call will help avoid accidental G-Os:

Example Warning: "Warning lights 83, and shift red"
Example Acknowledgement: "lights" "shift"

The standby is called 10–30 seconds before the cue will be called. This lets the crew members know that the G-O is imminent and to get their button-pressing fingers into position or be in their final ready position for a shift. Again, you may ask your crew to acknowledge your call, especially if you aren't in the same room. However, if you trust your crew and they always hit their cues, you may not need an acknowledgement. Large, fast cue sequences sometimes do not allow time for acknowledgements from everyone. In academia, crew members are often less trained and acknowledgements are helpful. Professional crews may respond negatively to a request for an acknowledgement, but sometimes you may still want to require it. Putting the word "standby" at the beginning of the call will help avoid accidental G-Os:

Example Standby: "Standby lights 83 and sound T"
Example Acknowledgement: "Lights Standing" "Sound Standing"

The windup is when you begin to speak leading up to the G-O; commonly 1–5 seconds before the G-O, but possibly longer depending on how many things you are calling. The windup allows you to get all the information out to the crew without rushing your words, but not too slowly as to lose the attention of your crew. The goal is for a seamless transition from the windup to the G-O:

Example windup; "Lights and Sound"

Finally, the G-O. At the end of your windup, you say "GO" indicating to all parties that they are to execute their assigned task. Be clear and even toned when you say

"GO"; don't shout it or whisper it, as you might startle your crew or they might not hear you:

Example Windup and G-O: "Lights and Sound … GO."
Example to Avoid: "Lights and Sound ……. GO."

Learning how each crew member responds to your G-O is something to pay attention to during tech and dress. Do they execute on the very first inkling of the "G" or is it at the very end of the "O"? During fast and complex sequences, this can make a huge difference in timing. Sometimes you may have a jumpy console-op who has a tendency to hit go too early or think they know when a cue is supposed to happen. As the stage manager, you have all the information and in a very complex show you might know that someone is in an unusual location that puts them in an unsafe position if a cue is called in "the usual" spot; so it's important your crew knows to always wait for your "G-O."

> There are moments where, at the discretion of the stage manager, someone may take a cue on a visual signal or during a large cue sequence without a "G-O" from the stage manager. This should be discussed between the stage manager and operator. Otherwise cues should only be taken from you.

Different stage managers use different words for the same meaning and may interchange warning and standby, and at times omit one or both completely. As you grow and evolve as a stage manager, you will find what works best for you in your specific production processes. The 2019 SM Survey[1] performed by David McGraw and Tara Patterson indicates that 85% of stage managers use the word "standby" with warning at 5%, ready at 4%, and 6% who do not use any announcement prior to cue calling. The 2019 survey also noted that 19% never use a warning, 30% rarely use it, 37% sometimes use it, 10% use it most of the time, and 5% always use a warning.

As you rehearse, you will become more familiar with the cues and it will be easier to call them more accurately. Don't get frustrated if you don't do it right the first time! Also remember that with live theatre, every performance is different. You may have to adjust some calls nightly depending on audience reactions, unexpected delays, etc. The important thing is to remain alert and constantly ready to adapt.

> As technology continues to grow, it is becoming more common to tie multiple cue systems together. The audio system may trigger lights or vice versa, lights may trigger media while sound is independent, etc. This can add a level of intricacy to the process that takes time to get used to.

Scene Shifts

Scene shifts will need to be set and rehearsed so they can be accomplished consistently in each performance. If the scene change will be seen by the audience, it may need to be choreographed to have specific things happen at specific times so the change does not look haphazard. You may run/choreograph scene changes during tech. However, if things are complicated or not going as smoothly as the team would like, a scene shift rehearsal may be scheduled.

Shifts during Tech

You should already have the basic shift assignments on your run sheet, but now is the time to finalize/adjust those assignments as movement patterns are getting locked in. Knowing what needs to move from where to where will make the rehearsal flow much more smoothly. Directors and scenic designers may also help with the flow and movement of the shifts. Scenic pieces need to be spiked before the shift can be completed. If spikes have been set before tech, try running into the shift without stopping. If spikes haven't been set, stop and set spikes with the designers and director. Once spikes exist, run the scene shift in appropriate light (if needed for safety, run the shift in brighter light before running it in performance light). You may need to run shifts more than once to get them right, and that's ok. It is important to balance the time you have in tech vs the time it may take to refine a shift. Remember that if a shift is close, you will have more opportunities to run it before you have an audience.

> **!** If any furniture or scenic elements have been moved during the scene and need to be re-spiked, be sure that you do so before running the scene shift.

Shift Rehearsals

If scene shifts are complicated or not going as smoothly as the team would like, a scene shift rehearsal may be scheduled to clean up any confusion and hone the shift(s). These rehearsals will typically involve only the cast and crew needed for the scene shifts. If the show has a lot of performer-driven scene shifts, the entire cast may be called. Come prepared to the shift rehearsal: bring all of the information about the shift gathered during tech (who is moving what, which spikes you're using, where units live backstage, performer traffic patterns, etc.) and have ideas for making adjustments to increase the efficiency and efficacy of the shift.

To start the scene shift, either give a loud verbal stand by and go, or, if a cue line is needed, read the cue line. Try to run the shift completely without holding, even if it is taking a longer time than is desired, so you know how long the shift currently takes. Watch for places where things can be done more efficiently. After the shift has been completed, talk through any needed adjustments or alterations, reset, and run it again. Once the run is successful, run the shift under performance lighting (if you are able) so the cast and crew know how much light they will have to complete the shift, and if any additional glow or safety tape is needed. The stage manager or an ASM should facilitate each shift and ensure that the shifts are happening in the safest and most efficient manner.

Facilitating Communication during Tech Rehearsals

One of the key components to a harmonious tech is keeping all lines of communication open throughout. Communication keeps things flowing smoothly and keeps everybody in good spirits. Keeping the cast apprised of what is going on during holds helps keep them calmer and quieter. A simple "we are holding to work through this shift" or "to set a cue" is all that's needed. Letting them know how this impacts them is also important (if you are trying to focus light on them, you need them to hold their position; if the director and designer are setting the level of a sound cue, the cast can probably relax). Don't lay blame or frustration on any department, "we are holding for lighting, <u>again</u>."

Facilitating communication with the design team is also important. You may have a director or designer come to you to request a change or modification to a moment; if that affects multiple areas, make sure to bring all areas into the conversation. If the director would like a light cue to happen later to hide someone exiting, bring the lighting designer into the conversation so they have input; cue placement falls squarely in their purview so a discussion between the director and designer is warranted. Similarly if a sound designer would like to alter the blocking of a performer (e.g., to better see the visual cue for a gunshot), make sure the director is part of that conversation. Much like the performers, the director isn't on headset and will not always be privy to the reasons for a hold; letting them know will help keep them in the loop and assure them that time isn't being wasted. Additionally, if you aren't sure if folks are still working, check in periodically on the status of the work.

As the communication hub during tech, you will often find yourself being inundated with conversations and requests. This is especially true when on headset, where you might be listening in on a handful of conversations whilst multiple people might be trying to get your attention simultaneously. Never be afraid to tell people to slow down, wait for a moment while you write down a note, or hold their question until you finish your current conversation. It doesn't help anyone if you try too hard to multitask and end up overlooking a safety note or becoming too overwhelmed to continue running rehearsal effectively.

Tech Notes

Tech notes will be given after each tech/dress rehearsal. This is a time to revisit any discussions that were tabled during the rehearsal, to confirm any specific work or notes that need to be accomplished, and to review the schedule for the following rehearsal (and revise if needed). Make sure that all crew heads, designers, directors, and any other personnel requested by the director stick around. Take notes during this discussion and include them in the rehearsal report. This consolidates the notes into one place and ensures that the design team has a reminder of the notes given.

Pre-Show Announcements

A pre-show announcement is either a live or pre-recorded announcement given immediately preceding each performance. Its purpose is to welcome the audience to the show, give them reminders about turning off cell phones (etc.), and inform them of any pertinent emergency information (usually just a quick note about where emergency exits are located). It may also include how long the performance will be and whether or not there will be an intermission. Near the end of the tech process (if you have not already), determine whether or not the show will have one and what it will be. This will usually require a conversation between the director, the producer, and the house manager (or other equivalent venue representative) to determine the need for a pre-show announcement and any specific information that needs to be included therein (often venues will have specific safety information that needs to be stated by law). If the announcement will be recorded, schedule the time and personnel to record it and determine cue placement with the sound designer. If the announcement is live, determine who will be delivering it at each performance (it may be the same person or different at each performance) and what they will require (handheld mic, light cue(s), etc.). Sometimes it will be given by a producer, the director, one of the performers, or one of the FOH staff members. Sometimes you will make the announcement over the god mic from the calling station. Regardless, once the decision has been made, loop in your lighting designer so they can arrange for correct lighting for the announcement.

A Note about Tech

Tech rehearsal is one of the more stressful times in a stage manager's process. Putting all the pieces together is both exciting and challenging. Lots of things need to happen all at once for the process to flow smoothly, but it is also important to remember to pause, take a breath, and smile. Don't let the stress of tech get to you. Remember it is ok to make mistakes, run something again, or ask for clarification. Remember that everybody on the crew is learning their role and how to perform it while juggling shared space with performers and scenery. Keep a level head, and remember diplomacy, poise, confidence, adaptability, compassion, assertiveness, discretion, and communication.

Dress Rehearsals

Dress Rehearsals are the next step in the process. Costumes are typically introduced at this time (although some theatres add costumes during tech rehearsals, if they are ready). The majority of rehearsal time at this point will be dedicated to run through of the show, incorporating all elements. When possible, these runs should be treated as though they were performances; performers and crew should act as though there is an audience in the house, performers should be in full costume, and crew should be in all black clothing or costume.

Depending on the complexity of the costumes and their impact on the timing of transitions, you may have a quick change rehearsal in order to run a few of the costume changes.

Quick Change Rehearsals

Just as scene changes must be choreographed and rehearsed with the stage crew, complicated and/or fast costume changes must also be choreographed and rehearsed with the performers and wardrobe crew (or whoever is executing the costume change). A quick change is any change where there is not enough time to make it to the dressing room and back to the stage. Quick changes may include very complicated or in-depth changes that have to be completed in a limited amount of time or they may be simple changes that have to happen very quickly. Performers often need assistance with changes that take place in under 1 minute. All performers and crew should be made aware of when and where each quick change takes place so they can stay out of the way unless they are involved in the change. Union contracts may have specific requirements for quick backstage changes.

If the costume is ready to be worked with, quick change rehearsals may take place during tech rehearsals. If not, time should be set aside during the first dress rehearsal for this. Quick changes may be rehearsed within the larger context of the dress rehearsal or a specific time may be set aside and dedicated to them prior to a dress run. For shows with many quick changes, a longer block of time may be set aside to practice these changes. Assign a dresser/crew member to assist with the change and give all involved a chance to talk with the wardrobe supervisor and/or costume designer to determine the best way to execute it. If needed, allow them to walk through the change a couple of times. Once a plan is in place, run the change exactly as it will happen during the show with as accurate timing as possible. Try to avoid calling hold during the change (even if it isn't complete in the allotted time) in order to get an accurate timing on the change. Even if the change took more time than it should have, knowing how much longer than expected it takes is very helpful. If the change ran 5 seconds too long, it is probably easily fixable with a few more rehearsals or small adjustments; if it ran 30 seconds too long, it may require rethinking the approach to the change or asking the costume shop to modify the costume with quick closures (e.g., velcro or snaps). Just as with scene shifts, balance the need for honing with the amount of time you have available. If the change went decently well, move on with the knowledge that they'll have more chances to run it. If it needs more time, don't be afraid to reset and run it again or set aside time outside of dress rehearsal to refine it. These subsequent runs are a good time to adjust the plan or to solidify the one they have. Encourage them to rehearse it during downtime.

Finding Your Stride

Dress rehearsal is the time to really get your flow down. During dress runs, holds may need to be called for changes that cannot be made, wardrobe malfunctions, or other safety reasons, but when possible, avoiding holds is preferable. While you have most likely called the show for a few tech rehearsals, getting to call a show with minimal holds really helps to lock in the timing in your mind. You will start to understand how your console ops respond to your calls, and you may start to be able to look up from your calling script to see the stage, allowing you to better understand how the cues interact with the staging.

Typically at first dress, you are still calling and working from the house/tech location. This allows you to keep easier communication with the technical/design team, and gives you easy access to the stage to troubleshoot any challenging moments if needed.

Second dress is a common time for the stage manager to move to the calling location. You can start to learn how things look and sound from that location. Find out if you have an obstructed view; can you see all the entrances and exits you need to see? Do you need an ASM to let you know someone is in place? If the calling location is especially challenging or if you are calling via video monitor, you may move to that location earlier in the process to familiarize yourself with those intracises.

Pre-Show Setup

When dress rehearsals begin, management should arrive in time to completely prep the performance space. The space needs to be accessible in time for performers to get into makeup and costumes. Some cast members may want early access to the dressing rooms to have enough time for hair, makeup, warm-ups etc., so make sure to communicate with the cast when the building will be unlocked and make arrangements if someone needs access before you will be in the building.

Pre-show for the stage management team means ensuring that all aspects of the production are in their proper place, on, and functioning for the run of the show. Just as during rehearsals, stage management arrives first to unlock doors and turn on lights. Next, the stage must be swept and/or mopped in preparation for preset. By this point, the crew has arrived and preset can begin. In accordance with the preset checklists, each crew member should be tasked with specific assignments that they complete for each show so that nothing gets missed. During this time, the stage manager will prepare their own area, ensuring that their promptbook is open and ready, all cue lights work, and headsets and monitors are on and functioning. If the show has minimal or no crew, the stage management team will be responsible for all preset tasks.

Once all scenic elements are in place, props have been set (both onstage and off), and quick change costumes have been set, stage management (or the stage manager and a crew member, if there are no assistant stage managers on the production) will perform "checks." This means to walk the set with the preset list in hand, checking that every element of the show is in its correct place for the start of the show. By doing checks with two people, one can read off the preset list while the second can put eyes on each item and verbally verify that it is accounted for. This greatly reduces the chance for something to be missed or skipped over. Whenever possible, prior to the start of each performance, the performers should also check that their props are set in the correct location. The house cannot be opened until stage management checks have taken place.

Sound/Light Check

Prior to opening the house for each performance, the console operators should run light and sound checks. The designers should instruct them on how to do this during tech rehearsals. This is to make sure that the cues are functioning and that levels are correct. It also checks that all lighting instruments are functioning and that the **focus** hasn't changed. This can be the stage manager's job if they are also acting as a console operator. Often this happens toward the beginning of call in order to have time to fix anything that might not be working.

Right before opening the house, it is beneficial to do a "blackout check." Usually, this entails executing a blackout cue from the show (if there is one, or else the console op should simply bring all channels down to zero) and double checking that all the lights are, in fact, out. This acts as a double check both for programming purposes on the lighting console and for any work lights that may have been left on by accident. Prior to executing the cue, be sure to yell "going dark onstage!" so that everyone is prepared for the imminent darkness.

Time Calls

The stage management team will be relied upon to keep track of time for the performers, crew, house manager, and audience members. As stage manager, it is your job to keep careful track of what time it is and call warning times backstage. Either in person, over a headset, or via a paging mic, call out the amount of time and what the countdown is to (e.g., "Five minutes to fight call," "Ten minutes to house open," or "Places"). When receiving a time call, it is proper etiquette to respond with "Thank you ____" ("Thank you ten," "Thank you places," etc.). This confirms that they have received the information. Maintaining this communication backstage is very important, so don't slack in this regard. The performers, crew, and front of house need to know the time calls in order to properly gage their preparation. It is up to you what you count down to, but be consistent (some people call "to places" while others call "to curtain," etc.). Typical calls are half hour, 15 minutes, 5 minutes, and places.

> Professionally, it is the stage manager's responsibility to collect and secure the cast's valuables once costumes are incorporated. Valuables can be put in quart- or gallon-sized plastic bags, pencil cases, or any other sort of container, as long as they are individually labeled for each cast member and can be secured either in the SM office or at the calling station. Valuables are typically collected at the 15-minute call. Be sure to return them at the end of the show.

Mic Checks

If microphones are used during a show, typically time must be set aside before the house opens for mic checks. These should happen as soon as possible after the performers arrive to allow time for any troubleshooting. The sound technician should arrive with enough time to get all mics prepped before the performers arrive. Have performers put on their makeup and then their mic (to avoid getting any makeup in the mic) and send them onstage for mic checks. It is important that performers do not reposition their mics after the sound/ mic check, as this will change the way their mic sounds. Often if a show has fights, dance, or intimacy, the performers should have their mics on for these calls to ensure everything is safe with the mic pack placement.

Fight/Dance/Intimacy Call

If the show involves any fights, you will need to have a daily fight call. This should take place prior to the house opening and will be supervised by yourself and the fight captain. Just like a fight call in rehearsal, each fight should be worked first slowly and then at show speed so that the cast feels safe and prepared. It is important that fight calls be taken seriously so that any safety issues can be addressed during that time. If an actor has a specific costume piece that affects their movement, they should wear it during fight call. An early call can also be given to review complicated dance choreography or lifts. For this, call all performers who are involved in the number as well as the dance captain. If a show has specific moments of intimacy, an intimacy call may be conducted to allow the performers to work that moment and ensure they are comfortable with their choreography.

Performer Notes

Following dress rehearsals, directors will likely gather the performers to give notes. Typically, performers are given 5–10 minutes to get out of costume and grab something on which to write notes. Keep careful track of this time and gather everyone as quickly as possible so as to release them at a reasonable time once notes have been given. Stay and listen to this notes session, both to keep it efficient and also to gather any notes that may apply to you or the crew. These notes can also be useful to remember as you maintain the show once it is in performances. If possible, hold notes sessions in a location away from the stage (e.g., green room) so that post-show cleanup can take place. If that's not possible, quiet cleanup can take place during these notes as long as it is not distracting to the performers and director. If there isn't time remaining before the end of the scheduled day, notes may be emailed.

> If the curtain call (bows) has not been staged at this point you should remind the director to do so.

Invited Dress and Previews

Some productions will have at least one if not multiple dress rehearsals for which an audience is present. Invited dress audiences are typically a select group of people (donors, sponsors, other casts from a show running concurrently), whereas previews are typically paying audiences who get a small discount to attend a rehearsal performance that may hold for an issue if needed. An audience presence allows the director and performers to hear live reactions to what is happening on stage and account for changes if needed. Having a live audience also allows you to learn where people laugh or applaud and how those things impact the timing of onstage action which may require small adjustments to cue calls so the cues happen as the designers intended them to. It is important to remember that these are still rehearsals and if you must hold, you should, but you should try to avoid holds if possible. If you do need to hold during a preview or invited dress, hop on the god mic, call hold, and let the audience know that you are holding for a moment to address technical difficulties. Once the issue is remedied, get the cast and crew set to as near to the hold spot as possible, and resume the show.

Post-Run Cleanup

After each run of the show, everything should be cleaned up and put away until the next call. Collect all props (especially personal props, which tend to walk away in performer pockets or be forgotten in costumes) and clean the stage of any spills or messes that may take place during the show. Dishes should be washed and any edibles must be disposed of or refrigerated if necessary. Just as with preset, assign specific tasks to each crew member that they will be responsible for throughout the run of the production so that nothing is overlooked. Use a checklist similar to the pre-show list to ensure that all tasks are complete, including all console and system shutdowns. Once everything is complete and everyone is out of the building, set out the ghost light, turn off the lights, and lock up.

Note

1. www.smsurvey.info

Chapter Twelve
Performances and Beyond

Looking Ahead

When everything has been made performance ready, it is time to start thinking about the run of the show. Once the show opens, the artistic team typically leaves the project for the remainder of the run, although they will continue to receive performance reports and are usually available for any questions or concerns. This means that the artistic integrity of the production will be in your hands (if you are working in the UK, this maintenance will fall to the assistant director). As intimidating as this may sound, it will be easy as long as you plan ahead and communicate with each person before they leave. In the days leading up to opening night, plan on meeting one-on-one with each designer and with the technical director to discuss the protocol for anything that may happen during the run of the show and whose responsibility it will be to address notes.

Depending on your production, an associate director and/or choreographer may stick around after opening night to help run **understudy** rehearsals and give performer notes throughout the run. We will go into more detail on this a little later in the chapter.

Maintaining the Show

Direction, Choreography, and Vocals

The directors will all be relying on you to maintain the show as they shaped it during rehearsals. At this point, you will likely be well acquainted with the commonly missed lines, the performer that likes to make up their blocking, the dance break that never quite got enough rehearsal time, and the harmonies that sometimes give you goosebumps, but other times sound like dying cats. These you will know to watch out for, but take the time to sit down with each director (stage, music, choreography, and fight) and talk through what they would like you to look for as well. The performance will evolve and reshape itself slightly throughout the performances, especially in long-running productions, as the performers discover and rediscover the play, and this is okay as long as it maintains the intentions of the directors. If things deviate too far from the director's intentions, you will maintain the show by giving notes to the performers between shows. If things begin to

DOI: 10.4324/9781003133049-13

vary too much from the original show, take note and seek feedback from the appropriate director about the evolution.

> When giving notes, give only ones necessary for maintaining the show. Don't be overly nitpicky or you will risk losing the confidence and trust of the performers and technicians and they will more easily dismiss you.

Costumes

The most prominent upkeep for this department will be laundry. Laundry duty will fall either to the wardrobe crew or to stage management, depending on the company. If laundry is your responsibility, discuss with your costume designer which pieces will need to be laundered and how (as well as how often), which should be **vodka-sprayed**, and which should be dry-cleaned. Put together a laundry schedule so that all laundry is complete and dry before the next performance. If laundry facilities are not available in the theatre, come up with a plan on where it will be done, as well as a budget and method of payment (petty cash, reimbursement, etc.).

The other item to discuss with this department is repairs. Determine who is responsible for minor repairs and who should be contacted to take care of any major repairs/damage. It is extremely beneficial for you or another member of the stage management team to be proficient in hand sewing to take care of minor repairs or for emergency fixes mid-show (in case the wardrobe crew is unable to take care of it). Request that a basic repair kit be left backstage that includes a variety of needles, thread that matches the costumes, extra buttons, snaps, hooks, and safety pins. If any costumes are rented, get a rundown of what can be done to the clothing and always ask before doing any repairs yourself.

> Take special note of cleaning instructions for any items that are dry-clean only or vintage. Never put these items through the regular wash. For short runs, it is likely that these items will only be vodka-sprayed (or similar). For longer runs or in emergency situations, periodic dry-cleaning may be arranged.

Scenic

Repairs and general maintenance are the big things to be aware of in this department. Have the scenic designer and technical director walk you through the entire set and point out areas to keep an eye on through the run of the show. Be sure to have a good working knowledge of anything that moves, flies, rolls, or has potential to cause injury. In particular, plan regular checks of all casters, brakes, and sliders on moving items, sturdiness checks on any furniture/scenic elements that are stood or danced on, and note any necessary paint touch-ups. Additionally, confirm that you have access to a basic set of tools (drill, screws, hammer, staple gun, etc.). As with costumes, establish who will be responsible for executing repairs during the run. Finally, discuss cleaning protocol for the set: what should be swept, mopped, vacuumed? How often?

Props

Props often require the most maintenance during the run of a show as they tend to break, go missing, or run out. This is where keeping a carefully organized prop table is to your advantage as this will help you easily identify any issues. If anything occurs immediately prior to or during a performance, it will fall primarily to the assistant stage manager(s) or deck crew head to solve in the moment. In any case, make note of any issues in the performance report and specify if any follow up is required by the props manager For expendable items, make a plan with your props manager on how these are to be maintained. Take note of where and how replacement/refill items can be obtained, how often consumables need to be replaced, recipes for colored liquids, etc. Additionally, determine who is responsible for obtaining replacement items once the show opens. If it falls to stage management, determine what the budget is and how payments should be made (petty cash, reimbursement, etc.). Keep particularly close watch on items that are rented or borrowed, as these need to be returned in good condition once the show closes.

On shows with weaponry, get in-depth training on how to properly handle, maintain, clean, and store all pieces. This information may come from the props manager or from the fight director. The fight captain should also be present for this discussion.

Electrics

Much of the maintenance for electrics will probably fall to your console operator or head electrician. If you are responsible for maintenance, have the lighting designer show you the location of the dimmer rack (tripped breakers), lighting storage (for replacement lamps, gels, etc. in case of burn outs), run you through channel check, and show you the basic focus of the lights (so you can note a focus issue in a report). Ask if there are particular instruments to watch out for: lights located on **booms** or on the floor that are likely to be kicked or bumped out of focus. If there is haze or fog being used, have them show you where it is located and what to watch out for if something malfunctions. Additionally, have a plan in place for what to do if you run out of fluid.

Sound

Like electrics, sound maintenance will also likely be taken care of primarily by the console operator. Sit down with the sound designer and make sure you know the plan for sound check and if there are any cues you should be keeping a special ear out for. If microphones are being used, familiarize yourself (and at least one assistant stage manager or backstage crew member) with basic troubleshooting should anything come up pre- or mid-show (know how to change a battery, replace an element, switch frequencies, and where mic tape should go). Monitor the supplies for microphones as well: batteries, mic tape, and saran wrap or condoms (commonly used to help protect body mic packs from sweaty performers; if it falls to you to replace them, make sure you get un-lubricated). If mic belts are being used, throw them in the laundry once or twice a week as well (make sure they are labeled first if they are performer-specific). If spare microphones exist, know where they are stored and how to put them into service if needed. Some shows will hire a crew member (sometimes called an A2 or "Audio 2"), whose responsibility is to be backstage helping with microphones and onstage sound equipment during the performance (including any mic swaps, troubleshooting, etc.) and all other mic maintenance.

Stage Management

Now that everything has been finalized, take the time to ensure that all paperwork within your promptbook is up to date, clean, and legible. All finalized run sheets from crew members (including wardrobe) should be submitted to you prior to opening night so copies can be made and kept in the promptbook throughout the run. If anyone is ever out sick or has an emergency, the person covering their track will have accurate and reliable paperwork to work off.

It is also the time to clean up the calling script so that it is detailed and precise. Not only will it make calling the show much easier and less stressful, but it will also guarantee an accurate and consistent show. This is critical not only for the safety of the performers and the company, but also for maintaining the artistic integrity of the designs. Calling a cue inaccurately is the same as a performer paraphrasing their lines. The general gist is simply not good enough. Just as a performer must strive to be word perfect, the stage manager must strive to be cue perfect.

> **!** During performances and throughout the production run, keep the promptbook in the theatre at the stage manager's station (or the SM office, if one exists). If something unfortunate were to happen (to you), this ensures the show can go on and another person can step in to call the show.

If you take these basic steps before opening, you will be much more prepared to maintain the show. More than anything, trust your instincts. You know this show better than anyone in the room, so you will be able to detect if anything goes wrong. Include any and all notes in the performance report (see Performance Report) so that designers can decide if further action is required for any given mishap. And when in doubt, ask!

Performances

It's time for the true public audience to take their place. All the steps and rehearsals up to this point in time have been to make it to this point – opening night.

Front of House

Now is the time to finalize performance protocols with your house manager. Determine the method of communication between you and the house manager; this may be a channel on headset, a walkie-talkie, or through in-person conversation and text messages. Regardless of the method(s), ensure that communication can happen between you through all points of the performance. If you have not already done so, discuss all house opening and closing procedures, intermission procedures, and all emergency protocols. Also discuss any post-show protocols (usually this just means establishing communication from front of house (FOH) letting you know that the house has cleared [emptied] so that work lights can go on and all systems can be shut down for the night). The house manager will also likely be the one to provide you with the house count (number of audience members who attended) for each performance, so establish how and when to obtain this information from them. They will also likely ask you for the running time of the show. Often the house manager will want to be included on performance reports, so get their email address.

If your show contains material or effects that may pose a health risk to patrons, the FOH staff may post warning signs in the lobby or in the program (or both). Most common warnings are for sudden or very loud sounds (e.g., gunshots), strobing lights, haze or fog usage, and cigarette smoke. These can also include possible trigger warnings (extensive violence, sexual violence, suicide, strong language, etc.). Arrange a conversation between FOH, the director, and the producers to determine if warnings of this nature are required. Another thing to discuss with all of these parties is what the late seating protocol will be in the instance of any late-arriving patrons. Often, a moment or two in the first 15 minutes of the show are identified during which the FOH staff can seat latecomers (usually during a transition or loud moment when the movement in the house won't be disruptive to the performance). Sometimes, however, the answer is that there will be no late seating for the show as it would be too disruptive to the performance (often this can be the case in very small houses or in shows where lobby entrances are being used by the performers or crew throughout the show).

Be sure to include the house manager in all time calls (via your arranged method of communication) so they have an idea of the progress backstage. Conversely, be sure to also coordinate your time calls with the status of the house. In some places, house management will have the final say as to when the show begins.

! "HOUSE IS YOURS"

This phrase is often used in communication between the stage manager and the house manager and is used to pass control of the house between the two. The house manager maintains control of the house during pre-show (when the house is open), during intermission, and during post-show while the audience is exiting. The stage manager has control of the house prior to house opening, during the performance, and after the house has cleared.

Opening the House

Opening the house refers to the time prior to a performance when the theatre doors are opened to allow the patrons to make their way to their seats. The house typically opens 30 minutes prior to the performance. You should give time calls to house opening during your pre-show time calls. Before the house opens, the preset checklist should be complete, as well as all fight calls, dance calls, mic check, and lights/sound checks. Be sure to check with everyone (house manager, performers, deck crew, and console operators) before allowing the house to open to make sure that everything is ready to go, including checking that all appropriate top of show cues are running. Unless it is part of the performance, the audience should not see any of the prep work, as this disrupts the illusion of the show. Once the house opens, no cast or crew should be visible unless they are staged to be. If the stage is blocked by a closed curtain, preset and other onstage activity can continue behind the curtain while the house is open as long as it is quiet and not noticeable by the patrons.

> If absolutely necessary (e.g., a technical problem or safety concern that needs addressing), it is okay to hold opening the house. Be sure to communicate this information to any FOH personnel. If possible, it is preferable for the work to be done upstage of the main curtain (if one is in use) so the audience can begin seating.

Intermission

Intermissions are run similarly to pre-show. You will hand house control back over to the FOH team. Just as before, you will give time calls to keep everyone on track. Your time calls will depend on the length of your specific intermission, but they are often "10 minutes," "5 minutes," and "places." The length of the intermission is usually determined by the producers or by the venue, with consideration taken into account for how long the cast and crew need to prepare for the next act. Typical intermissions run between 10 and 20 minutes. Once the audience has returned to their seats, the house manager will hand the house back to you for the remainder of the performance. You may end up extending intermission for FOH if there are long lines for the bathrooms or issues in the lobby.

Performance Reports

For every performance, the stage manager sends out a performance report to the same people as the rehearsal reports. You may also need to add additional personnel to the distribution list, such as the house manager or crew heads. This report should document the performance and contain any major mistakes, injuries, set, prop, and costume repairs, a house count, and the audience response. Always note any unusual occurrences; specify whether the item or moment has already been fixed or if it still needs to be addressed. Be as specific as possible, especially about the location of the item in question. "The USR Light" isn't all that helpful if there are ten USR lights, and "The bedroom unit needs paint touch-ups" isn't always specific enough. Like rehearsal reports, send this out by the following morning before the start of the workday, although preferably immediately following the performance (see Figure 7.7, p. 82).

Understudies and Swings

Depending on the company and length of the run, your production may have **swings** or understudies for various roles in the show. An understudy is a performer who is cast in the ensemble as a particular role, but learns the tracks for one or more other roles to fill in if someone **calls out** sick. A swing is a performer who is hired to learn the tracks for all the roles and is on standby backstage during all performances in case a performer needs to be replaced mid-show (due to illness, injury, etc.) or to fill in for an understudy who is covering a different track. Commonly, a production will hire one male swing and one female swing. Alternatively, the show may hire specific understudies for each principal character. This is more common on straight plays, whereas swings are common on musicals and operas.

If a production has hired understudy performers and/or swings, understudy rehearsals will become a regular part of the week once the show has opened. The specifics for this will be very dependent on your particular theatre company and production, but typically it will be a couple of afternoon rehearsals a week with just the swings/understudies and stage management to walk through their show tracks and prep them for the possibility of going on for someone. If there is an associate director, they will assist with these rehearsals as well. If the show is a musical, understudy rehearsals will also include the music director and the dance captain. If there is a fight, the fight director should be present to teach the fight to any understudies the first time. After that, fights can be supervised by the fight captain. These rehearsals most commonly take place on stage so the understudies can use the set and the props while rehearsing. However, tech (e.g., lights, sound, etc.) and costumes are not usually used during these rehearsals and no other crew is present.

In the event that one of the understudies needs to go on for a performance, a **put-in rehearsal** will take place. If time allows, the full cast (except the performer calling out) and crew gather to do a full run through with tech and costumes. Before the put-in rehearsal, consult with the costume department about the understudy's costume situation. Make sure they have been fitted for all necessary costume pieces and everything is on hand (including shoes and any accessories).

Photo Call

Photo call is an opportunity for the company (and designers) to take archival photos of the production. In most situations, it will be your responsibility to coordinate and run the photo call. Decide on a date and time as early as possible so that everyone (including performers and designers) know when to expect it. Announce it and add it to the production calendar. About a week prior to the photo call, send an email to the director and the designers requesting a list of the photos they would like. You should also remind the cast at this time (and again the day before). The deadline for receiving these lists should be no later than 24 hours before the photo call. Compile the responses and make a final list of about 10–15 shots (cut and combine the photos at your discretion to end up with as many different looks as you can, trying to keep as many of the photo requests as possible but also keeping the photo call to a manageable length, typically no longer than an hour).

Once you have a finalized list, go through and write down the setup of each photo. This includes set, props, costumes, and correct light cue number, as well as which performers are in each photo. The more detailed, the better! From there, organize the photo list in the most logical possible order, keeping in mind the time it takes to do set transitions, prop reset, changing costumes/hair/makeup, etc. Copies of this list should be posted prominently backstage for performers, as well as given to the light console operator and the assistant stage manager (or deck crew head). Have a physical copy for yourself as well (Figure 12.1).

> When organizing the photos, keep in mind that sometimes it is easier to move backwards through the show rather than resetting for the top and moving forwards. Also take special note of any moments involving large messes or specialty makeup that may take more time to either prep for or clean up from (e.g., blood effects, confetti, snow, etc.)

Photo calls should not last more than an hour, so plan accordingly. Also, if at all possible, take care of group photos and other full cast shots early so you can let people go as they finish (unless of course you are having a photo call before the show, then start small and work up to the full group shots). The entire cast and crew will be required to stay throughout the length of the photo call unless personally released by the stage manager.

Throughout the photo call, keep a running commentary on which shot will be taken next so anyone not currently participating in the shoot can be prepping backstage. Make

SMB   PETER THE STARCATCHER Photo Call List

PG	PHOTO	WHO	SET / PROPS	LQ	DONE
-	Cast/Crew photo	Full Cast & Crew	End of show	170	☐
137	Ready, Set, Go!	Full cast	End of show (no reset)	168	☐
135	Final Narration "Till we fly back home. Home"	Full Cast except Frank & Mickey	End of show (no reset)	163	☐
107	"The mission comes first. Get the trunk down to the beach. Now move it!" - umbrellas	Full Cast	Queen trunk, umbrellas, pineapple	140	☐
102	Grotto "And looking down fondly at Peter was - A mermaid!"	Full Cast	Stairs, Queen trunk, golden water, water sticks	136	☐
81	End of Mollusk Chant "Want that trunk!"	Full Cast	Sheilds, spears, pineapple	120	☐
1	Top of show - Prologue	Full Cast	Clear stage, boat in, walls in	5	☐
48	"There are only 6 and a half of us"	Sarah-Anne, Joel, Jordan, Brandon, Colin, Marc, Robert, Brian	Fulcrum, Plank, starcatcher lights, amulet	34	☐
49	Molly floats: "To have faith is to have wings"	Sarah-Anne, Joel, Jordan, Brandon, Colin, Marc, Robert, Brian	Fulcrum, Plank, starcatcher lights, amulet	36	☐
56	"Two ships make toward each other" / Walking the Frank	Full Cast	XL rope, model ships, stairs, Sand Trunk, mini flags,	50	☐
59	Boxing Match to "Crack! The sound of splintering wood"	Full Cast	XL rope, stairs, Sand Trunk, mini flags	64 - 66	☐
69	SAFELY HOME! (End of Act I)	Full Cast except Joel & Robert	Stairs	81	☐
40	Peter's Sorry monologue	Full Cast	XL rope, Chair	31	☐
32	Black Stache! (Stache entrance)	Full Cast except Sarah-Anne, Mickey	XL Rope, chair, union jack	22	☐
53	"It's the Wasp alright! Sally Lunn, she's a fast ship!"	Robert, Brandon, Joel, Andrew, Mickey, Jordan	XL rope, Ship wheel, Telescope	45	☐
73	Mermaid Outta Me "Shoop!"	Full Cast except Joel	Clear stage	108	☐

6/3/18   Pg 1 of 1

Figure 12.1 Photo Call List

sure any last-minute changes in the order of the photos are communicated loudly and clearly. At the end, thank everyone for their patience and participation. Be sure to do a thorough clean up with the crew before locking up for the evening, as props and costume pieces tend to be misplaced during photo calls.

AEA requires a 24-hour notice before any photographs may be taken, so ensure the cast is properly notified. Additionally, some theatres are beginning to discontinue separate photo calls. Instead, a photographer will come and capture pictures during a dress rehearsal. The 24-hour notification period still applies to this option.

> Remember that the more prepared you come for a photo call, the less difficult it will be. Sometimes, the director, lighting designer, or even the producer will be present – do your best to find a balance of getting them what they need and respecting the performers' and crew's time.

Archiving the Production

Once a show has closed, stage management's responsibilities will vary. One thing that should always happen is that you should do a final clean-up of your promptbook so that it is as neat and up-to-date as possible. Ideally, a company should be able to remount the production based off of your book. In fact, on certain professional contracts, your promptbook belongs to the theatre company so that they have all of the information for their archives. Even if the company does not require an archival promptbook, taking the time to do this right after the show closes gives you great portfolio materials for future employment.

> Don't put this off, you will tell yourself you will do it later, but it's best to do it when the information is foremost in your brain.

> Theatre folks are a superstitious lot. One of the most common superstitions revolves around saying good luck. It is considered bad luck to say good luck, so instead we say "Break a leg." There are a number of possible origins for this saying. Some people say that it originates from the idea of the cast bending their legs to curtsy/bow (breaking the straight line of their legs). Another possible origin is that it is a wish for the performers to have many encores and thus break the plane created by the leg curtains. Another theory posits that it stems from an ancient tradition in which the audience stomped their feet or pounded chairs on the ground to show appreciation (the hope being that the audience was so appreciative that they broke legs). It may also be a derivation of the German phrase Hals- und Beinbruch (neck and leg break).
>
> Australian performers say chookas, which may be a reference to chicken. Chicken used to be an expensive meal and "chookas" may have been a wish that the performers would be paid well and thus could eat well.

Chapter Thirteen
Unions

This chapter will touch on a variety of unions that you may encounter in the theatrical world with an emphasis on the American labor union Actors' Equity Association (the union for actors and stage managers). It will also highlight some of the more relevant associated rules of which a stage manager should be aware. There is a common misconception that being in a union is what makes one a professional. This is inaccurate, though often people will use professional and equity interchangeably when referring to a company. To be clear, if you are being paid for your work, particularly if it is your primary source of income, you are a professional whether or not you belong to a union.

A Very Brief Background of Unions

Unions exist to protect their members and provide an avenue for **collective bargaining**. A collective group of people has more clout than an individual. There are unions for any number of professions, from truck drivers to ticket takers to librarians and beyond. Labor unions have existed since the industrial revolution when factory workers joined together to demand safer working conditions and better wages. Unions in the United States negotiate contracts and moderate disputes between their members and the companies for which they work. There are some unions that allow their members to work both on and off a union contract, but the majority of unions require that once a person has joined, they work exclusively on union contracts. It is worth noting that some unions are international while others have counterparts in other countries.

Different Unions for Different Professions

Unions tend to be specialized or include specialized branches under the larger umbrella of a parent union. On Broadway, contracts are negotiated with at least 14 different unions and a guild. We won't talk about all of those unions but will hit some of the highlights. The more unions involved in a production, the more complex schedules become, as each union has its own set of standards and rules that govern its members.

DOI: 10.4324/9781003133049-14

IATSE

The International Alliance of Theatrical Stage Employees, Moving Picture Technicians, Artists and Allied Crafts of the United States, Its Territories and Canada is colloquially referred to by its acronym IATSE (Eye-Ot-See) because IATSEMPTAACUSITaC is unwieldy and wouldn't fit on their logo. IATSE is the parent union for hundreds of regional unions (**Locals**) as well as being an international bargaining entity in its own right. International IATSE supports the locals and sets international policies. They were founded in 1893 and represent most backstage workers as well as many front of house workers. Locals have a fair amount of autonomy from the parent organization.

USA 829

IATSE Local USA 829 is the United Scenic Artists of America. Although it is called a local, it is the national union for theatrical scenic artists, scenic designers, costume designers, lighting designers, projection designers, and a handful of film and television positions. USA 829 negotiates collective bargaining agreements (CBA) with employers, these agreements set salary minimums and protect workers at the companies that are part of the agreement. If a company doesn't have a CBA, they can hire individual designers using a Union Project Agreement or Standard Design Agreement.

AGMA

The American Guild of Musical Artists was founded in 1936 and represents opera performers and stage managers, ballet dancers and stage managers, and concert workers. AGMA members can work for both companies that have AGMA agreements and those that do not have an agreement. AGMA contracts are individually negotiated with each venue. AGMA provides predefined role classifications (leading, featured, mute bit) and minimum chorus numbers for productions at Opera companies via a document referred to as schedule C.

AGVA

The American Guild of Variety Artists was founded in 1939 to represent singers and dancers in theatrical revues and touring (**non-book**) shows, theme park performers, skaters, circus performers, comedians and stand-up comics, cabaret and club artists, lecturers/poets/monologist/spokespersons, and variety performers at private parties and special events. All of their contracts are individually negotiated.

SAG-AFTRA

SAG-AFTRA is the combined Screen Actors Guild and American Federation of Television and Radio Artists. These once separate unions merged in 2012. SAG-AFTRA covers television, film, commercials, music videos, news and broadcast, voice-overs, and sound recordings (like original cast recordings). Once you are a member of this union, it is expected that you will work under SAG-AFTRA contracts, but you are able to make this membership honorably inactive for a period of time if needed.

SDC

The Stage Directors and Choreographers society was founded in 1959. They set rules about intellectual property, travel and housing, and salary minimums as well as providing health and retirement benefits. There are two tiers of membership. Full members are required to file SDC contracts when they work; associate members do not file contracts with SDC but have access to the contract affairs office for help answering questions about individual contracts.

AFM

The American Federation of Musicians was officially recognized in 1896. They primarily deal with recorded music (including film and television) as well as symphonies and orchestras. In terms of theatre, the AFM comes into play primarily on Broadway/off-Broadway (Local 802), at larger LORT theatres, and most opera companies with a pit orchestra. Many of these companies have a negotiated minimum number of musicians that must be paid whether they are needed to perform or not. Like the other unions, they also negotiate fees, working hours and conditions as well as providing benefits like pensions and health care.

LORT (and the Broadway League)

LORT is the League of Resident Theatres. It is not a union but serves a similar purpose for the theatres involved (75 at the time of this printing). They work to bargain collectively with the unions. This has helped standardize working conditions in large swathes of the industry. There are a number of requirements that a theatre must meet to be a part of LORT and the theatres are sorted into categories from A+ to D based on size and ticket sales. As a group, LORT is the most prolific issuer of equity contracts. The Broadway League is similar but for Broadway theatres.

AEA (Actors' Equity Association/Equity)

In the not so distant past, producers could overwork and mistreat performers, put them in unsanitary dressing rooms, and abandon them far from home if a tour wasn't solvent. In 1913, a group of just over 100 actors gathered in New York and started to organize themselves into a union. By 1919, they joined with a few other unions and engaged in a strike for recognition. By the end of the strike, Equity was acknowledged as valid and had their first 5-year contract with the Broadway League. During this time, their numbers grew and the off-shoot Chorus Equity Association was created; they later merged in 1955. In 1920, stage managers were officially recognized as a distinct part of the union after a production closed and attempted to get out of paying the stage manager the same severance pay as the actors (stage managers and assistants had already been a part of the union since they often held small acting roles). Equity successfully defended him and acknowledged that stage managers needed to be formally recognized.

Just like the unions discussed previously, AEA negotiates on behalf of its members to provide safe, fair working conditions, minimum salaries, benefits, payments, and much more. As the union that stage managers and actors belong to, it is the most important union to have an understanding of as a young stage manager. As a representative of the union, AEA stage managers help ensure that all rules are upheld by the producing companies. It is not the stage manager's job to enforce the rules, but they are a conduit to the larger union which can, and will, defend the rights of its workers.

It is important to note that there are many different Equity contracts. Some of the most common ones are the Production Contract (Broadway), the LORT Contract, and SPT (Small Professional Theatres). There are also regional contracts like the CAT (Chicago Area Theatres) and the BAT (Bay Area Theatres) and contracts based on the type of theatre company like TYA (Theatre for Young Audiences), COST (Council of Stock Theatres), and Dinner Theatres. Many of these contracts have similar sections but once you are working on a specific contract, it is important to become familiar with the rules therein. All of the contracts are renegotiated every few years. Any rules referenced here are from the 2017–2022 LORT contract.

While most theatres that don't work under a union contract won't follow all the union's rules, there are several things that are more or less an industry standard, even within academia. The most common of these is related to rehearsal breaks – a 5-minute break is taken after working for no more than 55 minutes OR a 10-minute break must be taken after no more than 80 minutes of work. Many companies have also started to incorporate a cast deputy who speaks on behalf of the cast if there are problems that arise. On a union project, the deputy also reports to Equity as needed. Most of the union rules are irrelevant at the academic level, but it is worth being aware of the scope of the union.

In addition to providing rules governing breaks, the Union also provides rules establishing the span of day (7 out of 9 hours for a musical) and the amount of time between the end of one day and the start of the next rehearsal (generally 12 hours, though there are some exceptions). It also sets limits on the number of hours that can be worked in a week (stage managers are allotted more hours than actors to account for set up and shut down each day). There are specific rules about the number/amount of time that actors can be called for fittings, and a rental rates chart in the case that an actor is asked to use their own clothing.

Some of the most important things that the union negotiates are listed in a section of the rulebook called *Safe and Sanitary Places of Employment*. This section outlines the requirements for dressing rooms, stage conditions and inclines, aisles, bathrooms, usage of smoke and haze effects, first aid kits, etc. Prior to union involvement, producers often neglected many of these items, placing actors in danger during performances. The contracts also provide salary minimums (members can, and should, negotiate for more if the situation merits it) as well as compensation and requirements regarding publicity, photographs, recordings, or performing tasks outside the typical role.

Perhaps the most important early win for the union revolved around travel. As mentioned at the beginning of this chapter, prior to unions, a producer could strand the entire company hundreds of miles from their homes. Now it is explicitly stated that the producer must return the actors and stage managers to their point of origin. The contract also indicates minimum housing requirements (among them a private bedroom, high-speed internet, cooking facilities, salt and pepper, and a radio alarm clock) and how much baggage the company can be required to pay to transport (200 pounds at the start of the engagement and not more than an additional 100 pounds at the end).

When to Join the Union

This chapter barely scratches the surface of the 120-page LORT agreement and doesn't even touch other unions' rules, nor does it reflect the work that the union does for its members. That said, joining the union isn't for everyone. The trajectory of each individual's career is different, as are the circumstances in which one might find themselves. Living in the middle of nowhere doesn't provide many opportunities for union work and, in a larger city, breaking into the theatre community often involves taking non-union jobs and building a reputation within the community. Everyone has different opinions about the "right time" and "right way" to join the union. It is important to find the situation that works for you. It can be tempting to jump at the first opportunity to get your union membership (card) but if you don't have work lined up after that or if you tend to work for non-union companies as your main source of income, it might not be the right choice at the time. If you have worked consistently and built up a strong network and there are multiple or consistent equity opportunities near you, joining the union can be just the right thing.

How to Join the Union

There are a few ways to join the union and more information can be found on the Actors' Equity website. There are initiation fees and dues associated with all of them:

- Equity Contract – One can be offered (and accept) an equity contract, at which point one can join the union.
- The Equity Membership Candidate (EMC) program – The EMC program allows potential members to credit work at Equity companies toward future membership (these are specific companies that are part of the program, not just any equity theatre). After a certain number of weeks, the EMC is eligible to join equity and become a full member. The upside of this program is that one can work at non-union companies as well as with the union company providing weeks.
- 4A's Affiliation – There is a group of unions called the Associated Actors and Artists of America (the 4A's) which includes AEA, AGMA, AGVA, SAG-AFTRA, and the Guild of Italian American Actors (GIAA); these are known as sister unions. A member of any

one of these unions is eligible to join another sister union as long as they meet a certain set of requirements.

- Open Access – In 2021, Equity opened access to join the union to anyone who has worked professionally as an actor or stage manager within the United States. Applicants have to provide a copy of their contract, proof of payment, and pay a portion of the initiation fee. Access will remain open until May 1, 2023 at which point Equity will announce the permanent solution to equitable access to the union.

Chapter Fourteen
Opera

Stage managing opera has many similarities to stage managing theatre. In this section, we will primarily highlight the differences. Opera began in the late 16th century and is the Italian word for handiwork. Opera is entirely sung through with no spoken dialogue (recitatives are sung/spoken with accompaniment). There are three main types of opera: classical, modern, and operetta. Classical opera is broken into two subcategories: opera buffa and opera seria. The distinguishing feature is that opera buffa centers around the lives of ordinary people and opera seria centers on gods or heroes. An operetta is a short opera which may have some spoken dialogue (e.g., Gilbert and Sullivan musicals are often considered operettas).

Traits of a Good Stage Manager

All of the qualities of a good stage manager discussed at the beginning of this book also apply to opera stage managers. Here we have added a few and expanded on others that are particularly relevant for opera stage management.

Attention to Detail

Stopping and starting in music can be more challenging than stopping and starting in text. As such, it is imperative that the stage management team be ready to set and reset quickly and accurately when needed. Opera is at times more rote than theatre, and if a piece of furniture is off spike or a prop is reset improperly, it can derail things pretty quickly. Additionally, scenes are often rehearsed with different parts of the cast separately and the stage management team can be helpful in identifying complicated traffic patterns before it is too late to adjust them. Knowing when a group of people or piece of scenery is occupying a space even when they aren't physically present can be pivotal in avoiding issues once everyone and everything comes together.

Once you are in performance, attention to detail comes into play in knowing how the **Maestro** conducts so you can take cues from them. Being able to clearly identify and anticipate the signals for the upbeat, downbeat, and cutoffs will be integral to following the Maestro, as they may vary slightly from performance to performance depending on

DOI: 10.4324/9781003133049-15

the mood and energy of the audience and singers. For ASMs, attention to detail is the bread and butter of both rehearsal and performance for prop placement and singer cueing.

Respect

In some ways, this section is addressing formality more than respect, but they work hand in hand. No matter what genre of performing art you are working in, respect is paramount. In the opera world, formality is a key aspect of how respect is expressed. Performers are addressed using honorifics (or titles, e.g., Mr., Mx., Ms.) and the Maestro is treated with the utmost reverence. This doesn't mean you can't or won't make friends with the company members but official gatherings tend to be more formal and focused than many theatrical settings.

Tact

Opera, at times, has even larger personalities and egos than theatre, and learning when and how to discuss sensitive information will take you far. This can apply to anything from letting the director/maestro know when breaks are needed to conveying to costumes how a garment works in rehearsal. In theatre, the stage manager runs the room; in opera, the stage manager is still an integral part of the team but acts as more of a facilitator.

Processing Speed/Efficiency

In larger companies, there may be very limited rehearsal time with the principals. Most singers are expected to come in with the music learned and, in common operas, there may already be standard or typical blocking. So while in theatre you may have several opportunities to double-check your blocking notes and the director and performers may be figuring things out as they go (which gives you more time to write things down), in opera there may only be one rehearsal of some scenes, so you will have to be quick and efficient to keep up. It is atypical for the stage manager to slow the momentum by asking questions (though some directors are happy to answer questions between scenes or on breaks – this varies by person).

Selfless Leadership

It is your job to ensure the smooth flow of the production; if that means personal pre-show pages to the star dressing rooms or escorting singers to the stage, do what is needed (to the best of your ability). This doesn't mean that you are (or should be treated as) a doormat, but it does mean that you check your ego in service of the production. No one stage manages for the glory. There will be some tasks that are outside the scope of your job, but there shouldn't be any tasks (within reason) that you are unwilling to do or assist with.

Flexibility

In opera, the assistant director (AD) (if there is one) will take on a lot of the theatrical stage manager's traditional duties. Being prepared to step up or back as needed is integral to opera stage management. It can be challenging to work in a new medium, but having the flexibility to adapt will take you far.

Touring the Space

You will most likely be rehearsing in a different space than you will be performing in; so, if possible, tour both spaces and get to know them.

As you tour the performance space, find out where the calling station will be (almost always backstage rather than in a booth). Confirm that you will have video monitors of both the stage and the Maestro. You should also note how many dressing rooms there are and their locations in relation to the stage. Typically, the dressing rooms closest to the stage are assigned to the principals and those further from the stage are given to the chorus.

Questions for the PM/Person who hired you:

- Is there an AD?
- What is the company's typical rehearsal schedule?
- How will scheduling be dealt with?
  - What additional considerations are part of the schedule (coachings, publicity events, etc.)?
- Will the chorus be rehearsing separately from the principals?
- When will **supernumeraries** be joining the process?
- Are the costumes and/or scenery/props being rented as a package from another company?
  - If so, is there accompanying paperwork from that production?
- How does the music department/team work?
- If they are a union company, request a copy of their specific union agreement.

Additional Personnel

Maestro

The Maestro (conductor) is the most important/powerful person in the room. Since opera is primarily music and they are responsible for the tempi (plural form of tempo) and nuance of the music as it is played, they work very closely with the stage director and often have the final say in how a piece is performed. The stage manager needs to be aware of how the maestro conducts in order to take cues off their movements and gestures.

Assistant Conductor

This assistant conductor works closely with the Maestro and will run any staging rehearsals that the Maestro doesn't attend. The assistant conductor is also an additional set of ears taking notes at principal music rehearsals, noting problem spots so that they can be addressed. Once the orchestra is added, the assistant conductor may be out in the house checking the balance of the orchestra and voices. They are also often in charge of doing any conducting for an offstage chorus or banda. They will step in to conduct the opera in case of emergency.

Chorus Master

The chorus master runs the chorus, with lots of input from other members of the creative team. They confer with the Maestro about what tempi each piece that the chorus is involved in should be sung and the phrasing (when can the chorus breathe). They then rehearse the chorus to get them ready for staging. This position may also be combined with the assistant conductor.

Accompanist/Rehearsal Pianist (*Répétiteur*)

The *répétiteur* plays the piano for staging rehearsals. Most operas aren't written exclusively for the piano (for that matter, a large portion of the standard opera repertoire doesn't include a piano in the pit orchestra at all). The *répétiteur* is typically playing from a condensed orchestral score which can be pretty complicated. The conductor (or assistant conductor) or the stage director will often tell them where to pick up, but you should also be aware and ready to assist if needed.

Stage Director

The stage director is responsible for the blocking and movement of the singers. Opera seasons are often chosen many years in advance and directors may have very little input on the scenery, costumes, or even casting. They will work closely with the Maestro to guide the production. The stage manager's relationship to the stage director is similar to that in theatre, requiring trust and collaboration.

Assistant Director (AD)

Opera assistant directors are quite different from theatre assistant directors. The AD rather than the stage manager is responsible for taking and maintaining blocking. They also tend to function as a liaison between stage manager and stage director. You will likely work with the AD to create the next day's schedule. ADs also take a more active role in keeping the pace of the rehearsal moving and ensuring that the director is completing the day's scheduled staging. They may also work with the chorus and supernumeraries on their blocking. Once a production opens, the AD rather than the stage manager maintains the artistic integrity.

Performers

One way that singers are divided is by voice type. We will include general descriptions of the voice types, but you should know that there are exceptions to the "rules" laid out in the following section. It is also worth noting that there are subdivisions within the voice types that describe the quality of the voice or specialty of the singer.

Voice Types

Soprano

The highest of the "female" vocal types. They are typically the heroine or love interest in dramatic operas.

Mezzo-Soprano

A lower range than sopranos, they often play "trouser" roles portraying young boys or men. They also tend to be the villains or mothers. Notably, Carmen in the opera "Carmen" is a mezzo role.

Contralto or Alto

The lowest and rarest range for "female" voice types, they tend to play specialty roles like the Earth goddess in the ring cycle. Sometimes these parts are sung by mezzos with a lower range.

Tenor

Typically considered the highest vocal range for "male" singers. They tend to play the hero or the love interest.

Countertenor

Actually sings higher than the tenor with a range up into the "female" ranges. They tend to use a falsetto and can create an "otherworldly" tone.

Baritone

This is in the mid-range of the "male" voice and also the most common. They play a variety of parts. They may be the mischievous troublemakers, the hero who saves the tenor or soprano lead, or they could be villains.

Bass

The lowest of the "male" vocal ranges. They may play characters that provide wisdom and insight or they may provide comic relief.

The other way that performers are divided is by role type; we will describe a few of those roles in the following section.

Principals

Principals are the leading roles in an opera. These tend to be the named characters with solos longer than 24 bars. The AGMA schedule C document has a more detailed breakdown of this role type (it actually includes lead, feature, supporting, and solo bit parts).

Chorus

The chorus tends to sing as a group (unless there are chorus bit parts). They are the crowd at the party or the soldiers in the war. Choruses tend to be large (depending on the contract, there may be a minimum required). They may be divided into subgroups at various points throughout the opera. Crowd management in rehearsal can be challenging; assigning one ASM to work with the chorus specifically can be beneficial, so that the chorus has a dedicated point person and you have someone else helping keep track of them.

Supernumerary

Supernumeraries or "supers" are silent acting roles in an opera; often waiters, soldiers, guards, etc. There may be a few supers or an army of them. They don't usually join the full company until late in the process, though they may be rehearsed separately a couple of times before they join the rest of the company.

Dancers

Dancers are non-singing performers who, you guessed it, dance.

Banda

A musical ensemble in addition to the orchestra that plays music that the characters in the opera hear. They may appear on stage (banda sul palco) or play from the wings (banda interna).

Covers

Opera's version of understudies is much more common than theatrical understudies, and often have a variety of roles that they are familiar with and ready to cover. They attend all rehearsals to which their principal is called and may also have a smaller role in the opera.

Music Librarian

The music librarian is responsible for acquiring and distributing all of the needed music for a production. They may also make copies or scans for the conductor and/or orchestra.

The Orchestra

An orchestra is typically made up of five sections: woodwinds, brass, keyboard, percussion, and strings. You probably won't have a lot of interaction with the whole orchestra but you should be sure to introduce yourself to the concertmaster.

Concertmaster (Principle 1st Violin)

After the Maestro, the concertmaster is the highest ranking orchestra member. Before the Maestro enters the pit to start the performance, the stage manager will coordinate with the concertmaster to start **tuning**. The concertmaster will cue the oboe player to give the tuning note.

Pre-Production

One of the key differences between theatre and opera is that instead of a script there is only a score. While it is not imperative that an opera stage manager read music, it does make everything a lot easier. Prior to rehearsals, the stage manager should become very familiar with the story of the opera as well as the score. Frequently, operas are written in languages other than English, so you may need to look for a synopsis or a version with a translation or subtitles. You may also find some fun short video synopses online.

There are multiple versions of many popular operas, so it is important to have the correct edition. Once the correct edition is procured, the Maestro and/or the stage director may have a list of cuts or changes to the music which you should update in the stage manager's score prior to rehearsals starting. Another thing to be aware of are repeats (these are designated by two lines and two dots); if a section is repeated, make extra copies of those pages so that you don't have to flip back and forth. Just like the prompt book, you never want to flip back, keep moving forward.

As with the score, there may be a variety of recordings. Most likely the company will have a suggested recording; listen to that recording to become familiar with the music. Take the time to mark dynamic (volume) and tempo (speed) shifts in the music, as well as highlighting each system on a page for easy identification when you do timings. Listen to a recording while looking at the music to identify what the different sections sound like, and if you don't read music, listen/look for sections that you can recognize quickly to help keep yourself on track. You'll also want to check measure numbers between the conductor's score and the score the singers will be using. Sometimes they will match, but if they do not, you may want to create a score conversion chart for easy reference.

Once you have highlighted your score and listened to the music a few times, start at the beginning and follow along, marking 30-second timings throughout each act. Create a cheat sheet that details where each 30-second mark falls by noting the page, system, and measure.

! PAGE/SYSTEM/MEASURE

Because a score can be harder to read than a page of text, more information is given when identifying locations in the score. For 30-second timings, cues, etc., use Page/System/Measure (P/S/M).

The pages in a score are numbered like pages in any other printed work.

A system includes all of the musical staves that are played at the same time, they are often linked with a vertical line. (Staves is the plural of staff – a musical staff is a set of five horizontal lines and four spaces that each represent a different pitch or, in the case of percussion, different percussion instruments.)

Each system will be broken down into measures, indicated with a solid line. Each measure contains a set number of beats determined by the key signature. Measures are often numbered, starting at 1 and running for the duration of the song or movement. For paperwork purposes, you identify the number of the measure in the system, not the entire page or piece of music (you may have 26/2/4 but not 26/2/57) (Figure 14.1).

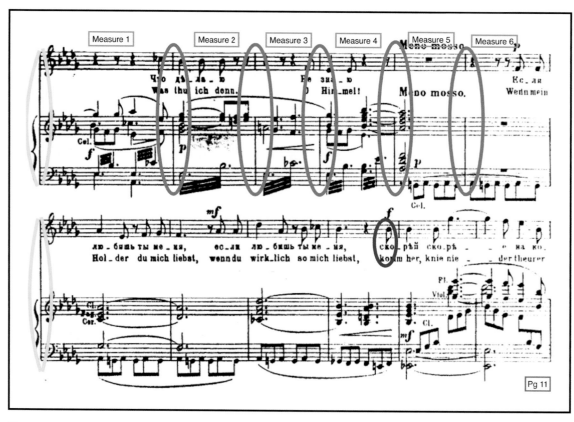

Figure 14.1 Example of Page, System, and Measure (P/S/M). The yellow circles mark the systems (notice that there are multiple staves in one system). The magenta circles show the lines marking each measure (which are numbered above in green boxes). The page number is marked in red in the lower right-hand corner. So the note/text circled in blue would be indicated as 11/2/4.

In addition to 30-second timings, you should begin marking any clear entrances, exits, and other relevant information. You will also want to start a lot of the same paperwork that we talked about in the pre-production and paperwork sections for theatre (report templates, prop information, etc.). One piece of paperwork that is very important in opera is the Who, What, Where (WWW). This is a combination of an entrance/exit sheet and a run sheet. It notes who is doing what and when they do it (more on this in Book and Paperwork).

Acquire hospitality supplies – room temperature water, hot water (or the means to make it quickly), coffee, lozenges, and tissues.

Make sure that you know who is covering whom and create a document for easy reference. Remember that if the principal is called for rehearsal, the cover is as well. This will impact the daily calls and sign-in sheets. Be sure that covers have any and all information specific to their tracks.

Just as in theatrical productions, it is important to meet early on with the director and the maestro. If the company has an assistant director, the stage manager may interact with them more often than the stage director; so it is important to meet with them as well. Use these early meetings to establish expectations. Many of the questions for the director from Chapter 5 are relevant for opera as well. Some additional questions to consider include:

- What sort of stool or chair does the maestro prefer?
- Who will primarily be in rehearsal, the maestro or the assistant?
- How would the team (maestro) like the room to be set up?
- How and who will coordinate rehearsal needs?

Scheduling for an opera can be a lot more complicated than a theatre production; as such, there is sometimes a dedicated scheduler or group of schedulers. There are a variety of different schedules of which the stage manager should be aware:

- The company schedule – the big picture schedule for the company, includes performance dates, technical rehearsals, and other company-wide events.
- The rehearsal schedule – the most important schedule for the stage manager.
- The daily schedule – a full rundown of what is happening on any given day.
- The coaching schedule – the singers will receive music coaching to work on pieces outside of rehearsal. Young artists often have a set number of coachings written into their contracts as part of an apprentice program.
- The music schedule – this is the schedule specifically for the music staff. It may include accompanists, coaches, the conductor, the assistant conductor, and the orchestra.
- The chorus schedule – exactly what it sounds like, the schedule for the chorus (they are often rehearsed separately from the principles until the groups are brought together later in the process).
- The super schedule – similar to the chorus schedule but for the supernumeraries.
- The fitting schedule – yep, it's the schedule for costume fittings.

The stage manager, maestro, and stage director/assistant stage director determine who is needed for rehearsals and send that along to the scheduler to coordinate. At smaller companies, the stage manager may be the person gathering and compiling this information.

Taping out happens the same way that it does in theatre. It is important to include the apron and the proscenium/curtain line (opera singers are often blocked downstage center for key moments and the **grand drape** is frequently brought in between acts). Once you have taped the floor, you should create color-coded versions of the groundplan for each act and scene that can be posted on either side of the rehearsal space so that the cast can reference them to know which color tape they should pay attention to for which scene.

Preparing the callboard and rehearsal props are much the same as in theatre at this point in the process.

Book and Paperwork

In addition to the typical paperwork for which the stage manager is responsible (see Chapter 7), there are a number of opera-specific pieces of which to be aware.

Face Page

The **face page** is a collection of headshots (or profile pictures) paired with the performer's name. This will help you, and the rest of the team, get to know what folks look like prior to rehearsals. In smaller productions this may be unnecessary, but with a large chorus or group of supers, it can be very helpful.

Name Tags

Name tags for the company feature the singer's last name (large enough to be read from the director's table) with the first name underneath and smaller. They should also include the singer's vocal part and character name. Name tags may be worn throughout the rehearsal process, not just at the meet and greet or first rehearsal, and as such, should be durable or easily replaced.

Singer Packets

These will have a lot of the same information as theatrical welcome packets but have to be as self-explanatory as possible. Unlike in theatre, the first rehearsal is less about paperwork and introductions and more about the maestro getting started with the singers.

Who, What, Where (WWW)

The WWW is the master document that records what happens throughout the show. It will include all entrances and exits (with special note of each singer's first entrance), prop hand-offs, prop catches, costume changes, and scenery moves (in opera all entrances are cued and all props are handed-off/caught). This document should answer the questions posed in its title as well as provide any needed clarifying notes. Additionally, it should include the P/S/M placement and approximate (and eventually accurate) timing. Once the WWW is complete, it can be utilized to create separate run sheets for each department as well as a first entrance list (which will be used when determining call times later in the process).

Score Conversion Chart

If multiple versions of the score are being utilized, create a chart that will allow you to give accurate information (particularly page numbers) to anyone in the space. This can be time-consuming, but especially helpful if the maestro is working from a full score and others are working from a vocal score. This chart is very similar to Figure 7.17 (p. 90).

Blocking Pages

In addition to the marking and timings we talked about in the pre-production section, there are some other considerations for getting your book ready for rehearsal. Opera scores tend to be significantly longer than musical libretti, and as such, it may be the best use of resources to print the score double-sided. Whether or not the stage manager is taking blocking, the stage management team is responsible for all people and prop tracking, particularly singer entrances and exits. Create a blocking page with room for entrances, exits, scenery, prop, and costume notes, as well as a couple of stage minis for bigger stage pictures, and room for miscellaneous notes.

> If you are using a double-sided score you should also consider using double-sided tracking sheets between each set of score pages.

Rehearsals

The two primary types of rehearsals will be music rehearsals and staging rehearsals. These may be broken down into subcategories based on role type (Principal, chorus, supernumerary, etc.). Typically, opera companies won't rehearse for more than 3 hours at a time and no more than 6 hours a day. The rules about breaks are also a little more flexible than in theatre.

The stage manager more formally starts rehearsals by calling the cast to places or announcing that the company is met before respectfully passing the rehearsal to the maestro to begin.

Room Setup

No matter what sort of rehearsal you are setting up for, the maestro (rather than the stage director) should be the most visible person and thus situated at the center front of the room. Typically, they will have a music stand and a tall stool or chair rather than a table. The piano will generally be off to one side of the maestro, while the director, AD, and stage management will be on the other side. Be mindful as you set up the room that you should avoid having to cross behind the maestro and you should never cross directly in front of them.

In addition to taping out the space, you should acquire tables for props and racks for costumes (the costumes for many classical operas are quite large and often rented, so taking good care of them in rehearsal is important). You may also need to ensure that there are stand (clip) lights available for the *répétiteur* and maestro. Be sure that the hospitality area is stocked and ready (water pitchers filled, coffee brewing, etc.).

Music Rehearsals

For music rehearsals, check with the maestro for their preferred setup. In general, rows of chairs and music stands arranged facing the piano will work. Singers may be arranged by vocal part, role type, or character relationship. At some companies, the chorus will rehearse music separately from the principals. If it is a principal-only rehearsal, the principals should be in the front row with their covers seated behind. As with a musical, follow along in the music as the singers work and be sure to note any changes that are made during the rehearsal.

Staging Rehearsals

Even in staging rehearsals, the Maestro should be front and center. At the first staging rehearsal, the stage director may talk/walk the cast through the set tape out. The ASMs should be on their respective sides of the stage and take notes about/facilitate entrances and prop hand-offs/catches. When working solely with principals, be sure to coordinate with the director and AD about how many chorus members/supernumeraries are in the scene and where they will be so that you can (a) have the ASM walk the parts as needed and (b) be helpful at the subsequent chorus staging rehearsals.

Chorus/Supernumeraries (Super) Rehearsals

These are rehearsals specifically for the chorus or supernumeraries. They are given their staging and are made aware of what the principals are doing during the scenes. Besides their time onstage, many operas have the chorus singing from offstage at various points. It is imperative that the stage management team know what the backstage traffic looks like so that the singers can be placed appropriately without being in the way of principal entrances/exits, scene changes, and/or costume changes. The chorus master will manage the chorus when they sing backstage, but they will need both an audio monitor of the orchestra and a video feed of the conductor accessible wherever they are going to be singing. Depending on placement and desired effect, they may also need amplification. If there isn't a permanent place that this can be set up, an additional tracking document may need to be created. This information needs to be communicated to the appropriate department as soon as possible so that arrangements can be made.

Many opera companies have very condensed rehearsal periods and the singers are expected to arrive knowing their music and with an idea about the character they are playing. There is much less organic discovery than in contemporary theatre productions (singers are sometimes hired years in advance). The shortened rehearsal period means that rehearsals may move at a brisker pace. As such, it is important that the stage management team be prepared to step in and support the process quickly and quietly without interrupting the flow of the room.

Room Runs

Once the entire opera has been rehearsed musically and staged, you will begin run throughs, which in opera are called room runs. The ASMs should be stationed on their respective sides of the stage and you should be incorporating all of the props, rehearsal garments, and stand-in set pieces that are available. Once room runs begin, time the runs to check for consistency and to have the most up-to-date timings as you move into tech. One of the room runs will act as a designer run (this is usually the last rehearsal in the rehearsal space). The lighting designer should attend and take notes and the other designers are encouraged to attend.

Orchestra Read

The orchestra read is a chance for the maestro to work with the orchestra. You probably won't have to be at these rehearsals, but it is good to be aware that it needs to happen and someone will have to schedule and prepare for it. It may impact your world if the read is happening in the same space as rehearsals, in which case things may need to be cleared away to make space for the orchestra. Chairs, music stands, stand lights and extension cords will all need to be set up (this is not typically stage management's duty, but may fall in your hands).

Sitzprobe (Sitz) or Wandelprobe (Wandel)

Ideally, this will take place in the performance space with the singers seated on stage and the orchestra in the pit. This rehearsal is a chance for the cast and the orchestra to work together without acting or blocking so that they can work out any vocal concerns. This is also the first time the stage manager will hear the orchestra and singers together and it is an important opportunity to confirm you know the music and can follow it – it may sound drastically different from the rehearsal space. The Maestro runs this rehearsal and may choose to work through all of the music or focus only on tricky/complicated sections.

Prior to Tech

After the final room rehearsal, everything will need to be transferred to the performance space. If the show is a rental from another company, it is especially important to keep track of all of the props even if your production isn't using all of them. Things should be labeled and packed up to transfer. If the performance space has a stagehand union agreement, stage management will have a lot less hands-on control once they are in the space; so it is vitally important that paperwork is clear and that the team is as prepared as possible.

Paper tech is similar to paper tech in theatre, but can be even more important. Opera tech rehearsals are much shorter than theatrical tech rehearsals, so planning and efficiency are incredibly important. If time allows, dry tech is also more beneficial in opera than in most theatrical settings.

Prepping the Space

Many of the tasks for preparing the space are the same as those covered in Chapter 10. Additionally, the stage manager should work with the wardrobe head to assign dressing rooms, taking into account any contractual stipulations about location/occupancy. Once dressing rooms are assigned, place the singers' names on the doors – traditionally opera is more formal than theatre and uses an honorific and last name format, so be sure that you know what honorific each singer uses. Place valuables bags at each singer's station.

Locate and set up the callboard, put up directional arrows to assist the company in navigating the space, assess wing space, confirm offstage lighting and sound equipment positions, and assist with spiking (in a union house, it is respectful to ask the union steward for permission to walk on the deck prior to doing so).

Make sure that the calling station is set up and ready; you will want two video monitors (one showing the stage and one showing the Maestro), a paging mic to backstage/dressing rooms, a god mic, a small audio monitor for the orchestra, the headset station, and cue light box (if using).

> In dryer spaces (most theatres), the crew may need to spritz the stage space to increase the humidity.

Tech

Tech rehearsals in opera are different from theatre. Rather than marathon days like the 10 out of 12s in theatre, opera rehearsals tend to max out at about 5 hours. As such, it is critical that rehearsals are run quickly and efficiently. Often, the lighting designer will work with the director, AD, and stage manager during the day to write light cues with the ASMs, volunteers, and/or crew walking the singers' blocking before the full tech rehearsal in the evening.

Paging, Cueing Entrances, and Prop Catching

One of the biggest differences between theatre and opera is that in opera the singers are called (paged) to places for each and every entrance that they make and all of their entrances are cued either by the ASM or stage manager. When you are preparing your promptbook, not only will it include standbys and G-Os for lights, sound, scenery, etc., it will also have places calls and entrance cues. Singers are typically paged to the stage four or five minutes before their entrance (the ASMs should let you know when they have arrived or if you need to make an additional paging call). You will use your 30-second markings and rehearsal timings to place these calls. Calling places is another instance where opera is more formal than theatre; these calls tend to take the form of "Places please, Mx. Singer Name, Mx. Singer Name to (location) please." You may also be calling wardrobe and makeup crew to the stage for quick changes. Ideally, there will be two ASMs, one on each side of the stage. They will have their scores with them and, between any running duties they have, they will cue the singers to enter. If there is only one ASM, they will be on the opposite side of the stage from you and you may have to cue singers on your side. The other paging calls that stage managers make in opera are end of act warnings (usually 10 minutes until the end of the act and 5 minutes until the end of the act). At first, this may seem like overkill, but working in a foreign language with no dialogue can be difficult to follow even with the music in front of you, let alone if you are in the dressing room changing.

Another difference from theatre is that, typically, every prop is handed off and caught by the crew. Again, this may seem excessive at first but it comes from a place of practicality – opera costumes are often large and ornate and can make reaching over a prop table hazardous. It is also helpful when a large number of people are entering or exiting at the same time to not have them all crowded around the tables and in each other's way.

Piano Tech/Dress

Piano tech is exactly what it sounds like; you tech the show without the orchestra. Piano tech gives the singers more time to work on stage (once the orchestra is called rehearsal are generally limited to 3 hours per union agreements). Piano tech can be boring for the cast and difficult for the stage manager (if you are planning to cue off an instrument other than the piano, they won't be there), but thorough preparation and efficient planning will help you utilize this time effectively. If there are scene changes that are problematic, it will be beneficial to schedule a scene shift rehearsal during the day before the following night's tech.

Sometimes, the second piano tech will actually be a piano dress and include costumes (although generally not wigs or makeup). This is an opportunity to run quick changes. Additionally, if they haven't already been added, follow-spots will join the rehearsal process on this night. If you weren't paging the performers already, start at this point in the process. During piano techs/dresses, it is okay for the stage manager and director to stop and fix things.

Orchestra Dress

Orchestra dress will add any remaining elements (wigs, makeup, tuning, Maestro bow, top of show curtain cues, etc.). Once the orchestra is in the pit, no one stops the rehearsal except the Maestro, unless there is a safety concern that can't be fixed in the moment. If a hold must be called, the stage manager should announce it over the god mic and on headset and then get out on stage to hear what is happening and find out from the Maestro where the rehearsal will need to resume. This information is relayed to the company using the P/S/M style we talked about earlier (p. 186). Quickly and efficiently get the technical elements standing-by and restart the rehearsal. This rehearsal may have an invited audience, so all paperwork and running information must be updated and show ready (pre-show checklists, intermission lists, etc.). If there is an invited audience, you may also need to coordinate with the front of house staff before starting.

> To help preserve voices, the day before opening is usually a day off for the singers but may well be utilized by the technical staff to continue fixing and refining before opening. Often the day before any performance is a day off for the singers; for this reason operas are frequently double cast if the schedule requires back-to-back performances.

Performances and Beyond

All of the pre-show tasks are similar to theatre. You'll make sure everything is set and ready, check in with the house manager, and make time calls. At most companies, you'll start the performance at the listed curtain time (it is unusual to hold for front of house due to the previously discussed strict time constraints of the orchestra). There may be more than one intermission, and they are frequently longer than the 10–15 minutes typical of theatrical productions. You'll call cues and page performers like you rehearsed during tech. After performances, you will send out reports and will help facilitate giving notes and maintaining the show.

Bows

The curtain call for operas can get complicated. If the chorus appears in the final act, they will take the first bow (if they aren't in the final act they will typically bow after the act containing their final appearance). As with all things, bows may vary by company or director, but typically at the end of the final act, the main curtain will be flown in and the principals will clear the stage while the chorus (and supers, dancers, etc.) get into position upstage of the curtain. Once everyone is set, the curtain flies out and the chorus bows, any soloist or bit parts may have an individual bow, and then they all bow together. After the chorus bow, the main curtain is flown back in. Then, if the main curtain has a center split, the crew will page the curtain as the principals enter one by one and bow before returning upstage of the curtain. After the last individual bow, the curtain goes out and there is a group bow (or two). If the main doesn't have a split, the principals will enter one at a time (often alternating from each side of the stage) and bow, then step back until everyone has bowed before forming a line or lines for a group bow. Meanwhile, in either case, the Maestro will make their way from the pit to backstage. Once the group bows have happened, the lead soprano will bring Maestro on from the wing. Maestro bows, acknowledges the orchestra, and then joins the company for additional group bows. The stage manager is often responsible for deciding how many bows the company takes depending on audience response.

On opening night after the maestro bow, the lead tenor will bring the director and designers onstage before the company bows. These are sometimes called "penguin bows" because, for most of history, this group would be a bunch of men in tuxedos. Once bows are completed the main curtain flies back in. Your curtain call may be more or less complicated but the maestro bow and penguin bows are industry standards.

Archiving the Production

Once the production is open and things are set, it is important to update your script and all of the paperwork and send it to the production manager (or equivalent). This provides an accurate record of the creative team's work which can accompany any future rentals or be included in the return if your production is a rental.

Strike/Prior to Strike

Once the opera is closed (or closing), the stage management team should compile any notes that need to be shared with the folks doing strike. There may be items from a rental package that your production didn't use – they will need to be gathered and added back to the return package or there may be items that your production added that shouldn't go back with the rental. You may have a few borrowed items that get sent to a different location while everything else goes back to storage. You don't necessarily need to know where everything goes, but you should have notes about what is rented, borrowed, or owned.

> Opera singers are no less superstitious than theatre folks. They also don't wish each other good luck. Opera singers say either "toi, toi, toi" or "in bocca al lupo." Toi, toi, toi comes from the Yiddish tradition and imitates spitting over one's shoulder to ward off the evil eye. In bocca al lupo is Italian and means "in the mouth of the wolf"; the traditional response is "crepi il lupo" (may the wolf die).

Chapter Fifteen
Dance

Traits of a Good Stage Manager

All of the traits of a good stage manager discussed at the beginning of this book also apply to dance stage managers. Here we have expanded on a few that are particularly relevant for dance stage management.

Attention to Detail

Entrances and exits vary by dancer, based on length of leg, how far their turns travel, etc. Pay enough attention to each dancer's individual style that you notice differences and can distinguish between average day-to-day variances and those that may indicate illness or injury. Maintenance for dance applies only to technical (as opposed to artistic) elements, and it is imperative that you know when light, sound, and deck cues happen as well as what they do.

Adaptability

Often dance performances include many distinct and potentially unrelated pieces. Dance stage managers must know the program backwards and forwards because the program order can change from night to night depending on casting, injuries, etc. Casting can change at the last minute or even mid-performance. This can cause a small headache with reordering cues or switching costumes quickly, but it's the nature of the genre.

Neutrality

The biggest difference between theatre and dance is that dance stage managers are mostly viewed as technicians. Of course, we know that our work takes the touch and approach of an artist, but the creative team and performers will consider you a technician. Neutrality is actually pretty easy in dance because no one will ask you your artistic opinion. It's important to understand and accept this before working in dance.

DOI: 10.4324/9781003133049-16

Discretion

A large amount of the work in dance involves discussing bodies. You'll know more about the dancers' bodies than you ever wanted to and that information can never be shared. Sometimes dancers will not know that you have been told about their injury or menstruation (yes, really) and unless they bring it up, you should not. You have to be ready to protect and prepare for them without disclosing personal information.

Types of Theatre

Most dance performance happens in proscenium theatres, though it is important to note that site-specific work is very common, too (particularly in museums and outdoors). Again, this factor's into adaptability.

Touring the Facility

Touring the theatre should be an early priority in the process. Most dance companies do not own their own theatres, so they are often renting performance space and it may vary between productions. Because of this, you may not be able to physically tour a theatre. In that case, someone else will have advanced the site and written documents to help you find this information. Additionally, site-specific dance is common and unconventional spaces raise unusual questions. Knowing the specific parameters of every venue is essential to your success in planning and executing technical rehearsals and performances.

In addition to the questions you would ask during a tour for a theatrical production, this is a list of dance-specific questions to ask the technical director or venue manager:

- Is there a way to control the temperature, specifically the heat? Dancers have to stay warm (for their health and safety). Some companies have temperature requirements written into their contracts, so it is important to know how or who controls the temperature.
- Where do artists enter the building? Is there security and is any specific identification or personnel list required? Who makes those?
- Is there a curtain between the stage and the audience?
- Is there a booth for the lighting console operator?
- Is it possible to call from backstage? (This is preferable in dance to allow you to anticipate entrances.) If that is not possible, from where does the stage manager call?

For site-specific/outdoor works:

- What is the size and shape of the performance space?
- What is the material of the floor? How hard is it? Is it even or are there any notable inclines, bumps, etc.?
- Is there a backup plan for inclement weather?
- How will sound and lights be powered, if needed?

- Is there any ambient sound that could interfere with the performance?
- Where will laundry and wardrobe set up?
- Where will the dancers dress? Are there showers available? Are there bathrooms available to only the dancers from which the audience will be restricted?
- Is there a warm-up space for the dancers?
- Is there a space for a stage management office?

Stage Directions

Stage left and stage right are the same in dance, though you may also hear the ballet terms below. Specifically, if you hear that a dancer will end a phrase "en face," you know you're looking for them to stop while facing the audience. Same with hearing "croisé" or "efface"; look for them to be on the diagonal.

- **En face** (/ähn-fäs/) – dancer facing the audience, hips and shoulders squared
- **Croisé** (/craw.ze/) – dancer on diagonal, legs crossed to audience
- **Effacé** (/e-fah-say) – dancer on diagonal, legs open to audience
- **Devant** (/day-vount/) – to the front, toward the audience
- **Derrière** (/deh-ree-heir/) – to the back, away from the audience

If you have trouble remembering these terms or are new to ballet, keep a note with these key terms nearby to reference quickly.

Types of Dance Productions

There are two primary forms that a dance program (production) might take. **Mixed Rep** is a series of shorter, often unrelated, dance pieces. The order that the pieces are performed may be changed or adjusted as needed (in the event of injury, substitutions, etc.), though, typically, they aren't reordered arbitrarily.

The other typical format is a **full-length** or story ballet that follows a storyline from beginning to end. You may also find companies that run two (or more) full length ballets in repertory, alternating productions at each performance. In any of these configurations, there may be double or even triple casting and, if that is the case, the artistic staff determines who will be going on in each role nightly.

Personnel

Dance company staff are usually divided into three departments: Executive, Artistic, and Education. The executive departments mirror theatres with staff in finance, development, marketing, patron services, and ticketing. Artistic departments are very different.

Artistic Staff

Artistic Director (AD)

The artistic director is the head of the company and is often an accomplished choreographer or retired dancer. In a modern company the AD may perform with the company. The AD guides the artistic vision of the company by selecting the ballets for a season and hiring all artistic staff.

Ballet Masters or Mistresses

Ballet masters serve many functions in a company, including teaching a daily ballet class to the company of dancers and rehearsing ballets. They work directly under the AD. Ballet masters support choreographers by taking choreographic notes and fine-tuning the steps during a rehearsal process. After the opening performance, the choreographer may not return to watch subsequent performances, so it is then the job of the ballet master to maintain the artistic vision of a dance. They are also responsible for daily schedules.

Choreographers

In dance, the director is replaced by a choreographer. The choreographer is the one to provide the artistic vision that guides the designers and creates the steps for the dancers. Choreographers are often guest artists hired to make or rehearse one work but may be in residence at a company to create or recreate multiple works. In this case, the title is Resident Choreographer.

Stagers

If a company is producing something they have never done before but the work is old, a stager will be hired. This is someone who was trained by the original choreographer to teach new dancers their piece. Consider the stager a proxy for the choreographer, and anywhere in this chapter that the word choreographer appears it could also refer to the stager.

Dancers

Dancers are essentially professional athlete artists. They also tend to be perfectionists. In large companies, dancers are hired for a season of work and they function as a company. Dancers are ranked within the company, usually starting as Apprentice. After an apprenticeship, they may be hired to the Corps de Ballet. Promotions from the Corps go through the ranks of Soloist (sometimes divided into Demi and First) and, finally, Principal. Dancers are cast in various roles in many ballets throughout the season that coordinate with their rank. Dancers that are part of a company, audition each year and may move up or down through the ranks.

The Corps de Ballet

Often shortened to "corps," this is the group of dancers who work together as a group with synchronized movements. These are the lowest ranking members of a professional ballet company.

Archivist

The archivist in a dance company is responsible for acquiring, organizing, and preserving documents, photographs, and videos to maintain a complete record of the company's history.

Music

Music Director

The music director mirrors the responsibilities of an AD, directing all musical components of a company. They choose arrangements and orchestrations, hire musical staff, and coordinate with choreographers.

Company Pianists

Sometimes called rehearsal pianists, they are staff members that play for all rehearsals, both in the rehearsal studio and on stage. These pianists are occasionally, though not always, performance pianists too. It is preferable for dance to rehearse to live music, so whenever it is possible a company pianist is used. Notable exceptions include recorded performance music, sound effects or soundscapes, and cases where the music will sound too different on piano for dancers to follow.

Music Librarian

They are responsible for licensing music and compiling and distributing sheet music parts for each musician. If you want to call a ballet from the score, the music librarian will give you that music.

Therapy, Massage, and Conditioning

Physical therapy, massage, and conditioning via pilates and cross-training are important tools to maintaining a dancer's body, so these staff positions are vital to the success of any professional or academic dance company.

Education

Education departments at a dance company are often very large and include their own leadership, administrators, teachers, pianists, parent volunteer coordinators, and community education. Dance schools are essential to the training of future dancers and are essential in any company.

Safety

Be aware that dancers regularly experience injuries that vary greatly in severity and consequences. Since most dance companies employ physical therapists, they will most often be the one to treat a dancer if first aid needs to be administered. In the event that the therapist is not on-site, this responsibility falls to stage management.

A specific place that dance stage managers need the quality of compassion is around injuries. While it is undoubtedly important to be swift and direct when managing a crisis, it is imperative to keep in mind that an injury can be completely devastating to a dancer. A sprained ankle may mean up to three months of restricted movement, after which it could take another couple months to get back into performance shape. With their short careers and perfectionist natures, injuries are just as emotionally challenging as physically. Keep this in mind when administering first aid, know that often holding a hand or wiping tears may be all you can do while waiting for an ambulance.

Another significant change in administering first aid to a dancer is that often dancers will rally around each other in these moments. Stage Managers are trained to clear the area and maintain privacy, but the reality is that dancers are very well trained to care for their bodies and can often be a help. Additionally, they often best know what to say to keep another dancer calm. Use your best judgment to always best protect the injured dancer, but stay in touch with your humanity and allow them to find comfort in those crushing moments.

Pre-Production

Script (Source Material)

As you may have predicted, this is the most significant difference between working in theatre and dance. There is almost never a written text. So how do you prepare? Video. Dance is a very old art form and part of its appeal to many artists is working on pieces that have been performed and celebrated for decades. The ratio of new works to remounts varies widely between companies and dance genres.

When you are stage managing a dance production that has been produced before, archival videos and paperwork will be the best resource. All professional dance companies, and nearly all academic dance programs, record video of their performances, and most choreographers today record video of their rehearsals. Asking to see and study this video is standard in the dance industry, but it is important to follow the company's restrictions around saving and sharing these videos. Online resources for video sharing are often used to distribute links to recent run throughs or performances to study. YouTube, Vimeo, and Dropbox are often used, but keep in mind the storage limitations with Dropbox. YouTube and Vimeo will be password protected and the links may expire, so be clear with the company about those restrictions.

The First Watch – An Enjoyable Watch

Even though there is no script, the concept of an initial read/watch/listen remains true. This first interaction with the piece is to get the general feel or mood, to see what the audience will see. If possible, watch a video from a performance.

When working on a full length, it can help to read any program notes or a scene-by-scene explanation of the story before watching a video. Without text, these stories can be complicated to follow and it will help you to know the plot and characters in advance.

The Second Watch – A Structural Watch

Learning to recognize the sections of a dance can help you understand how the music and movement work together. Classical dance often has prescribed sequences that adhere to a strict structure. In contemporary or modern dance, the structure is not as strict or defined, though the work is usually still very structured. Choreographers may create 'movements' or 'sections' to delineate different parts of their piece. Take notes on the sections while watching the dance. You may identify the different sections using specific ballet terms but you can also make simple notes like group dance, man's solo, fast music, women's dance, finale, etc. These sections will help you know where you are in the piece and help clearly communicate with the artistic team about a specific section in the dance.

One classical sequence you may run across is a **pas de deux**, a dance for two people; it consists of four main parts:

- Entrée – the entrance of the two dancers. This is a short prelude of pageantry for the dancers to enter the stage, acknowledge each other, and set in place for the next part of their dance.
- Adage or Adagio – the graceful, elegant, languid part of the dance featuring a lot of partnering for the two dancers. The adagio is usually slow in movement and romantic in mood.
- Variations – after the adagio, the dancers separate and perform solos. Usually the male variation is first with the ballerina offstage. The variations usually highlight the dancers' jumping and turning skills.
- Coda – after the second variation, the dancers come back together to perform the final segment. Often movements from the adagio or variations repeat and build up to a grand musical finale.

A **pas de trois** (a dance for three people) is similar to a pas de deux with an entrée, adagio, three variations, and coda. Pas de trois usually consists of two women and one man, though there are popular pas de trois examples with two men and one woman.

A **pas de quatre** (a dance for four people) or **pas de cinq** (a dance for five people) do not follow those same structures. They most often are only one segment and do not include variations.

Classical productions may also include Corps dances which do not have a specific or singular name but are often referred to by the type of music. Examples include Waltz, Mazurka, Polonaise, Moderato, or Cortège.

> The terms **pas d'action** (dance action) and **pas d'ensemble** (ensemble dance) refer to a block of dances usually involving the **corps de ballet** that may advance the plot of a story ballet.

The Third Watch – A Technical Watch

A full length requires a more theatrical third watch. If paperwork exists relevant to the production, you have a major advantage. Likely, there will already be a calling script as well as prop and deck tracking. If preparing to call a piece, watch the performance video while following along with the calling script. This is to familiarize yourself with the cues, not to learn them, so there is no need to start and stop the video. At this point, you should start to notice the cues aligning with the structure of the work, like a light change for the corps entrance or new music for the pas de deux coda. These trends will become more predictable and familiar to you the more dance stage management you do. If preparing to be on deck for the piece, watch the performance video while following along with the prop and deck tracking. The goal is to see how accurate, readable, and thorough the paperwork is. If paperwork does not exist, start making notes about props, scenery, costume changes, and lighting changes as applicable.

A remount of a smaller work follows the same process as a full length, though most likely there will be little to no information on the deck and props. Since dance rarely uses props or scenery elements, the information recorded on those is often sparse. Make your own notes as you watch about any props, scenery, and internal costume changes (this is rare). If preparing to call the ballet, watch the performance video while following along with the calling script.

New Works

A new work often takes months or years to develop and a lot of that work happens before the stage manager joins the process. Preliminary discussions about concept and design do not usually include stage management. When stage managing a new work, there may not be video of a run through when you join the process. In that event, you should meet with the choreographer to discuss the movements. They may not have the movements complete, but they almost always have an idea of what will be created. Watching small segments can help you get a sense of the work, even if it is incomplete. If there is no video at all, it can be useful to listen to the music. If the music is not complete you simply have to wait. Preparation in this scenario moves on to discussions and meetings to evaluate the technical needs of the production. Adaptability comes into play again.

```
SMB          CINDERELLA - Scene Breakdown - 1/13/20
                        ACT I (45:30)
00:00  OVERTURE (2:05)

2:05   OPENING – VISION PAS (1:50): Cinderella Double, Cinderella, Prince

3:55   1ST FAMILY SCENE (3:30): (Cinderella Double & 2 Servants @ beginning only),
                     (2) Stepsisters, Stepmother, Father, Cinderella

7:25   BEGGARWOMAN (2:05): (2 Servants @ beginning only), Cinderella, Beggarwoman

9:30   CINDY SOLO (MEDALLION DANCE) (1:50): Cinderella, (Beggarwoman @ Fireplace)

11:20  CINDY & FATHER PAS (1:25): Cinderella, Father, (Beggarwoman @ Fireplace)

12:45  MEMORY FAMILY SCENE (2:30): Memory Mother, Memory Father, (6) Memory Kids
                     (Cinderella & Father @ Fireplace in Dark)

15:15  BALL PREPARATIONS (7:10): Cinderella, Father, Stepmother, (2) Stepsisters, (2) Servants,
                     Dress Maker, Dress Maker's Assistant, Wig Maker, Modiste,
                     Dancing Master, Harpsichordist

          15:15  BALL PREP – Fittings (1:55)

          17:10  BALL PREP – Dance Lesson (3:55) (Dancing Master & Harpsichordist Join)

          21:05  BALL PREP – Get Dressed (1:20) (Dancing Master & Harpsichordist Exit)

22:25  CINDERELLA LEFT ALONE (2:10): Cinderella (+ Fairy Godmother set Upstage in Cape)

24:35  FAIRY GODMOTHER REVEALED (1:30): Cinderella, Fairy Godmother, (6) Bugs

26:05  ATTENDANTS & SEASONS JOIN (1:40): Cinderella, Fairy Godmother, (12) Attendants,
                     (4) Seasons (6 Bugs @ End Only)

27:45  BUGS DANCE (1:05): (6) Bugs, (Cinderella & Fairy Godmother Stand DR)

28:50  SPRING VARIATION (1:05): Spring, (Cinderella & Fairy Godmother Stand DR)

29:55  SUMMER VARIATION (2:15): Summer, (Cinderella & Fairy Godmother Stand DR)

32:10  AUTUMN VARIATION (1:20): Autumn, (Cinderella & Fairy Godmother Stand DR)

33:30  WINTER VARIATION (1:45): Winter, (Cinderella & Fairy Godmother Stand DR)

35:15  FINALE (3:25): Cinderella, Fairy Godmother, (12) Attendants, (4) Seasons, (6 Bugs @ End Only)

38:40  TRANSFORMATION (3:05): Cinderella, Fairy Godmother, (12) Attendants, (4) Seasons, (6) Bugs

41:45  CLOCK CHILDREN (1:30): Cinderella, Fairy Godmother, (12) Attendants, (4) Seasons, (6) Bugs
                     (12) Clock Kids

43:15  ACT I ENDING (1:20): Fairy Godmother, (12) Attendants, (4) Seasons

44:35  ACT I BOWS (0:50): (12) Clock Kids, (6) Bugs, (6) Memory Kids

                        (Page 1 of 3)
```

Figure 15.1 Dance Scene Breakdown

Scene Breakdowns

Scene breakdowns are useful in dance, though they function differently. Use the structure notes you made on your second watch to create the breakdown. The important information is the time when the section begins, the name of the section, how long the section is, and who is in the section (Figure 15.1).

- To know the name of the section ask the choreographer how they refer to it. They may be numbered or have names inspired by movement or the music. If the choreographer does not have names for the sections, use your own.
- Knowing the length of the section will later help decide how much tech rehearsal time should be devoted to it.
- Knowing who is in the section can help decide who to call to a rehearsal as well as help the costume and wardrobe departments evaluate quick change times.

First Meeting with the Choreographer

Unlike in theatre, dance stage managers do not regularly schedule or attend studio rehearsals. This means that while the first meeting with the choreographer is an important step in the process, it may happen much later than it would in theatre.

Think of choreographers like musicians or painters. They are fine artists and, by nature of the job, stage managers quantify their work, so these relationships can easily become fraught. To avoid this, learn their language. Show them that you care about the art, not just the technique or product. Keep in mind that dancers are some of the hardest-working people in the entire performing arts industry and choreographers expect that level of training, discipline, focus, respect, and work ethic from all of their collaborators. This includes stage managers.

The timing and content of the first meeting will vary based on many factors. Stage managers often meet choreographers late in their artistic process when stress levels are rising. A good amount of grace and understanding will go a long way to having a strong, smooth relationship with a choreographer. This is a list of sample questions for that first meeting. It is not comprehensive but should serve as a good starting place:

- Discuss the concept of the piece. An in-depth discussion of what they are creating will help you to earn their respect and teach you the motivation behind the work.
- What does the choreographer expect from you? This is a good time to feel out where you will operate on the artist-technician spectrum.
- How do they prefer to be addressed?
- What is the best way to reach them and when is it acceptable to do so?
- Discuss the other collaborators, including designers, composers, technical director, etc., to understand the conversations they have already had.
- What materials do they need to work? Examples include a music stand, table and chairs, a singular chair, or a bare room. Do they want the mirror uncovered or covered? Sometimes choreographers teach with the mirror uncovered, and then at a certain point in the process, the mirror should be covered to get the dancers used to spacing themselves without it. Ask when that point is for them.
- How are they giving breaks? The industry union standard is a 5-minute break after 55-minutes of work, working no more than 3 or 3.5 hours consecutively without a meal break.
- When would they like to start using rehearsal props and do any props need to be the final performance prop?
- Are there any stage division markings needed on the floor? Typical division marks include center, quarter, and eighth marks, as shown in Figure 6.21 (p. 72).
- Who will be making the rehearsal schedule and will it be made daily or weekly?
- To whom should performance reports be distributed?
- Are there any special concerns or specific worries they have about this piece?

It is important to note that not all works will have choreographers. If a company is producing something they have never done before but the work is old, a stager will be hired. If a company is producing something they have done before, the work will be taught by a ballet master. In all of these circumstances, a meeting with this individual will help build a healthy relationship between you.

Auditions

Professional dance auditions happen without stage management present, though it is common for stage managers to organize and facilitate dance auditions in an academic setting.

While character breakdowns and sides are not necessary for dance auditions, forms and schedules are still expected. It may also be the responsibility of the stage manager to provide numbers to be worn by dancers during the audition, though sometimes those are kept in stock by the company and only need to be distributed and collected. These are often safety-pinned to the dancers, so make sure an ample supply of pins is available.

Most dance auditions happen in large groups, and sometimes dancers are dismissed as they are cut from the audition process while others stay to continue working with the choreographer. Stage managers are not often in the room for the audition. The amount of time a group is in the audition varies from 20 minutes to an hour or more.

Study Videos and Study Casting

Dancers and ballet masters learn previously performed works by studying recordings (often referred to as study videos), and in some companies, the distribution of those videos is the responsibility of stage management. If a company has performed a piece many times, check-in with the AD about which version they want to reference for this production. It may be the original or it may be the most recent. It may also be a production from another company, which requires permission and cooperation in sharing that video securely to the artists involved at this company. Sometimes the choreographer (or ballet master) will decide it is best to distribute a video filmed in the studio instead of onstage, especially if the stage lighting is dark and the movement is hard to see.

Once the correct version is decided upon, turning the raw footage of that performance or rehearsal into a shareable video may require some file conversion and editing. It is useful to be familiar with basic video editing software to be able to create these study videos. A couple of video editing software options are iMovie and Davinci Resolve. These have slight differences but are user-friendly and easy to learn with online tutorials.

Every company distributes and shares these study videos differently, so ask the production manager how to do that. All companies will have policies about not sharing the videos with the public and some companies may require encrypting, password protecting, or restricting the videos to only being watched on the premises via DVD or iPads.

Some dancers like to watch video of themselves performing a role and others want to watch a different dancer. This means that often multiple study videos of a single piece need to be prepared.

To keep these study videos separate and clearly labeled, study casting is often included in the distribution. Study casting is simply the cast list from the performance or rehearsal in the study video. If you are compiling the study videos, you will also be responsible for creating the study casting. It is best to include all feature roles in the study casting or the full company in an ensemble piece. This can better help dancers and choreographers reference different videos without confusion.

Scheduling Rehearsals

It is very uncommon for stage management to make rehearsal schedules for dance productions until onstage rehearsals begin. Who creates these schedules varies depending on the size of the company, budget, building ownership, etc. Typically, ballet masters make the daily schedules, which may include studio rehearsals, costume fittings, physical therapy, and publicity and media engagements. If there isn't a ballet master, the schedule is a collaboration between the choreographer and dancers, studio managers, wardrobe, and musicians (if they are being used in the creation of the work). In the event that stage management is responsible for scheduling studio rehearsals, follow theatrical protocol and include the individuals listed above for devising and distribution.

Prepping the Rehearsal Space

Even though stage managers are not physically in the room during studio rehearsals, it is a common expectation that they will be available for questions and assistance. Therefore, it is a typical duty of dance stage managers to prepare the rehearsal space on a regular basis.

Since dancers and ballet masters learn previously performed works by studying video, a media station with video and sound playback is needed in every rehearsal studio as well as the study videos applicable to the current pieces being rehearsed. If a dance involves a lot of scenic elements or props that are being used in the studio, daily set up and clean-up is necessary. If a mixed rep is being rehearsed in which one or more pieces involves scenery or props, a reset of the studio may need to happen every time the company switches between pieces. If a new work is being created, choreographers will likely want video recordings of their rehearsals. In this case, the stage manager will likely be responsible for ensuring a camera with charged batteries and adequate memory is set up for each rehearsal. Learning and meeting the needs of each production is a conversation that needs to happen early in the process between stage management, ballet masters, choreographers, and production management.

Tape Out

Dance companies that perform regularly in the same venue usually have the floor of their rehearsal studio permanently taped to match the stage, including the front edge of the stage, the standard wing placement, and the standard stage division marks included in Figure 6.21.

For those dance companies that do not have a home venue, it will be necessary to tape the dimensions of the stage and standard spike marks in the rehearsal studio. A common unit of stage depth is "Marley panels." Marley is the industry standard material for dance floors and the rolls come in widths between 5' and 6'. The technical director will determine how many Marley panels will fit in a performance space and then the studio will be marked to reflect that decision.

In addition to the stage dimensions and standard spike marks, all scenery elements will need to be taped out on the floor. Since companies are almost always rehearsing more than one piece, it is useful to color-code each piece so the choreographers, ballet masters, and dancers know which spike marks apply in any rehearsal.

> In the United States, Marley panels are typically run SL to SR. In Europe, Marley panels are often run US to DS. This can be disorienting for touring dancers and stage managers.

Rehearsal Props/Furniture/Costumes

Depending on the staff size of a dance company, rehearsal props and furniture may be handled by the carpenters and prop department. In this case, stage management needs to provide a list of rehearsal props and furniture needed and then check them in when they arrive at the theatre. If those departments do not exist within a company or are not engaged on a contract before rehearsals begin, rehearsal props and furniture will be the responsibility of stage management.

Rehearsal costume pieces are commonly needed in dance as they greatly affect movement. Performance shoes are expected at the first rehearsal, which should be coordinated between the costume designer, choreographer, and dancers. Other pieces may be added to rehearsals in subsequent weeks, so check in with the choreographer or ballet master regularly to see when pieces will be needed. It is common for the wardrobe or costume department to provide items like classical and romantic tutus, capes, hilts, hats, and the Mother Ginger rig (during *The Nutcracker*). Knee pads may be distributed by wardrobe or stage management, so make sure to ask this in advance if there is a lot of floor work in a piece. Union rules may require that even in rehearsal, a wardrobe union member dress the dancers in costume pieces instead of stage management, so check with your director of costumes before rehearsals begin.

> The easiest way to store and protect these rehearsal pieces is to keep a costume rack in the studio tucked out of the way with a list of pieces attached to the rack. Costumes pieces are expensive and custom-fit to each dancer, so consider them irreplaceable and take checking them in and out daily seriously.

Sound Systems

Sound systems are an important part of every studio since music and dance are tightly interconnected. Nearly all dance companies share their studios with other companies and/ or dance schools, so many different people with varying understandings of sound technology will use these sound systems every day. An important part of a stage manager's pre-production training should include learning about the studio sound systems. Each day when you set up the room, ensure that the system is in good working order and ready for the choreographer to use.

Basic Tools and Supplies

In addition to the basic tools and supplies needed in theatrical stage management, you will need two stopwatches. Stopwatches are a key component of dance stage management and often you will have two running at the same time, so make sure you are familiar with them and that the batteries are not dead. It can be helpful to disable any noise-making features. Depending on the type of production, you may also want to stock a loud mini speaker (could be bluetooth) in case you have to play sound for rehearsal in an unconventional setting.

Stage Management Kit

While dance stage managers do not attend studio rehearsals, stage management kits are still essential when you're in the venue. The contents are very similar to theatrical kits, with a few notable exceptions:

- Pens, pencils, highlighters, and notepads are only used by choreographers and ballet masters; so significantly less are needed.
- Dental floss and clear tape are sometimes used on pointe shoe ribbons, so stock more than you would expect.
- Acetone-based nail polish remover is the best way to release the super sticky glue dancers use on their pointe shoes. Keep a good supply of this in your kit to help with unwanted residue.
- A large supply of tissues.

Dancers use tissue to remove glistening sweat from their faces, necks, and arms while offstage, so it is standard to attach a box of tissues to the offstage booms in several places. The best practice is to also attach a trash can below each box of tissues, so they are easily disposed of and not thrown on the floor.

Paperwork and Promptbook

A lot of this paperwork should look familiar, but we have included it here so that you won't have to reference back and forth if you are compiling information for a dance project. You should take special note of the calling script section since this is one of the major differences between theatre/opera and dance and one of the most difficult undertakings in dance stage management.

Paperwork Checklist

- Contact Sheets – staff, artistic team, dancers, orchestra, and stage crew
- Dancer Cheat Sheet (usually created by stage management, this is a document with the headshot, name, and rank of every dancer in the company)
- Emergency Contact Forms (in professional companies, these may be compiled and kept by company management, human resources, or department managers)
- Emergency Procedures
- Company Handbook
- Applicable Union Agreements (AGMA, AFM, IATSE, and SDC are the applicable unions)
- Production Calendar
- Daily Rehearsal Schedules
- Run Orders (usually this comes from the production manager or artistic director; Figure 15.2)
- Prop and Deck Tracking
- Line Schedule and Rail Sheet (the list of what is on each line set and the run paperwork outlining each fly [AKA Rail] cue)
- Lighting Cue Sheet and Plot
- Sound Cue Sheet
- Scene Breakdown
- Performance Reports
- Production Meeting Agendas and Notes
- All archived paperwork from previous productions

The Promptbook

Across all art forms, stage managers must be organized and prepared. Though the term promptbook is not often used in dance, dance stage managers do compile and carry pertinent production information. If using a view binder, ½″ for a mixed rep or 1″ for a full length should be a good size, though dance stage managers regularly use manila folders or expandable files instead.

Prepping the Calling Script

In addition to the aforementioned paperwork, the "promptbook" should also include the calling script. In the absence of both a score and a pre-existing script, it will be up to you to create a roadmap of each piece to help guide you through tech and eventually the run of the production. There are myriad ways to document movement from written descriptions to stick figures to more archaic foot pattern notations or formalized style notations.

SMB
STAGE MANAGEMENT BASICS

REP 1 – JEWELS

Running Times (approximate) - Total Evening (Opening Night Only): 2 hours 0 minutes
Running Times (approximate) - Total Evening (Rest of Run): 2 hours 10 minutes

6:30pm Performance (Opening Night Only)		
EMERALDS (Fauré)	6:35pm - 7:09pm	34:00 min
Pause/Speech	*7:09pm - 7:14pm*	*5:00 min*
RUBIES (Stravinsky)	7:14pm - 7:35pm	21:00 min
Intermission	*7:35pm - 8:00pm*	*25:00 min*
DIAMONDS (Tchaikovsky)	8:00pm - 8:35pm	35:00 min

2:00pm Performance		
RUBIES (Stravinsky)	2:00pm - 2:21pm	21:00 min
Intermission	*2:21pm - 2:41pm*	*20:00 min*
DIAMONDS (Tchaikovsky)	2:41pm - 3:16pm	35:00 min
Intermission	*3:16pm - 3:36pm*	*20:00 min*
EMERALDS (Fauré)	3:36pm - 4:10pm	34:00 min

7:30pm Performance		
DIAMONDS (Tchaikovsky)	7:30pm - 8:05pm	35:00 min
Intermission	*8:05pm - 8:25pm*	*20:00 min*
RUBIES (Stravinsky)	8:25pm - 8:46pm	21:00 min
Intermission	*8:46pm - 9:06pm*	*20:00 min*
EMERALDS (Fauré)	9:06pm - 9:40pm	34:00 min

SM: L. Andrews   *2/24/18*   *1 of 1*

Figure 15.2 Dance Run Order

However you choose to work, watch the videos and rehearsal (as allowed), listen to the choreographers, and use your notes about the sections or movements from your previous watches to create a "script" of sorts that will help you follow what is happening on stage and know what is coming up. If the pieces are using pre-recorded music, you may be able to work almost exclusively off timestamps, at which point your stopwatch becomes your best friend.

Making each piece a self-contained document can be very helpful. You may not tech the pieces in order and, depending on the needs of the company, they may not always be performed in the same order, so having the flexibility to rearrange the "script" as needed can be useful (Figure 15.3).

Meetings

Production Meetings

The occurrence of production meetings varies greatly in dance depending on the scale of the production elements. In a mixed rep that does not have any quick changes or scenic elements other than soft goods (legs, borders, and backdrops), there may be only one or two production meetings during the entire process. A full-length ballet or new work with

Upon Awakening (Barragan) ~11 min 30 sec

Electrics	Scenic/Props/Costumes	Company
No Gel Changes LQ#s: 400s	Curtain Closed Red Silks Rigged Traveler OUT Skrim IN Legs OUT Haze (as soon as curtain is closed from previous)	16 Dancers -Preset onstage in semicircle

Time	Movement/Action	Cue
Standby LX 400-402, SD 22, & Curtain Open		
Stop Timer	Scene Shift Complete-Dancers at Places	**LX 400 GO**
	Curtain Warmers Out	**LX 401 GO**
Start Timer	Curtain Open	**Curtain GO**
	Curtain at 1/4	**SD 22 GO**
	Once Curtain Open; Dancers Preset onstage in Semi-Circle	**LX 402 GO**
0:15	Arms raised to sides; duo backs into semi-circle	
	Arms raised above heads	
	Duo meets CS	
Standby LX 403 & 404		
	All face in	
0:48	Semi-circle breaks in half; form two lines SL & SR	**LX 403 GO**
1:12	Lines space out; move towards CS	**LX 404 GO & Haze OFF**
	Lines completely break apart (leaps); Duo on floor CS	
Standby LX 405		
	Duo walks UC (then off)	
1:31	Second duo moves CS	**LX 405 GO**
2:00	Leaps toward DR then US and off	
	Dancers enter SL & SR (Enter one at a time)	
Standby LX 407 & 407.5 & Silk		
2:25	3-4 onstage; back-roll into airsplits (TRUMPET!)	**LX 407 GO (anticipate!)**
2:30	Second Trio enters DL (others Ex); Crazy arms	

11/6/11   1 of 4

Figure 15.3 Sample of a Dance Calling Page

projections, scenery, special effects, and sound effects may need weekly meetings. Again, flexibility and adaptability are essential qualities in a dance stage manager.

Running a Meeting

There are a couple of things about the culture of dance that should be kept in mind during production meetings. The work happens very late. Choreographers are big dreamers with great imaginations. They like to propose many ideas to their collaborators and these ideas tend to change. Until they begin making the piece with the dancers and seeing the work come to life, choreographers may have a hard time envisioning the physical world of their dance. This may mean that all production elements will continue to change until the week or two before performances. If everyone knows this at the beginning of the process, it is not too difficult to manage. Remain adaptable and do not pressure anyone in the process to commit to a final product until it is truly necessary. You will learn to find this line with practice and experience.

Since everything will be changing constantly and rapidly, do not rush to say no. Production meetings should be a productive, creative time for the design team and choreographers. As they propose ideas, allow them to dream big even if you know it is not possible in this venue or on this timeline. They will usually come to this conclusion themselves or find a compromise when reminded of those constraints by the technical director or a shop head. However, it is always the responsibility of stage management to keep safety in mind, so near the end of a conversation you should point out any safety concerns.

Rehearsals

Dance productions can vary just as much as theatrical productions. Rehearsal periods can be as little as 2 or 3 weeks if the company is familiar with the material or as long as 8–12 weeks if a new work is being made or rehearsal hours are limited. Academic dance usually falls in the latter category.

Class

Dance companies offer class to their dancers before every rehearsal and performance. This is an instructor-led period to prepare the dancers' bodies for their work. Class typically lasts 60–90 minutes and takes place in the rehearsal studio before a rehearsal or on stage before a performance. Dancers prefer class to be consecutive to their rehearsal or performance with only a short break between so their bodies stay warm. Class begins with barre and then moves to center, where the floor is completely open and the dancers move across the floor. Dancers set up and strike the barres themselves. Class is almost never mandatory and stage managers are never in attendance. However, class can be a good time for a stage manager to make an announcement to the entire company. You may miss a few folks, so a follow-up email is necessary; but gathering all the dancers in a production in one place is difficult to do, so class is a good time for that.

The scheduling of class can make studio preparations tricky. Scenery, props, costume pieces, and choreographer requests cannot be set out before class as they will be in the way. This means the small break between class and rehearsal is when all studio prep needs to occur. Arrive early and have a plan, so set up can happen swiftly after class.

Music in the Studio

In ballet, it is usually preferred to rehearse with a live pianist. However, occasionally a piano cannot replicate the orchestra appropriately or in a way that is useful to the dancers, so recorded sound is used. In contemporary or modern dance, a variety of music may be used in rehearsal. If the performance will be using recorded sound, then the recorded sound will be used in rehearsal, too. Sometimes a combination of live piano and recorded sound is useful. Sometimes a drummer, violinist, guitarist, or string quartet will play in rehearsal. Know in advance what will work best and make accommodations in the rehearsal studio for whatever musician(s) will be present.

Running Rehearsal

Since stage managers do not attend studio rehearsals, keeping time and administering breaks falls to the choreographers and ballet masters. Some companies have closed rehearsals which do not allow guests, including stage management, to attend without permission.

Run Throughs

In a lot of cases, run throughs are the only time when stage managers are present in studio rehearsals. Remember to ask the choreographer's permission before attending a run through, as they may be trying something like a new order or piece of music that they do not think it will be helpful for you to see yet. Studio run throughs are the best time to practice calling or running the deck with a live company of dancers before being on stage. Keep in mind that you will be the only crew in the room, so you may be asked to run sound, hand off props/costume pieces, or move scenery. Be prepared by having all paperwork complete and readable before you come into the rehearsal studio and bring a pencil to make corrections and changes to the paperwork in real time. It can also help to bring sticky notes or flags to easily mark any places in the piece where you got lost or need further practice outside of the studio.

Attending run throughs, even if they are only running one complete section, helps stage managers become familiar with the piece. You learn the pacing and build up endurance alongside the dancers. Practicing to a video can only prepare you to a point. Often the music will sound different when played by a piano or it can be harder to see a particular movement without stage lighting. These things can trip you up in an onstage rehearsal, so practice in the studio until you feel comfortable and prepared.

When watching a run through, it is advisable to watch from the audience's perspective the first time, so you can see the work the same way you saw it in the video. After that, if possible, watch from where you will be calling or running the deck. It will help the transition to the stage if you have seen the piece from that perspective before. Always ask the choreographer if your preferred location will be in the way to ensure they are comfortable.

If a lighting designer or composer is attending a studio rehearsal, stage management may also be requested to attend. This can be a very useful time when developing a new work to become familiar with the piece alongside those who are building it. Sitting with them in a studio rehearsal will also help build rapport before technical rehearsals begin.

Video Recording

Video recording is a major component of the creation of new works. Since there is no official written language for dance to describe each gesture or expression, the best way to document it is with video. Rehearsal video is especially useful for documenting because you can hear the choreographer's original instructions and corrections to a dancer. Recording video is often the stage manager's responsibility, so even though you may not be in the entire rehearsal it will be necessary to set up the camera and start and stop recording. The processing and organizing of all this video footage sometimes falls to stage management, but may also be the video or archival department. The important thing to know is how quickly the video needs to be ready to be viewed by the choreographer. Some want it that night to review before the next day. Some like to review a whole week of work over the weekend. Some want it after opening so they can teach the piece to another company. Ask that question early, so you can be prepared for what the daily needs will be.

After Rehearsal

There is no daily reporting of what happens in a dance rehearsal since stage managers are not in the room. This means, all production elements and decisions made in rehearsal are not being shared outside the rehearsal studio. Therefore, it is absolutely essential that stage managers regularly check in with choreographers and ballet masters to ensure that everyone is up-to-date and on the same page. This takes practice. It may be difficult in the beginning to remind choreographers to meet with you after each rehearsal or before the next day begins. They may have a hard time remembering any production questions that arose during rehearsal. With practice, both parties can become accustomed to working without daily reports in a manner that is efficient and productive.

One way to ensure production notes are getting to stage management is to ask specific questions when checking in with a choreographer. Below are a few examples of such questions. Take notes on these conversations so you can follow-up with the creative team appropriately:

- Is the music working out during rehearsal? This will prompt them to think about any music changes that are being made such as cuts, new pieces, or a new order.
- How do you feel about the props/scenery/costumes in rehearsal? This will allow them to remark on any changes that need to be made for safety or aesthetics. Often these notes will go directly to the department involved and skip stage management, so check-ins ensure that you are always informed.

- Does the tape on the floor make sense? This will prompt them to think about the distance between objects or the size of objects. Maybe they have not noticed dancers moving beyond the limits of the tape and now they will see that and make an adjustment.
- What are you planning for the rest of the week? It is helpful to know if a choreographer is working toward a run through or is finishing a section of the piece that they may not return to for a while. This question may also remind them that their next section needs something they do not yet have in the studio.
- Is there anything else you need in rehearsal? This reminds them to communicate with you regularly and that you are there to serve the production. The answer may be something as small as a notepad, but it could be that they want to change where the entrances are onstage.

Cleanup

Since most companies are not the sole users of the rehearsal studio, it is common for another company or school to use a rehearsal studio immediately following the end of rehearsal. This means that all cleanup and resetting of the room must happen expeditiously to keep the studio schedules running on time. This does not excuse errors in checking in props and costume pieces as they could be scattered across the studio or accidentally taken into a locker room after rehearsal. Be thorough but quick.

Tech Rehearsal

In many ways, tech for dance is the same as tech for theatre. The stage manager is in charge of these rehearsals and facilitates the collaboration between the choreographer(s) and the designers. These rehearsals may also be boring for the dancers.

While much of the rehearsal will be focused on the cued design elements, it is also necessary to "dry tech" scene changes before trying to run them in time to ensure safety and to set traffic patterns.

The time constraints of tech can be challenging for choreographers who have been working at their own pace for an extended amount of time. The amount of information that has been provided to the designer prior to tech will greatly impact the tech process. If they have seen full runs of pieces (either live or via video) or recordings of previous productions (if the performance is a rental or remount), they may have cues already created that just need to be tweaked. If videos have been incomplete or unclear, they may be starting from scratch. Sometimes the choreographer may have very specific thoughts or ideas about what they want the lighting to look like and other times they will have no preconceived notions and will rely on the designer to provide looks and options. If you can ascertain how the choreographers and designer work in advance, it will ease this process, though that may not always be possible.

Clear communication with the designers is critical in dance for a number of reasons. For mixed rep shows, it isn't unusual for dances to be teched out of order. As such, each piece may be assigned its own chunk of numbers for cues (piece #1 may be cue numbers that fall between 1 and 99 while piece 2 will be cue numbers between 100 and 199, etc.), or they may be set up as separate cue lists in the console. If you are working out of order, you will need to make sure that the appropriate cue numbers are being recorded. Another consideration is that it is significantly harder to stop and start to adjust cueing (it is difficult to find a reasonable place for the dancers to pick up and communicate that place to them). Additionally, depending on the length and intensity of the pieces, it may not be practical for the dancers to run pieces more than once or twice due to endurance/fatigue/safety. You also don't want the dancers standing idle for too long because their muscles need to stay warm so they can perform safely. For longer, story-based works, tech may be more like a theatrical production, though stopping and starting/repetitions may still be challenging.

Tech will also be the time that the ASM joins the production. Their tasks are basically the same as in theatre. They set up the space, manage the crew, and run the deck (this can be a HUGE job in ballet). Some of the key tasks include cleaning the floor (we do this in theatre but the need is amplified in dance), checking boom heights (making sure that the lights haven't been knocked out of place), and setting leg trim (particularly in mixed rep, the curtain legs may move on and off stage depending on the piece). An additional run responsibility that doesn't often come up in theatre is changing the gels in the boom lights between pieces; a separate gel tracking sheet may need to be created to ensure that the lights are always as they are intended to be. One of the major differences for a dance ASM is that they are responsible for using the sign-in sheet to check the dancers in and confirm their role assignments (as this may change on a performance by performance basis).

SIGN-IN SHEET

Sign-in sheets have a particular weight in dance because the casting for each piece and the order of pieces can change with each performance, and that information is indicated on the sign-in sheet. It is essential to double-check with artistic staff and wardrobe before posting.

Dress Rehearsal

Costumes are often introduced earlier in the process to allow the dancers to become accustomed to them. Therefore, dress rehearsals are less focused on the addition of costumes and more about endurance, timing, and music. Dress rehearsals should be run like performances. The crew will come in to prepare the space and then the company will have their class to get warmed up. Afterward, the dancers will get into costume and makeup while the crew finishes the preset. Once everyone is ready, the show should be run in as close to performance conditions as possible, holding only if absolutely necessary. In both mixed rep and full-length pieces, it will be important to address any quick costume changes before getting to them in real time.

Dress rehearsal is often the first time the dancers get to hear the music performed by the orchestra and it may be the only time before performances. In the event that there are multiple casts, each cast may want to try sections that sound very different from the piano-only version.

TIME CALLS

In addition to the typical pre-show calls of half hour, 15 minutes, 5 minutes, and places, a "Stage is Yours" announcement is often made to the dancers after the pre-show checks are completed. Dancers need to keep moving to stay warm and they often like to practice certain sections with their partners or around scenic elements before the performance begins. To ensure that can happen safely, dancers are asked not to use the stage until the crew has completed their presets and stage management has checked them. Once checked, crew and stage management should avoid the stage space so that dancers can prepare.

Performances and Beyond

Unlike in theatre, after opening, the dancers' daily schedule remains the same. They will continue to take class, rehearse, and perform every day. Performance periods are often short (2 weeks or less), but notable exceptions include touring, repertory seasons, and *The Nutcracker*. Touring dance productions can be on the road for months, though it is common to have week-long breaks on tour for bodies to rest. Repertory seasons may run for 4 weeks, alternating two different productions during that time. Almost every ballet company of every size in the United States runs *The Nutcracker* in November and/or December. Productions of *The Nutcracker* run anywhere from 1 to 100 performances.

Opening Night

Opening nights are a huge deal in dance, no matter the production. If a new work is being premiered, it is often the accumulation of years of collaboration and preparation, so a large celebration is expected. If there are multiple dancers cast in each role, every time a new lead dancer or new cast performs, the backstage energy is as if it is opening night.

Bows

The curtain call for dance varies greatly depending on the style of the production. For a full-length production, the company will bow at the very end of the performance. The bows follow the hierarchy of the company with the apprentices and the corps bowing first, then the coryphée (junior soloists), soloists and character dancers, and finally the principals. Commonly, once the last dance is completed, the main curtain flies in and the corps assembles upstage, then the curtain flies out and the corps cross downstage and bow.

After their bow, they move upstage and either the curtain comes in and then back out for the next group or the next group comes in from the wings. Soloists and principals take individual bows (sometimes called run-ons, because the dancers run-on from the wings). There may also be a full group bow. In a mixed rep there will likely be a set of bows after each piece, but they will run similarly with the curtain flying in and out. The stage manager determines how many encore bows are taken based on the audience applause. In ballet, you should be aware that it is traditional for the prima ballerina to receive a bouquet of flowers during the principal encore bow. It is typically delivered by a stagehand or the conductor and then the ballerina takes a flower from the bouquet and gives it to the leading man. On opening night, choreographers, composers, and designers are also brought onstage for bows.

Maintaining the Production

Just like in theatre, the stage manager is responsible for maintaining the artistic integrity of the various design elements. Contrastingly, in dance, the stage manager doesn't give maintenance notes to the dancers unless something they are doing interferes with technical elements (e.g., exiting in the wing where a large scenery piece is waiting to enter or being out of the light).

Archiving

Archiving all of the information about a dance production is even more important than archiving for theatre. Choreographic work is reproduced verbatim far more often than theatrical productions (the notable corollary may be theatre companies that produce the same version of *A Christmas Carol* each year). It is your responsibility to make sure that all of the paperwork is up-to-date and accurate. You may also be responsible for video archiving.

> Just like in theatre and opera, dancers are superstitious. Instead of good luck most dancers say "merde". Merde is the French word for shit, and the use of the phrase dates back to 19th-century Paris when people arrived at the dance venue via horse-drawn carriage; the more carriages the larger the audience, and thus merde was a wish for a good show in front of a full house.

Special thanks to Leigh'Ann Andrews for the Dance Chapter Framework.

Conclusion (Standby)

Stage management is a field that takes time and experience to really master, but the information contained in this book provides the building blocks to become a successful stage manager. A lot of becoming a good stage manager is learning to work collaboratively within any context. Learning to communicate clearly and concisely will save you many headaches down the road.

As made clear by the previous chapters, much of stage management as a job is endless logistics, precise organization, and exemplary communication. All of these things can be learned, practiced, and improved upon with each new production. Even the personality traits discussed in the first chapter exist on a sliding scale. Some creatives work best when allowed to do their own organizing, while others will need you to provide them with structure. Some performers need firm, clear instructions and tangible consequences. Other performers may need a little extra care and an open ear to listen to their frustrations. Some designers need strict deadlines and many little reminders, while others will shrink away from too much communication and will be less efficient as a consequence. Your particular traits will mesh perfectly with some teams while another stage manager may be a better fit for others.

Traits alone do not define a great stage manager. What separates a decent stage manager from a truly great one is drive and joy. Each new production should be an exciting prospect – a chance to practice and improve your skills, learn new ones, and to tackle new, unexpected challenges. If you cannot love your work, stage management is a job you may quickly come to resent and none of the stress will be worth the reward. It will be difficult at times – scheduling may seem unmanageable, transitions may seem impossible, and each hurdle you overcome may lead to three more you didn't see coming. But the joy of looking back, seeing all that the production was able to overcome, and being such a critical part of a team that puts together something beautiful and meaningful makes the whole process worthwhile.

Use the examples in this book as a jumping-off point for your own forms and templates. Check out the suggested readings on the companion website to expand your knowledge base and make you a better stage manager and theatrical artist/collaborator. Never stop learning, never stagnate or stop evolving the way you do things, and most importantly, never stop enjoying the work that you do – take pride in it, take care of yourself and have fun.

GO!

DOI: 10.4324/9781003133049-17

Glossary

Actors' Equity Association (AEA) The American union for theatrical actors and stage managers, commonly referred to as Equity or AEA.

AED Automated External Defibrillator. A portable device used to shock the heart in case of cardiac distress. Training is recommended (but not necessary) before utilizing an AED.

Apron The area of the stage floor downstage of the plaster line. In a proscenium theatre, it commonly extends over the pit and is often curved.

Architect's Scale Ruler (Scale Ruler) This tool is used to measure scale drawings in order to translate it into full scale measurements. The stage manager will primarily use this for taping out the set for rehearsals. These differ from an Engineer's scale ruler, so be careful when purchasing.

Arena A theatre in which the audience surrounds the entire stage. There is no "upstage" and "downstage" but rather the action takes place in 360 degrees to cater to the whole audience. Also commonly referred to as "theatre in the round".

Audition Form The form that prospective cast members fill out prior to an audition. It typically includes information such as contact information, physical traits (height, hair color, age range), performance traits (vocal range, special skills), and scheduling conflicts.

Aural Related to the sense of hearing.

Batten Long pipes hung above the stage, used to hang scenery, curtains, and lighting instruments. These can be dead hung (permanently hung at a specific height) or rigged to fly meaning they can be brought in and out via the fly rail or automation computer (if the theatre uses electric winches).

Blackbox A typically square or rectangular room usually painted completely black created to be a "flexible" space (designed to be set in any of the different types of stage configurations).

Blocking/Staging The movement or path of the performers throughout the production. This term is used both as a definition of the type of rehearsal in which the director and the performers discover the movement of the production (a blocking or staging rehearsal) and as a definition of the movement itself (blocking notes or the blocking).

Blocking Key A list indicating the shorthand that will be used in your blocking notation.

Blocking Sheet/Slip Sheet The pages on which blocking for a show is recorded. These are usually printed on the back of each script page or on a separate sheet that "slips" between the script pages (hence "slip sheet").

Boom A vertical pipe mounted on a base plate used for side light fixtures.

Booth This is the room or place in the theatre, where the light board and sometimes the sound board are located. Typically, this is found at the back of the house, often above the audience.

Brush-up Rehearsal/Pick-up Rehearsal A rehearsal that is scheduled to let the cast refresh the material if there are several days between performances. At times these may also be scheduled if performances have gone especially badly and the stage manager feels that the performers/crew may need a "brush-up" on what they are supposed to be doing.

CAD Computer-Aided Design. Programs such as Vectorworks and AutoCAD are commonly used by set designers and lighting designers to draft their designs digitally.

Callboard The callboard is where the company goes for important information regarding the production. It is often a bulletin board and is placed in a centralized location easily accessible in the theatre. Online callboards are steadily increasing in use, although usually in addition to a physical callboard.

Calling Out This is the term used when a performer or crew member has a planned scheduling conflict or is unable to do a performance, usually due to injury, illness, or an emergency. When someone calls out of a show, the production must make adjustments to cover that person's absence, usually by having an understudy, swing, or sub step into the role.

Calls Refers to a specific time or chunk of time that a performer, crew, or other production team member is expected to arrive and be present at a rehearsal or performance.

Caster Wheels used to allow for the movement of scenic pieces on and off stage. Casters can either be swivel ("smart") meaning they are free to swivel in any direction or fixed ("dumb") meaning they can only roll along a fixed line depending on the direction they are mounted.

Catches When a crew member or performer stands ready backstage to grab a prop or costume piece from a performer with a quick transition who doesn't have time to return it themselves.

Catwalk (Cat) The area above the audience that provides additional lighting positions. Depending on the theatre, spot lights may also be located and run from the catwalks.

Center Line The imaginary line that runs vertically upstage to downstage along the center of the stage, splitting the stage in equal halves. Commonly used by stage managers as the y-coordinate in conjunction with the Plaster Line to help with accuracy in tape-out, as well as for marking dance numbers and quarters. This line is commonly marked on groundplans with a CL.

Character Breakdown Character breakdowns provide basic information regarding the characters in the show: name, relationship to other characters in the play, age, brief description. Typically distributed or provided during the audition process.

Cold Reading When a performer is asked to present a piece of text that they have not prepared before the audition. They may be given a few minutes to review or may be asked to read it on the spot. This is especially common during callbacks.

Collective Bargaining When an organized group negotiates for wages and other conditions of employment.

Company Manager A position common in many theatres and especially on tours. This person is responsible for managing the company as a whole and is often responsible for maintaining the physical and mental well-being of the company. This position includes handling logistics such as housing/accommodations, food, coordinating travel, etc.

Concept Meeting Meetings for which the focus is to discuss the artistic vision of the production. This is the time during which the director presents their concept and the designers discuss ideas for their various design elements to help achieve that concept. These tend to be more brainstorming sessions rather than a time for final decisions and logistics.

Console (Board) The shortened term for the light and sound control consoles or "boards". The "console ops" operate these under the direction of the stage manager.

Corps de ballet The group of dancers who work together as a group with synchronized movements. Also the lowest ranking members of a professional ballet company.

Costume Plot A piece of paperwork that tracks each performer's costume pieces throughout a show. It notes when costume changes occur and outlines what each character is wearing at each moment. This can be used to help identify moments when complicated or quick-changes will be happening and if additional crew members will be needed to assist.

Costume Shop The space in which costumes are created and/or altered. This is often where fittings take place.

Croisé Dancer on diagonal, legs crossed to audience.

Crossover Paths that performers can take backstage to get from one side of the stage to the other without being seen by the audience. This can be a hallway just outside of the theatre, a space behind a curtain upstage or even outside the building.

Cue (1) Something that signals a performer or crew member to begin or enter. (2) A lighting look, sound effect, video, etc. that the stage manager calls for an operator to actuate.

Cue Light A light mounted offstage that serves as a visual cue. It is controlled by the stage manager at their station and can be used to cue anyone from stage crew to performers to fly crew to the conductor. These are especially common when a vocal cue is not possible (lack of headsets or backstage communication) or on productions with a large number of simultaneous or quick sequence cues. Typically, the light is turned on to indicate a standby and switched off to indicate a GO for the cue.

Cue-to-Cue (Q2Q) A technical rehearsal in which the show is worked through in order skipping from cue to cue.

Cueing (1) When a stage manager or ASM indicates that a performer, crew member, or console operator should enter, begin a transition, or execute a cue. (2) The time during which designers create the cues for the show (relevant specifically for lighting, sound, and media designers). This is typically done during "dark time" or "quiet time" when all the work lights on the stage can be turned off and no one is working onstage. These levels are usually programmed for recall later during the process and show. *In a perfect world this happens and is completed before the tech process because tech is for all technical areas, not just one.

Cyclorama (Cyc) A seamless piece of fabric (usually muslin) stretched tightly and cleanly along the back edge of the stage and used for lighting and/or projection. Typically white, although light gray and blue are also common colors.

Daily Call The rehearsal or performance schedule for any individual day.

Dance 8s A way to record choreography that relates the movement to the count of the music.

Dance Call A part of the audition process for productions that involve dancing. The auditionees are taught a dance sequence and then the choreographer and/or director watch them and decide who they want to cast.

Dance Numbers A visual marking on the stage floor used in musicals and other shows with dance or choreography. Numbers are displayed at consistent increments along the downstage edge of the stage, starting with 0 at center stage and growing larger as they move offstage in both directions. This allows the choreographer to easily space the performers evenly and enables consistency in performance by giving a specific reference point of where to be on the stage.

Deck Another term for the stage. Used commonly in reference to the stage crew (aka deck crew).

Derrière To the back, away from the audience.

Devant To the front, toward the audience.

Downstage The part of the stage closest to the audience. Stages used to be raked (at an incline) and the lowest end was closest to the audience (as performers moved toward the audience they were literally moving down the incline).

Dramaturg A person who provides information about the script, time period, writer and anything else relevant to the production. They may provide a glossary if there are a lot of unusual words or find articles that give context to an aspect of the setting of the play.

Dress Rehearsal (Dress) A rehearsal that takes place after tech, in which all elements of the production are put together, including the costumes. These rehearsals are meant to simulate a performance but without an audience.

Dresser Wardrobe crew members who assist performers with getting dressed at any point before or during a show.

Dressing Room The area where the cast puts on their costumes and make-up to prepare for the performance. They often have mirrors and make-up lights.

Dry Tech A technical rehearsal in which the creative team works through the show cue by cue and (if necessary) scene shift by scene shift in the space. This gives the director a chance to look at and listen to each cue. It also allows the stage manager to become familiar with the cues and where they will be called.

Effacé Dancer on diagonal, legs open to audience

Electrics (1) Another term for ""lighting". The department that handles lighting needs. (2) Battens that hang above the stage and are designated for hanging lighting instruments. Typically are numbered from downstage to upstage (Electric 1 being most downstage). In some theatres, these are always the same, in others they are flexible and can be moved anywhere.

Elevation A term used in drafting to indicate a front, side, or rear view of scenic elements.

Emergency Information Form A confidential form outlining an individual's contact information, emergency contact, and allowing them to disclose any relevant medical information (including physical limitations/previous injuries, underlying conditions, and allergies) in case of emergencies.

En face Dancer facing the audience, hips and shoulders squared.

Endstage A theatre that has audience on one side of the stage but no proscenium arch.

Entrance/Exit Plot Very similar to a French Scene breakdown, this tracks every entrance and exit of every character throughout the show. This can be very useful for determining when performers are offstage and where they exit during the production.

Face Page (Who's Who?) A document that displays names and photos of company members as a way to help connect names to faces as people are getting acquainted. Used commonly in Opera, but is becoming more prevalent in theatre as well.

Fight Call A practice run of all choreographed fights in a production. It typically takes place 15–30 minutes (depending on the number of fights) before the house opens and is run by the stage manager and the fight captain.

Fire Curtain Only found in larger proscenium theatres, this curtain is made of a flame retardant material, it lowers typically around the plaster line. The curtain can usually be triggered manually in case of a fire, most fire curtains also have a fusible link (link that melts at a relatively low temperature) and will trigger automatically if the heat reaches a certain point. The fire curtain line (where the curtain will fall) may not be obscured by any permanent scenery or props, anything placed on the line (furniture, hinged flat/wall) must be easily movable in the event of a fire. If something will be placed in the fire curtain line a plan should be made with the crew during technical rehearsals about how to clear the fire line in the event of a fire. Fire curtain regulations vary by local legislation.

Fire Proofing Coating a scenic element, costume or prop with a fire retardant to reduce its flammability. This is especially important if the item is near open flame (Candle, lit match, etc.).

Fitting(s) The time during which a performer (or crew member, as applicable) tries on their costume to see if/how it fits. These typically take place in the costume shop. The stage manager is usually responsible for scheduling fittings, acting as communication between the performers and the wardrobe department.

Flat A piece of scenery that typically makes up a wall. Hollywood flats are hard flats covered with Lauan and Broadway flats are soft flats covered with muslin. Flats can be constructed in all shapes and sizes but typical stock sizes are 2×8, 4×8, 4×10, 4×12.

Fly Rail Area in the wings where the machinery controlling the fly system is housed and where the fly crew will run the show.

Fly Space The area above the stage used for storing hung scenery and curtains. Not all theatres have a fly space and height of the fly space varies from space to space.

Focus The time when a lighting designer points and positions the lights where they need to be focused for the show. If an electrics crew exists, this will be done by the crew with the designer indicating proper placement and location.

Foley Sound effects that are created live, rather than with pre-recorded sound effects.

French Scene Breakdown French Scenes are delineated by any entrance/exit of a performer (There may be multiple French scenes in a single book scene). This type of breakdown is also useful for plays that are not broken down into acts and scenes.

Front of House (FOH) This refers to both the area of the theatre through which the patrons are taken and the staff that manage it. This includes the box office, the lobby, the bar or concession area, etc. The personnel includes box office managers, house manager, bar staff, and ushers.

Gaffers Tape Colloquially known as gaff, this is one of the most commonly used tapes in the theatrical world. It is a fabric tape, which allows it to be ripped cleanly and easily on two planes. It comes in a variety of colors and typically doesn't leave residue. However it is a strong adhesive and can easily pull off paint or other surface finishes. Gaff tape, especially cheaper off-brands, can get very sticky in hot weather.

Gel A colored piece of polyester or polycarbonate that is placed in front of theatrical lights to color them.

Ghost Light A single bulb, typically on a stationary or rolling stand, that is left illuminated on the stage of a theatre when no one is actively using the space. Practically, it is there for safety purposes so no one trips over the set or off the stage in the dark. The name originates from the theatrical superstition that ghosts inhabit all theatres. It is said the light is left illuminated to allow the ghosts to perform, thus appeasing them and reducing the likelihood of supernatural mischief.

Glow Tape Glow tape is specialized tape coated with photo-luminescent pigments that absorb and store energy from ambient light. In a blackout, the tape glows, allowing performers to see without needing to wait for their eyes to adjust. Most commonly used for safety purposes. Glow tape only works when it has been exposed to ambient light (e.g., stage lights), so it is best for use on stage where there is consistent exposure. When used backstage with limited light exposure, the tape must be "charged" in order to glow (a flashlight works well for this).

Go The magic word in all theatrical performances, during techs, dresses and performances used by the stage manager to indicate the execution of a cue. It should never be used unless the command to "GO" is actually being given. To avoid confusion over headsets and intercoms spelling the word "G-O" is the best way to avoid prematurely moving forward.

Gobo (Template; Pattern) A lighting accessory used in theatrical lights, commonly made of either cut metal or etched glass, used to project an image or pattern.

God Mic A handheld microphone used by the stage manager and/or director during technical rehearsals and performances to communicate with the entire company without the need for shouting. Sometimes referred to as a paging mic or abbreviated to VOG, short for Voice of God.

Grand Drape (Main; Rag; Act Curtain) The main, downstage most curtain in a proscenium theatre.

Green Room A lounge area for the company. Typically located backstage of the theatre. This is a common area to house the callboard, to gather the company for announcements, and may sometimes double as an extra dressing room.

Grid (1) In smaller theatres, the structure used for hanging lighting instruments and sound equipment (often a pipe grid). (2) A metal or wood support structure of a theatre that supports a fly system.

Groundplan The birds-eye view of the set, drawn to scale. This will be provided by the scenic designer and will be used for taping out the set for rehearsals and for reference throughout the production process. It can also be scaled down and used in the blocking script.

Half Hour This refers to the 30 minutes prior to curtain time for a performance. On many professional productions, it is the time when performers are called and is often also the time when the house is opened to start seating the audience.

Hand Prop Props that are handled and moved on/off stage by the performers (e.g., cups, books, pencils). See also Personal Prop and Prop.

Handoff When a crew member or performer stands ready backstage with a prop or costume piece to be handed to a performer with a quick transition who doesn't have time to grab it themselves.

Heads A common warning called out when someone working overhead drops something. The proper response is to cover one's head with their arms and move away from the direction of the "heads" call. Do not look up and watch what is falling.

Headsets/Comm Intercom equipment utilized to communicate between stage management and departments.

Headshot Headshots are professional quality photos provided by the performers.

Hospitality This is the common term used to refer to the snacks and drinks provided by a theatre for its company members (and the area in which this fare is staged). This can be as simple as a place to brew coffee or as elaborate as a full kitchen. Stage management is often responsible for brewing coffee and providing hot water for tea, as well as general maintenance of the area.

House The term used to refer to the audience and/or the area in the theatre in which the audience is placed for a performance.

House Lights Used during pre-show, intermission, and post show to light the audience to help with seating.

Incident Report A report that's filled out in the event of an incident or injury. The blank reports are usually provided by the theatre company, but stage management is often involved in distributing and archiving forms as needed over the course of the production.

Knap A term used in fight choreography. Because violence is often staged without actual physical contact for things such as slaps, punches, etc., the sound that would normally occur when contact is made must be created artificially elsewhere. This is referred to as a knap.

Legs Vertical curtains, typically black, used at intervals on the sides of a proscenium to help mask the wings from the audience.

Libretto The combined script and vocal score used for most musicals. Plural form is Libretti.

Light Plot A graphic representation of the layout of the lighting instruments for a given production. The light plot includes information such as type of instrument, color, channel, dimmer, and other relevant information. This will be provided by the lighting designer or the head electrician.

Line (1) The words spoken by a character in the text of the play. (2) Request from a performer for a prompt when they have forgotten their words.

Line Notes Notes taken by the stage manager once performers are off-book, tracking any errors made in the text, including paraphrasing, skipped words, and inaccurate ordering of words or phrases. Some stage managers will also take note of when a performer calls for line. These notes are distributed on an individual basis after each rehearsal off-book.

Lineset A batten that moves or flies. Each lineset is identified by a number with 1 being downstage and numbers increasing as they move upstage. Linesets may also be referred to as flylines.

Load-In The day (or days) in which the technical elements of the production are brought into the theatre. This is when the set is installed, the lights are hung, the sound is set up, and the costumes, props, and furniture are moved into the theatre. Typically takes place a few days to a week before tech rehearsals begin.

Maestro The Maestro (conductor) is the most important person in the room in an opera production. Since opera is primarily music and they are responsible for the tempi (plural form of tempo) and nuance of the music as it is played, they work very closely with the stage director and often have the final say in how a piece is performed. Maestro is a proper noun when referring to a specific person.

Mark (Marking) When a performer does not use their full voice or full range of actions during a rehearsal, either due to illness/injury or in order to save their voice for an upcoming performance. Performers (especially dancers and singers) may mark when they are required to run a sequence many, many times during tech in order to prevent injuries.

Marley Marley is the industry standard material for dance floors and the rolls come in widths between 5' and 6'.

Marley Tape Translucent tape named for its original use of taping the seams of Marley floors used for dance. The most common use for stage managers is to help protect spike marks from wear and from pulling up from the floor. This tape comes in multiple different colors, for this use clear is the best option.

Model (White Model) A fully designed miniature 3D version of the set. A white model is typically one color and simply represents the shapes and functions of the set. A full production model will also include accurate textures and colors of the final set for reference.

Monitor An audio or video device that allows the performers to hear music/orchestra or sound effects or see the conductor while onstage. When off-stage, monitors are often mounted in the dressing rooms, hallways, and/or green room for everyone to follow the show and be ready for their cues. Depending on the calling location, a video and/or audio monitor will be mounted at the stage manager's podium for use in calling cues.

Music Rehearsal A rehearsal in which the music of a show is learned/reviewed. These are typically run by the music director.

Naloxone The drug used in first aid to help reverse an opioid overdose.

Not To Scale (NTS) This abbreviation is commonly found on drawings and indicates to the observer that this drawing is not in any scale. It has simply been sketched out for quick reference or design concepts. Be careful not to use NTS drawings for tape-out!

Off-book Refers to when performers are expected to have fully memorized their lines (and music, as applicable) so they no longer have their scripts in hand during rehearsal.

On Book The act of following along in a script during a rehearsal in order to prompt performers with lines and actions as needed. Usually done by stage management or a PA.

OSHA Occupational Safety and Health Administration (OSHA) is a regulating body that sets and enforces safety standards.

Page (1) To hold a door or curtain open to allow for smoother exits/entrances by performers or crew members. (2) Can also refer to the use of a paging mic or system to transmit messages to performers or backstage crew.

Paper Tech A meeting involving the stage manager, director, and relevant designers at which you talk through the script in order and take notes about cue names, placement, and intent.

Park and Bark Theatrical jargon for any moment in a show where a performer plants themselves in a single spot for a long time and delivers their lines or song without moving around a lot.

Pas d'action Dance action

Pas d'ensemble Ensemble dance

Pas de cinq A dance for five people

Pas de deux A dance for two people

Pas de quatre A dance for four people

Pas de trois A dance for three people

Patron A paying audience member.

Performance Report A report generated to note what happened during a performance. Performance reports should include a brief overview and evaluation of the performance as well as relevant notes for each department, noting broken items and absences or injuries if they occur.

Period Piece A production which takes place during a very specific time period in history. Although it could refer to any time period, this term is commonly used for pieces taking place during the romantic era and usually indicates the need for elaborate costumes and sometimes wigs.

Personal Prop Props that are kept in a performer's possession throughout the show (e.g., pocket watches, fans, canes). See also Hand Prop and Prop.

Photo Call A dedicated call used to take staged production photos, usually for use in portfolios and archives. Commonly takes place during dress rehearsals or sometime during the run of the performances and typically lasts around one hour. This call is often arranged and run by the stage manager.

Pit (1) The orchestra. (2) The area in the theatre designated for the orchestra. In proscenium theatres, this is commonly located below the apron, underneath the stage with the conductor positioned facing upstage so they can see both the orchestra and the performers. Alternatively, the orchestra may be positioned in a separate room and the sound piped in through the system.

Plaster Line In proscenium theatres, this is an imaginary horizontal line that runs the width of the stage at the proscenium arch (mimics the line of the grand curtain, whether one is present or not). In non-prosceniums, this line can be arbitrarily designated. Commonly used by stage managers as the x-coordinate in conjunction with Center Line to help with accuracy in tape-out. Commonly notated on the groundplan with a PL.

Platform A piece of scenery that is walked on and used to create an additional level on stage. Typically a wood frame with a plywood top.

Practical An audio, lighting or scenic element of the set that functions as it would in the real world- a bedside lamp that lights up, a cell phone that rings, window that opens, a radio that plays from its own speaker, an LED "Open" sign on a shop door, etc. This may be controlled by the performers on stage or the light/sound console.

Pre-show The time prior to the start of a performance. This is the time during which all performers and crew members prepare for the show, including setting props and scenic elements, getting into costume, hair, and makeup, and checking lighting and sound systems to make sure everything is running smoothly.

Prep Week The week preceding the start of rehearsals during which a stage manager prepares for the productions (including paperwork, rehearsal space prep, creating the promptbook, and any communication with the company in preparation for rehearsals). This may be longer or shorter than a week, depending on the company and the specific production.

Preset Checklist A checklist outlining the exact location of each prop, costume, and set piece as it should be set for the top of the show.

Preview Essentially a trial performance in front of an audience. These performances take place prior to opening night, allowing the cast to perform for an audience and the creative team to continue to make adjustments to the show to make the best performance possible. Typically tickets are sold for a discount and the audience is warned that it is possible the show might be stopped mid-performance for adjustment or technical difficulty, although this rarely occurs.

Principal A term used for starring or lead roles.

Production A specific company's interpretation of a script (a fully realized performance of a particular text). The performance as a whole, including all technical elements.

Production Analysis A detailed breakdown of the text that accounts for all design and technical elements mentioned in the script. This is created by the stage manager during prep week.

Production Meeting Meetings held to discuss the logistics and progress of the production. Typically they take place once a week during the rehearsal period with the whole creative team in attendance. This is the time to check in on progress of plots, set and costume building, the prop search, budgets, and to answer/clarify any questions that have arisen during rehearsals.

Promptbook The promptbook, sometimes called the "The Book" or "Show Bible" is a binder containing any and all important information pertaining to the show as well as the script. This book is created and maintained by the stage manager.

Prompting The act of feeding a line or action to a performer in the event that they have forgotten what comes next.

Prop (Property) Any item that cannot be classified as scenery, electrics or wardrobe falls under this category. Furniture is considered a prop in most theatres, although there are some exceptions. See also Hand Prop and Personal Prop.

Prop Table A table (or other flat surface) designated to hold props. It usually falls to the ASM to organize and maintain these tables throughout rehearsal and performances.

Proscenium This type of theatrical stage is easily identifiable by the proscenium arch that frames the opening of the stage and the audience seated on only one side of the stage. These theatres typically have wing space and fly space, which allow for large productions with elaborate sets.

Proscenium Arch Refers to the architectural archway framing the opening of the stage in a proscenium theatre.

Put-In Rehearsal This type of rehearsal is scheduled to allow a new cast/crew member to run through the show prior to having an audience. These are common if a last minute change in crew or casting occurs (injury, sickness, family emergency)

Quarters Another type of visual marking for a stage, similar to Dance Numbers, used to help dancers place themselves accurately for choreography. For this, the stage is broken up into equal quarter sections, with center stage marked and then halfway offstage on either side. Some choreographers may request 1/8th marks as well for more accuracy.

Quick Change A costume change that must take place in a constricted amount of time. These commonly take place in the wings or behind the set, rather than in the dressing rooms, and often require an extra person or two to assist.

Raked Stage A stage built on an incline. Rakes with the area of the stage closest to the audience being the lowest and gradually rising as it moves to the back of the stage were common long ago when the audience were all seated or standing on the same level, so the raked stage allowed for more people to see the action. Raked stages can be a safety hazard and often have regulations on their allowed incline.

Read Through (Table Read) The action of reading through the full script as an ensemble (each performer reading their individual role and someone reading the stage directions) while seated. This usually takes place in the first week of rehearsal and allows the group to hear the script out loud before jumping into rehearsals.

Rehearsal Prop A stand-in prop of similar size, shape, and weight of the final prop that is used during rehearsals. The stage manager is often in charge of finding and keeping track of the rehearsal props.

Rehearsal Report A report generated to note what happened during rehearsal as well as any questions or changes there may be. It should be comprehensive in the information it includes and be distributed to the production and design teams immediately following every rehearsal.

Rendering A digital or physical drawing depicting design elements.

Run Light (Clip Light) Colored light bulbs or dark gelled lights (traditionally blue) used to help ease navigation and provide illumination at necessary points backstage in the dark during performances.

Run Sheet Serves as the backstage "task" list during the run of the show. It outlines every action that happens backstage to make the show happen (transitions/scene changes, costume quick-changes, prop handoffs or catches, curtain pages, etc.).

Run Through A rehearsal in which large sections or the full show are run with minimal or no stops. The intent is to build continuity and allow the cast and director to get a feel for the show as a whole.

Running Order A simple list of all the scenes in order. Helpful for posting backstage or around the rehearsal room for people to keep track of the flow of the show.

Scale A term used in drafting to indicate the size of a drawing or model in relation to the real size. Common scales are 1/4" and 1/2" in US Standard, 1:5, 1:10, and 1:20 in Metric.

Scene Breakdown A piece of paperwork created by the stage manager that gives a quick reference of each scene in a script. It details such information as Act/scene, page numbers, characters in the scene, location of the scene, and a brief description of the action for easy identification.

Score The sheet music for a musical. The conductor's score is the most complete and will include all music in the production. Many rented scripts will provide chorus-vocal books per character that include only the musical numbers that that character sings.

Script The text of a play or musical, including the dialogue and stage directions.

Set (1) The scenic elements that create the physical world in which the production takes place. It may be one single unit that stays the same throughout the production or be made up of many different pieces that move, change, and transform throughout the show. (2) A term meaning to place an item or items on stage in a predetermined location.

Set Dressing Prop items that are used for the purpose of decorating the set and lending to the design, rather than for practical use by the performers (e.g., mirrors, lamps, picture frames, window dressing, rugs).

Sides Selected scenes or portions of scenes from a play to be used as audition material. Usually only involve a few characters and are only a few pages long.

Sign-in Sheet A sheet for performers (and crew, when applicable) to sign-in upon arrival to the rehearsal or performance space. This allows the SM to track attendance and easily identify when individuals are not present.

Sing Through A rehearsal in which all of the music of the show is sung-through by the performers. This usually takes place during the first week of rehearsal, after the music has been taught, and is typically accompanied by the pianist or by rehearsal tracks. This may be in combination with the reading of the script (a read-sing through) or just the music, skipping from song to song.

Site-Specific A performance that takes place at a non-traditional venue that is specific to the content of the performance (e.g., a bar, a park, a particular restaurant, etc.). This choice gives the audience a fully immersive experience.

Sitzprobe A seated musical rehearsal that takes place prior to tech in which the orchestra and the performers work together for the first time. This is a chance to set tempos, volume, and other musical adjustments as necessary. This rehearsal should be the musical director, with input from the director.

Soundscape Sound design that creates the audio world of the show. Different than sound cues (such as a gunshot, doorbell, phone ring, etc.), this is the ambient sound of the outside world (the background sound of battle, gunshots, men shouting, and shells in a war; birds chirping, dogs barking, children playing and wind blowing at a park, crickets chirping at night) and helps to give body and realism to a show.

Spacing Rehearsal Typically the first rehearsal in the theatre in which the director and choreographer takes time to take the blocking and spacing found in the rehearsal space and translate it to the actual stage, especially as it relates to the set. Blocking may be changed and spike marks may move in order to best fit the space.

Special A light focused to illuminate a very specific area on stage. Stage management may need to provide spike marks to assist in objects or people landing in the correct spot for the light to function as designed.

Speed Through A rehearsal or run in which the cast speaks the lines (and perhaps marks the blocking) as fast as they can. These help continuity, timing, and line retention.

Spike A semi-permanent indication of where a prop, set piece, or person is meant to be set on stage, marked with tape to ensure consistency from performance to performance.

Spike Map A guide created to track the precise placement of all spike marks on the floor. Used primarily as a tool to transfer spikes from a rehearsal room to a performance space.

Spike Tape A type of gaff tape, usually cut to 1/2 inch width that is used for taping out sets and for spiking furniture, props, and set pieces for consistent placement throughout the run of the production. It comes in a large variety of colors, including neon and glow, to allow for color coding and easy identification.

Stage Directions (1) Within the text of a play, Stage Directions are the notes included regarding action, sound or lighting effects, and other details regarding the visual aspects of the production not portrayed in the lines. Typically given in italics. (2) The areas of the stage (Upstage, Downstage, Stage Right, Stage Left, and Center).

Stage Management Kit A toolbox (sometimes literally) of basic supplies that might be necessary in rehearsal or in performance. Depending on the theatre a stage manager may use a personal kit or the theatre may have one for use by the stage manager.

Stage Manager's Station The area in the theatre where a stage manager is stationed during the performance to call their cues. Depending on the theatre and the production, this may be in the booth or backstage in the wings. Commonly this is a podium with space for the promptbook and has a headset, a monitor, and cue light control. Sometimes known as the Calling Station.

Standby A warning call given over headset to crew members to indicate an upcoming cue. Standbys are typically given about 1/2 page prior to a cue being called.

Start and Stop A type of technical rehearsal that is meant to acquaint everyone with the technical elements of the show and allow the stage manager time to learn the correct placement of all the cues. These are typical on shows that are heavily cued, like musicals.

Strike (1) The time following the closing performance during which all elements of the production are taken down and the theatre space is cleaned out and reset for the next production. Commonly takes place immediately following the final performance or in the day or two afterwards. (2) A term meaning to take something away or remove.

Stumble Through A rehearsal in which large sections or the full show are run for the first time as a full unit and tend to be clunky and have mistakes, hence the name "stumble".

Supernumeraries Supernumeraries or "supers" are silent acting roles in an opera; often waiters, soldiers, guards, etc.

Swing A performer who is hired to learn the tracks for all the roles and is on standby backstage during all performances in case a performer needs to be replaced mid-show (due to illness, injury, etc.) or to fill in for an understudy who is covering a different track. Commonly, a production will hire one male swing and one female swing.

Table Work Rehearsals in which the goal is to work slowly through the script, stopping to talk about character, pacing, story background, tone, etc. These most commonly take place during the first week of rehearsal and ideally include the full cast.

Tabs (Curtains) Curtains that mask the wings from view of the audience.

Tape Out The groundplan for a set represented in full scale by tape on a rehearsal or stage floor for use in rehearsal until the set is available. This should be completed by stage management prior to the first blocking rehearsal and should include all major elements of the set.

Technical Rehearsal (Tech) Rehearsals that are used to integrate all technical elements of the production, with the exception of costumes.

Thrust A stage that typically has audience seated on three sides.

Tracking (1) The term used for monitoring where props, set pieces, costumes, and sometimes performers travel throughout the run of a show. (2) This can also refer to the act of moving something from one location to another in order for it to be in the correct location for its next use. Sometimes tracking of a single item is impossible, so multiple of the same item will need to be acquired.

Tuning The act of musicians tuning their instruments as a group in preparation for a performance. On operas and certain musicals, this is done at the very start of the show immediately preceding the overture and is an expected part of the performance, indicating to the audience that the show is about to begin.

Turntable A piece of scenery that rotates around a stationary central axis and can contain multiple scenes or scenic pieces depending on its size and layout.

Understudy A cast member that is responsible for learning the lines, blocking and choreography of an assigned character in case of injury, emergency etc.

Union A group of people that work in the same industry and join together to practice collective bargaining.

Upstage The area of the stage furthest from the audience (or the front-facing audience in a thrust stage). In an arena space, "upstage" is usually chosen arbitrarily by the production team for ease of communication.

Ushers Front of House personnel who assist with checking tickets, seating the audience, answering questions, and giving directions around the theatre.

Vamp A musical term referring to a short section of music that can be repeated as necessary until the performers are ready for the next section of music. These are helpful during moments of a show when an action or section of dialogue may not reliably take the same amount of time each performance and are commonly found near the start of a song or in the music covering a transition.

Visual cue (1) A cue that an operator takes on their own rather than from a verbal cue from stage management to ensure perfect timing. (2) A cue called off of specific blocking (e.g., picking up a phone, flipping a light switch) rather than from the text or more general blocking (e.g., Joe crosses DS).

Vodka Spray A concoction of cheap vodka and water in a spray bottle used by wardrobe departments to freshen and sanitize costume pieces between performance.

Vomitorium (Vom) An aisle that runs through the audience that acts as an entrance/exit for the performers during a show. These are most commonly found in thrust and arena theatres.

Wagon A rolling platform mounted on castors, which typically houses a set piece.

Wandelprobe A rehearsal involving the performers and the orchestra/pit during which all songs in the show are run through, while the performers mark through their action onstage.

Weekly Call The detailed rehearsal or performance schedule broken down by and distributed on a weekly basis

Wings The offstage right and left sides of the stage, unseen by the audience. The wings are typically blocked from view by a combination of walls and curtains and used to store props, set pieces, and performers waiting for their entrances.

Work Lights (Works) Overhead lights in a theatre or other performance space used during working hours (not during the performance).

American to British English Glossary

American	English
Bells, chimes	Barbells (chimes that play in the lobby five minutes before show comes down to alert FOH staff)
House closed	Clearance (FOH gives to SM when lobby clear and ready to start show)
Curtain warmers	Tab warmers (lights on the house curtain before it rises)
Blackout curtain, full stage black	Full black
(list of props to check before house opens)	Tick check
Board, console	Desk
Booth	Box
Building the set onstage	Fit up
Call the half-hour at 30 minutes to curtain	Call the half-hour at 35 minutes to curtain
Calls include Half, Fifteen, Five, Places	Calls include Half, Quarter, Five, Beginners
Consumables, perishables	Comestibles
Cueing	Plotting
Masking softgoods	Blacks
Flashlight	Torch
Gaff	Gaffa
Glow tape	Lumi
House curtain	Tabs
Intermission	Interval
Load in	Load in (or simply In)
Monitors in dressing rooms	Show relay
Monitors in dressing rooms, God mic	Tannoy (speaker system in dressing rooms used by SM to communicate backstage)
Opening night	First night
Paper tech	Cue synopsis
Performance report	Show report
Places	Beginners
Plaster line	Setting line

Pre-show checklist	Checks
Production calendar	Provisional schedule
Prompt book	Book, prompt copy
Headsets, radios, walkies	Comms, cans
Raised platform of any shape or size	Rostra
Reset	Reset (at end of show before next)
Reset (props, set, costumes, lighting, etc)	Setting back
Run sheets	Running plot
Scrim	Gauze
Special thanks	Credits
Spikes	Marks
Stage Left/Right	Prompt side/Off prompt (P and OP, Usually P is SR but this can vary
Stage manager's podium (down stage left)	Corner, prompt corner
Stage Right	Opposite prompt
Strike	Get out
Tape out	Mark out/Mark up
Tech (Tech rehearsal)	Technical
Tech week	Pre-production week
Theatrical housing	Digs
Traveler	Split curtain
Turntable	Revolve
Wagon	Truck
To forget a line	To dry

Index

Page in *italics* refer to figures.